Sport in the Global Society

Running Cultures

Running is one of the world's most widely practised sports and recreations but until now it has tended to elude serious study outside of the natural sciences. John Bale brings the sport into the realm of the humanities by drawing on sources including literature, poetry, film, art and sculpture as well as statistics and training manuals to highlight the tensions, ambiguities and complexities that lie hidden beneath the commonplace notion of running.

The text explores both local and personal, as well as communal and global aspects of running. It deals with the runner's body and also with the globalisation of running and its practitioners. It examines the streets, tracks and stadiums where athletes run, the races in which they compete, and running relationships such as exist between the athlete and the coach, between runners and between the athlete and spectator. It discusses the importance of speed and records, how running has been used to symbolise resistance and transgression, and the extent to which it can be associated with 'the good life'.

Running Cultures provides new ways of seeing a familiar sporting phenomenon. It will appeal to both students and researchers with an interest in running in particular, and sport and leisure cultures more generally.

John Bale obtained degrees from the University of London and currently shares his time teaching and researching between the University of Aarhus, Denmark and Keele University, UK. He has been a visiting professor at the University of Jyväskylä, Finland, the University of Western Ontario, Canada, and the University of Queensland, Australia. Among his books are *Sport, Space and the City, Landscapes of Modern Sport, Kenyan Running* (with Joe Sang) and *Imagined Olympians*.

Sport in the Global Society

Series Editor: J.A. Mangan

SPORT IN THE GLOBAL SOCIETY

General Editor: J.A. Mangan

The interest in sports studies around the world is growing and will continue to do so. This unique series combines aspects of the expanding study of *sport in the global society*, providing comprehensiveness and comparison under one editorial umbrella. It is particularly timely, with studies in the political, cultural, anthropological, ethnographic, social, economic, geographical and aesthetic elements of sport proliferating in institutions of higher education.

Eric Hobsbawm once called sport one of the most significant practices of the late nineteenth century. Its significance was even more marked in the late twentieth century and will continue to grow in importance into the new millennium as the world develops into a 'global village' sharing the English language, technology and sport.

Other Titles in the Series

Cricket and England
A Cultural and Social History of the
Inter-war Years
Jack Williams

Sport in Australasian Society
Past and Present
Edited by J.A. Mangan and John Nauright

Freeing the Female Body
Inspirational Icons
Edited by J.A. Mangan and Fan Hong

Footbinding, Feminism and Freedom
The Liberation of Women's Bodies in
Modern China
Fan Hong

Superman Supreme
Fascist Body as Political Icon –
Global Fascism
Edited by J.A. Mangan

Shaping the Superman
Fascist Body as Political Icon –
Aryan Fascism
Edited by J.A. Mangan

Scoring for Britain
International Football and International
Politics, 1900–1939
Peter J. Beck

The Race Game
Sport and Politics in South Africa
Douglas Booth

The Games Ethic and Imperialism
Aspects of the Diffusion of an Ideal
J.A. Mangan

The First Black Footballer
Arthur Wharton 1865–1930: An Absence
of Memory
Phil Vasili

France and the 1998 World Cup
The National Impact of a World Sporting
Event
Edited by Hugh Dauncey and Geoff Hare

Sporting Nationalisms
Identity, Ethnicity, Immigration and
Assimilation
Edited by Mike Cronin and David Mayall

Making the Rugby World
Race, Gender, Commerce
Edited by Timothy J.L. Chandler and
John Nauright

Rugby's Great Split
Class, Culture and the Origins of Rugby
League Football
Tony Collins

Runners by Alexandr Deineka (1899–1969)
State Russian Museum, Moscow

RUNNING CULTURES
Racing in Time and Space

GV
1061
B334
2004
VAN

JOHN BALE
University of Aarhus
and
Keele University

Routledge
Taylor & Francis Group

LONDON AND NEW YORK

First published in 2004 in Great Britain by
ROUTLEDGE
11 New Fetter Lane, London EC4P 4EE

Simultaneously published in the USA and Canada by
ROUTLEDGE
29 West 35th Street,
New York, NY 10001

Routledge is an imprint of the Taylor & Francis Group

British Library Cataloguing in Publication Data

A catalogue record of this book is available from the

ISBN 0-7146-5535X (cloth)
ISBN 0-7146-84244 (paper)
ISSN 1368-9789

Library of Congress Cataloging-in-Publication Data

A catalog record of this book is available from the Library of Congress

Typeset in 10.75pt on 12.5pt Times New Roman by Cambridge Photosetting Services,
Cambridge
Printed in Great Britain by MPG Books Ltd, Victoria Square, Bodmin, Cornwall

'Human facts are always ambiguous'
(Yi-Fu Tuan, *Morality and Imagination*, 174)

Contents

List of Illustrations   x

Series Editor's Foreword   xi

Acknowledgements   xiii

Introduction   1

1.   Ways of Running   9

2.   Running Ways   37

3.   Beyond the Arena   61

4.   Athletes as Pets   77

5.   Running as Transgression and Resistance   109

6.   Escape: Runners as Cosmopolites   131

7.   Running and Racing: Moral Dilemmas and a Good Life?   147

Notes   166

Bibliography   192

Index   209

Illustrations

1.1. 'Sun and youth'   11
1.2. 'The Song of the Ungirt Runners'   13
1.3. 'Upright human body, space and time'   20
1.4. Hannes Kolehmainen, Kuopio   30
1.5. Grete Waitz, Oslo   30
1.6. 'The crash site became an instant memorial'   32
1.7. 'To an athlete dying young'   33
2.1. The track as a metaphor for the motorway   45
2.2. The Olympic Stadium, Stockholm   53
2.3. 'The 27th Olympic Games in the year 2000'   59
3.1. Running course used by Gunder Hägg at Vålådalen, Sweden   62
3.2. A typology of sensory relationships in running   76
4.1. Paavo Nurmi as machine   88
4.2. 'A spectre is haunting Europe: Rationalization on the march'   90
4.3. Paavo Nurmi   94
4.4. Interval training as a group activity   98
4.5. 'After defeat at Turin, an affectionate embrace from
      jubilant Luigi'   104
5.1. Carl Lewis, photographed for a Pirelli advertisement   119
5.2. Alf Tupper   124
6.1. Zola Budd by Chumbawumba   142
7.1. Emil Zátopek   148

Series Editor's Foreword

As a sleepy young schoolboy, like most having crept like a snail unwillingly to school, one morning I was once made to read aloud in class C. H. Sorley's 'The Song of the Ungirt Runners' from a battered school text book, *English Verse, Old and New An Anthology for Schools*,[1] inherited from an earlier – first former – one Michael Savage.

The poem puzzled me greatly.

Only now, perhaps, have I the words to say why – those 'ungirded hips', the lightened eyes, the strange insecurity, the uncertain destiny, the forlorn purpose and yet the joyful intoxication possessed only quixotic messages for an eleven-year-old preoccupied with autumn conkers:

> We know not whom me trust
> Nor whither ward we fare,
> But we run because we must
> Through the great wide air.[2]

Years later, I came closer to Sorley, in my research for *Athleticism in the Victorian and Edwardian Public School*, and closer to an understanding of his strange poem and its now clearer meaning. Sorley was a pre-Great War Marlborough schoolboy,[3] whose radical spirit was irked by the period public school conservatism. Paradoxically the compulsory 'sweats' (runs)[4] over the glorious Marlborough Downs freed him from it. He loved the, sometimes sunny, often wet and windy outings:

> We run because we like it
> Through the bright broad land[5]

'The Song' was, in fact, a celebration of the 'sweats'. Schools intended that they diminished the libido, strengthened the limbs and lungs and produced fitness for the places of moral exercise – the playing fields.

Sorley found in the 'sweats' something else – spontaneity, individuality, freedom and pantheism.

Running Cultures, quite properly, in rather more sober academic style than the 'Ungirt Runners', probes Sorley's discovery: 'Running is not mere perambulation ... it can invoke the notion of speed – of running wild', of escape, of indiscipline ('running wild, lost control')'.[6] *Running Cultures*, in fact, is an interpretative exploration of running that considers its specific sensory effects. And it is more. It involves a singularly original approach to this exploration based on the humanistic-geographical writings of the geographer Yi-Fu Tuan. Furthermore, the suggestion in it is that Tuan's insights have a wider relevance to sports studies well beyond running. Tuan, it appears, uses sport to shine a light on broader ideas and its use, de facto, 'unwittingly illuminates sport itself'.[7]

Tuan's view of sport and life is mostly positive. The vitality, grace and playfulness of the athlete pleases him as it certainly pleases Sorley. However, Tuan considers somewhat less fully 'the darker side of sports – the exploitation, the pain and the ugliness'.[8] Sorley was rather more aware of these things on public school playing fields.

Running Cultures' 'humanistic' approach to running – 'mostly ... racing, its participants, and its environments'[9] is defined in *Running Cultures* as 'the desire and the ability to see afresh those ordinary objects and motions of life, to take delight in them for what they are, as they appear, then to dive under the hidden relations and meanings, and finally present both – surfaces and depths, the seen and the unseen'.[10] This approach covers sites, senses, motions, relations and statistics depicted in numbers, human figures, words, pictures and stone within their political economic and social constraints and notions of space and place.

Running Cultures is a challenging book. Its radicalism would have fascinated Sorley if he had been able to read it warm in the school library after 'running without a cause/ Neath the big, bare sky'.[11]

J. A. Mangan
IRCSSS
De Montfort University (Bedford)
October 2003

Acknowledgements

I would like to thank my colleagues and friends at the Institute for Sport Science, University of Aarhus, for support and help during the writing of this essay. The Institute provided a friendly and stimulating milieu in which most of this book was written. I must also thank Kevin Wamsley and Bob Barney for facilitating a visiting fellowship at the International Centre for Olympic Studies, University of Western Ontario. Here I was able to garner material in the early stages of research. Likewise, Kenth Sjöblom provided very helpful assistance at the national sport archive in Helsinki. I must especially thank those who have commented on various parts and versions of the manuscript, in particular Anthony Bale, Susan Bandy, Jim Denison, Jens-Ole Jensen, Ejgil Jespersen, Jeff Hill, Sigmund Loland and Tiffany Muller. I also obtained encouragement for this project from David Howe. Additionally, Sine Agergaard, Olav Ballisager, Mette K. Christensen and Niels Kayser Nielsen have been congenial colleagues who have always been available to discuss ideas. Help with the reproduction of visual material was provided by Mike Daniels at Keele University. The staff at the Bodleian Library, Oxford, and Birmingham University library were, as usual, extremely efficient. Most of all, however, I must thank Yi-Fu Tuan for not only providing the inspiration for this book but also for reading critically an almost-finished version of the text. I sense that he is much more than the amateur and outsider that he claims to be when it comes to sports studies.

I am pleased to acknowledge those who have given me permission to reproduce illustrations. However, it proved impossible to track down permissions for some images. If contacted I will acknowledge these in subsequent printings of this work.

Many people have contributed to this work but the usual caveat applies: I take full responsibility for what follows.

Introduction

After walking, running is the first technology of the body that, through human agency, seeks to compress time and space.[1] Although the collapse of time and space has become a major theme of writers focusing on late modernity,[2] few have recognized that breaking into a run has, in the span of human time, been as important in the history of time-space compression as the stagecoach, the railway, the aeroplane and the telephone. Each of these technologies seeks to bring closer together in time two discrete points in space, overcoming the constraint on interaction caused by distance. I run to close the distance between myself and the train waiting to pull away from the platform; I run rather than walk from potential threats, hoping to place distance between the threats and myself. Running as a means of time-space compression is breathtakingly illustrated in the stunning German movie *Lola Rennt* (*Run Lola Run*), written and directed by Tom Tykwer in 1998. In it, Lola has 20 minutes to reach her boyfriend or he will be killed. Given no other means of transport, she has to run as fast as she can given the time available to her. It is an example of space being (or attempting to be) devoured by time.[3]

Running is not mere perambulation or 'rushed locomotion';[4] it can invoke the notion of speed – of 'running wild', of escape, of indiscipline ('running wild, lost control'). The sensory effect of running is different from that of walking, and from movement by vehicular-aided transport. Yet as a body-cultural phenomenon running has eluded serious study in the humanities and social sciences. Of course, this is not to deny that a substantial number of publications have been written on the techniques of running, on the history of running and on the biographies of runners. Running also features in novels and movies. But interpretative studies of running remain limited.[5]

In this book I attempt an exploration and an excavation of running and its representations. I do this through a lens that has been crafted in the humanistic-geographical writing of the Chinese-American geographer, Yi-Fu Tuan. The book is what might be broadly called a 'Tuanian' approach to the study of sport. By this I mean that I take a general theme, running, and 'explore its various dimensions through extended analysis of several concrete examples', though Tuan's lucid writing 'is impossible to imitate'.[6] Running is my example, but much of what I write could be readily applied to other sports. Tuan's views, I believe, inform sports studies, particularly those of a geographical, social or environmental nature.

I expect that a good proportion of those who read this book will not have heard of the man who has inspired it. Yet Yi-Fu Tuan has been a prolific writer in the field of humanistic geography and one of his admirers, the historian Simon Schama, feels that it is time that Tuan 'was recognized as one of the most remarkable and creative figures in the intellectual life of our time'.[7] Another devotee describes him as 'the consummate geographer'.[8] It is further claimed that 'few if any contemporary geographers can match his intellectual range'.[9] Tuan's first major and perhaps most well-known book, *Topophilia*, has been rated as one of the classics of Human Geography.[10] At the same time, however, it is possible to see Tuan's œuvre as 'idiosyncratic' and the man himself as a 'geographical maverick'.[11] Tuan's work has been applied in a rather small range of sporting contexts.[12] One of the aims of this book, therefore, is to alert a wider audience to some of his thoughts and to their applications to the serious study of serious sport.

Tuan and Sports

What Tuan – a humanistic scholar more than a social scientist – might see in running can be contrasted with a positivist view that, through experimentation, seeks scientific generalizations. There is little obvious 'theory' in Tuan's writing. But theory would be unlikely to be explicated by someone primarily concerned with writing geography into the humanities rather than the social sciences. This is not to say, however, that the contents of 'Tuanian' studies are necessarily irrelevant to theoretical debates in sports, and other social scientific studies.[13] Readers of this book possessing a strong theoretical bent are therefore invited to 'spot the theories' in the pages that follow.

Sport is one of several subjects about which Tuan manages to convey important ideas without saying very much about them.[14] He would hardly call himself an expert on sports, yet his life story and his corpus of writing reveal a number of sporting connections and allusions. For example, having arrived in England and waiting to enter Oxford University, he was a spectator at the 1948 Olympic Games in London.[15] And on his bookshelf he admits to having Allen Guttmann's *From Ritual to Record*, Norbert Elias and Eric Dunning's *Quest for Excitement* and Joyce Carol Oates's *On Boxing*.[16] I suspect that he also has Roger Bannister's *First Four Minutes* (published in the United States as *The Four Minute Mile*) as he refers to Bannister's writing in at least two of his books, allusions I shall return to later.[17] Additionally, he refers to sports in several other contexts. He talks about his playing of cricket at school in Australia and to his somewhat reluctant recruitment as coxswain to his college rowing eight while an undergraduate during his Oxford days.[18] He ponders the sensation of speed on drag strips for hot-rodders and reflects on the ice hockey player Eric Nesterinko, formerly of the Toronto Maple Leafs, as he experiences physical vitality and spatial expansiveness while skating, not on a rink but on a huge sheet of ice on the street.[19] He refers to the need for brain as well as brawn in the skills of the triathlete; to the problem of identity for Iranian-Americans during the USA–Iran soccer match in Los Angeles in 1999; and to the novelty of an 'authentic golf prodigy' in the from of Tiger Woods.[20] Tuan also makes passing reference to the golfer who, in his swing, illustrates how the means to sports success can possess elegance and economy.[21] He relates a tale from the locker room, as told by Bill Bradley, basketball player and US senator, about how the most mundane of sporting experiences can contribute to the quality of life.[22] He alludes to what he considers the wonderful aesthetic 'fit' between male and female as evidenced in ice-dancing, and cites Joyce Carol Oates's evocation of pugilism as a site of homoeroticism – 'part dance, courtship and coupling', a kind of warmth different from that generated by heterosexual sex.[23] And in his autobiography, Tuan alludes to his decision to play the part of goalkeeper in a game of soccer during his childhood in China, staying put in his goal, holding his ground. He chose this position because of what he saw as his lack of vitality, a quality that, along with youth, he was later almost to idolize. He also recalls the shame of being unable to throw a ball like other boys did.[24] But the boy to whom he was attracted as a youth was an athlete, a not uncommon form of schoolboy affection.[25] And there are other, more substantive, Tuanian observations about sport that I will refer to in later chapters. So Yi-Fu Tuan is not such an outsider to sport as he might suggest but, having said that, he uses sport to illustrate broader ideas. However, I sense that he also unwittingly illuminates sport itself and it is this approach that I try to take in what follows.

Tuan's broad view of sport (and life itself) is generally positive. He is attracted to the playfulness, the vitality, the beauty and the grace of the athlete. However, he pays rather less attention to what I regard as the darker side of sports – the exploitation, the pain and the ugliness. Even so, in recalling his visit to Wembley Stadium in 1948 to witness the London Olympics, he can still remember watching 'with bursting excitement' the women's 100 metres final:

> The athletes *looked* beautiful to me from a distance, but if I could see their faces I would no doubt see them twisted and ugly. But then the same could be said of ballet – how elegant the dancers look from a distance, how ugly from up close. And how close this elegance is to violence! At the end of a performance, the ballet slippers are stained by blood.[26]

Tuan's interest in sport is evident but he has been 'an occasional spectator' rather than 'a practitioner' and, in his view, this explains why he fails to 'give proper weight to pain and perhaps too much weight to beauty'.[27] However, most sports participants would, I think, feel the same way, reminiscing more about the ecstasy than the agony.

Based on Tuan's writings (and to some extent on his approach), this book is a humanistic study of one body cultural practice: running. More specifically, it is, for the most part, about the sporting practice of racing, its participants and environments. I follow Tuan's view of what is meant by 'humanistic'; that is, the desire or ability 'to see afresh those ordinary objects and motions of life, to take delight in them for what they are, as they appear, then to dive under the hidden relations and meanings, and finally to present both – surfaces and depths, the seen and unseen'.[28] This approach is reflected in Tuan's observations about the 1948 women sprinters and the ballet dancer.

The 'ordinary objects' that form focal points in this book are the streets, the tracks and fields, the stadiums and arenas, and the meadows, beaches and forests, where athletes run. The 'motions' are the various runs and races that take place in these environments. The 'relations' I deal with include those between athlete and coach, the races between one runner and another, between athlete and spectator, and the links between those possessing power and those over whom power is exercised. Humanists learn to read between the lines and to take note of not what is said so much as what is left unsaid. This study highlights the tensions, ambiguities and complexities that lie beneath the certainties and concreteness often associated with the common-place notion of running. As John Pickles comments, 'human behavior is complex and unpredictable. Laws of behavior cannot be established. Instead inquiry is to investigate the richness of lived experience or the meaning given to behavior by social actors.'[29]

Humanists are also concerned with the senses. '*Experience* is a key word in the humanist geographer's lexicon', writes Tuan;[30] 'people are always feeling, willing, thinking and making decisions. This is the natural emphasis of humanist scholars.'[31] Running can be a source of feelings and sensory experiences, positive and negative, pleasurable and painful. Humanists might also argue that an appreciation of running's sensory geographies – 'the *felt quality* of the human world'[32] – and the runner's perspectives on the world, might best be obtained through the close reading of literature, seeking insights from texts that include (auto)biographies, novels, histories and other writings.[33] An objective of literary art is to 'present possible modes of experience', which 'is more complex than that of which a social scientist is normally aware'.[34]

Likewise, Hans Lenk and Gunther Gebauer have suggested that 'narratives in sport literature have a greater flexibility than historical reports'.[35] By this they mean that the 'mere report' fails to adopt anything approaching a critical perspective and, indeed, is supportive of the status quo. They argue that 'trivial sports stories' often 'depict day-to-day legends in their compliance with common, all-too common expectations'. On the other hand, other creations of sports literature depict and explore 'elaborate collisions with unusual expectations'.[36] So literature need not follow or mirror the banal events of modern sport but include 'detours' and even 'inversions' of the conventional way of seeing. I believe that Tuan's writing also does this. But this is not to say that statistics, biographies and other mundane representations are of no value since they inform the banality of sport itself by mirroring it. Nor is it necessarily the case that 'high-level' works in sports studies are subversive. My use of literature (in a broad sense and from a wide variety of sources) in the search for experiences of running is a response to the growing interest in representation in sports studies.

But sport is a world of statistics. Where do these come in the humanist approach? Tuan's reply is that a humanist 'looks at this world of facts and numbers and asks, what does it mean? And what does it say about oneself?'[37] Additionally, statistics can be humanized by supplementing them with other kinds of figures – those representing human beings in words, pictures and stone.

Humanistic approaches have been criticized for focusing on the individual, the privileging human agency, and fetishizing experience and subjectivity.[38] However, the emergence of a *critical* humanism, by recognizing the presence of ideology and emphasizing contradictions and tensions, is able to accept that notions such as 'sense of place' may be constrained by a variety of structures – social, political and economic.[39] Additionally, as with Tuan's work which often deals with ethical questions, I try to adopt a grounded and concrete perspective, unlike that of some sports philosophers.[40]

Autobiographical Exegesis

Compared with Tuan I can claim to be relatively well versed in running and its lore. To be sure, both he and I must have run as children, freely frolicking in the open air. And later in life we were both surely compelled to run as part of our schooling. But unlike him I took running seriously; I was not simply a runner but a racer. For about ten years of my life I took running – track, cross-country and road – very earnestly, both as a fan and as a competitive athlete. Although I was never a successful athlete (by whatever criterion 'success' is measured) I think I can identify with the world of elite athletes, partly because I dreamed of being one, partly because I read voraciously about them, partly because (at my own modest level) I behaved like them, and partly because I met and knew some of them. Like the huge majority of aspirant athletes, I never reached the upper echelons of sport. At the age of 22

I had hit my peak and achieved my personal best time over 880 yards of 1 minute 58.4 seconds: Note the precision of the timing – to a tenth of a second. This personal record was the result of serious training and considerable discipline for I was far from being a 'natural athlete'. I gave up track running a year or two after this moderate achievement for a life focused on different kinds of achievements. Yet I never really stopped running and, rather pathetically, at the age of 40 returned to racing – as a sad 'veteran'. I really believed, at this rather advanced age, that I could run under 2 minutes 10 seconds for the (by then, de-imperialized) 800 metres. I never did. I moved on to longer distances to keep fit, to improve my physical well-being. But I could not resist the seductive lure of the 'prison of measured time'[41] – the timed race over a prescribed distance, the challenge of time over space. Despite further efforts at training during the road running boom of the 1980s, I never reached my target of 1 hour 40 minutes for the half-marathon. Now, at over 60 years of age, my running has almost come to an end. When does running – having long stopped being racing – become jogging, hobbling, stumbling? Will I soon become an object of grotesquery, an old man aping a youth, struggling to lift his legs in much the same way as those old Hollywood film stars try to lift their faces? Am I 'exhausting the energy of a body that has, in [my] eyes become useless'? Am I running on and on because I 'have lost the formula for stopping', like society itself?[42]

These autobiographical notes reveal me as something of an insider. I know how it *feels* to run 400 metres in 60 seconds and I know what it is like to train until I feel physically sick. I have also experienced running, sometimes exuberantly, in the forests of Småland in Sweden, on the beaches around Noosa Heads in Queensland, in the humidity of downtown Suva in Fiji, and in the winter temperatures of snow-covered central Finland. However, by having been there and done it I cannot claim to represent the feelings of all runners. Each athlete will have different stories to tell, of glory, disappointment, success, failure, exhilaration and pain. Was training and racing a waste of valuable time, a form of social control or a spiritual experience where even the disappointment of losing was, as the British runner Chris Chataway said, 'all rather good for my soul'?[43]

My various personal engagements with running and my knowledge of what it is like to train and compete do not necessarily mean that I more easily access scientific objectivity. As implied above, in this book I do not seek to present a theory of running but instead place more emphasis on the 'dense textured facts of experience' that lie below the surface of the taken for granted, and indeed, of scientific generalizations.[44] To obtain insights into running – to read running – is not always compatible with the scientific view. By excavating running and its representations I attempt to improve understanding.[45] To do this is a personal project but may also be relevant to anyone involved in running or sport per se, from whatever perspective or form of involvement. Tuan argues that the approach of the cultural-humanist writer is similar to that of a storyteller. I know well the subject whose story I tell (as an insider) but in the very act of telling it I become an outsider for the duration.[46] This means that I am consciously trying to avoid writing this work from a runner's perspective since this could amount to 'going native'. Instead, I can draw on my own experience of running reflectively, reading it as a text in much the same way as I read biographical texts and other writings on running – and, of course, running itself.

Plan of this Book

This book is structured around a number of themes, each of which has been inspired by Tuan's writing. In several cases his thoughts provide the basis for a chapter's content. In others, his ideas stimulate exemplifications. I do not treat Tuan's writings as absolute truths but as ideas and suggestions. Additionally, I take stimulus from the work of other humanist cultural geo-graphers such as Edward Relph and Robert Sack.[47] I also draw on several studies from the perspectives of sports studies, history, geography, sociology and philosophy. The book is centrally focused around notions of space and place, from the scale of the sports field to that of the globe. But in a world of sport where geography and geometry meet it would be impossible to avoid introducing concepts such as lines, segments, directions, landscapes, envi-ronments, movements and interactions, all quite traditional interests of geographers. Such terms are used both literally and metaphorically. So places, such as running tracks or arenas, can be directly experienced and concrete, or can be metaphorical, such as in knowing 'one's place' or being 'out of place'.[48]

Chapter 1 focuses on different ways of running. I differentiate between various configurations of running, basing my approach on the work of writers in geography and sports studies. Central to their thinking, however, is the connection between the body and the place in which it is engaged in running. I concentrate on achievement running (that is, serious running) or racing and some of the themes associated with it – statistics, time-space compression, records, speed and slowness, for example. Some of Tuan's ideas are central to these themes. Having cleared some of the conceptual ground, chapters 2 and 3 look at the landscapes – the spaces and places – in which running takes place. My Tuanian approach to a geographical view of sport is mainly based on his books *Space and Place, Segmented Worlds and Self, Dominance and Affection, Topophilia* and, to a lesser extent, *Landscapes of Fear*. Running landscapes include tracks, arenas, meadows, forests, woodlands, sand dunes, beaches, streets and fitness studios. How may such places be read? Can a progression from the pre-modern to the late-modern be identified among them and where is the place of running in such sites? And where is nature in these landscapes? Have sites become, in some instances, sights – places to be gazed at and admired? Has the track and the field been turned into a mixture of architecture and horticulture – a sort of garden, as a reading of my favourite of Tuan's books, *Dominance and Affection*, might suggest? Does the arena as garden make athletics basically anti-nature? Or does the arena increasingly resemble space rather than place, an isotropic plane – placelessness – or a landscape of anaesthesia? I also explore a tendency for athletes to seek alternative sites for running, away from the arena and track, in forest and meadow, on beach and dune. However, in some contexts I suggest that running be read as a devalued version of walking.

Dominance and Affection also inspires Chapter 4. If arenas can be read metaphorically as gardens, can the athlete be read as the garden's zoological analogue, the pet? What are the power relations that runners encounter? And what other human groups surround the runner and lend meaning to running? I deal with trainers and coaches, an athlete's competitors and the spectators that attend the track meets, watch running on television or read about runners in books and magazines.

Chapter 5 draws on some thoughts derived from Tuan's books *Cosmos and Hearth* and *Escapism* and examines the ways in which running can be read as a form of escape. But escape from what? Perhaps the world of the routine and the mundane – or perhaps runners run because much running *is* routine and matches the work-like character of much day-to-day life. This chapter focuses, then, on the migration of athletes. Such migration produces new experiences but at the same time raises questions of representation and identity. To an extent, *Escape* also informs Chapter 6, which grapples with notions of transgression and resistance through running. I include some brief biographies in order to examine the possibility of transgressive behaviour in sportized running. I also explore the extent to which the running track could be a site for resistance. Finally, in Chapter 7 I draw on Tuan's books *Morality and Imagination* and *The Good Life*, and question whether racing is compatible with a good life and consider the variety of moral and ethical dilemmas runners face during their careers. Some dilemmas exist in relation to their lives as athletes, others occur in their off-track activities. But the main feature of this chapter is a consideration of whether serious runners are good people.

Is this book a geography of sport? If it *is* a geography, it is one that is interested in the production and breaking of bodies through the highly spatialized and specialized demands of different configurations of running, a body-culture which I see as ambiguous and complex, even problematic.

1

Ways of Running

Two people are running down a street. One has committed a crime and is attempting to distance herself from the police; the other has committed herself to the London Marathon and is attempting her first 30-kilometre training run. A sports-philosophical response to this scenario could be that 'in each of these cases the agent's physical movement may have displayed the same external form'.[1] Likewise, a Tuanian reading might be: 'If we observe only the behaviour, nothing perhaps distinguishes the one from the other'.[2] Yet the worlds in each of their heads are radically different. Or, as W.H. Auden put it,

> The camera's eye
> Does not lie,
> But it cannot show
> The life within,
> The life of a runner...[3]

An understanding of running cannot be achieved by simply looking at runners. Or, as C.L.R. James might have asked, what do they know of running who only running know?[4] Understanding is visceral and even visceral writing cannot be the experience itself.[5] Running can assume many forms. It can be spontaneous; it can be enforced. Sometimes running is a necessity; it may be an occupation, an exploitation, a relaxation, a ritual, a race, a recreation. It may be imposed and painful; it may be free and exhilarating; it may even be imposed and exhilarating. To an extent, individuals and society have a choice about which form to adopt. In this chapter I want to briefly consider some ways in which forms of running can be differentiated.

There is no single, agreed classification of the configurations of running.[6] For purposes of economy and convenience I will use the trialectical model proposed and developed in numerous contexts by Henning Eichberg.[7] Why do people run? Simply put, the reason for running may be for fun, for fitness or for achievement. Fun can be regarded as aproductive; fitness and achievement can involve the accumulation of cultural, social and financial capital. None of the three configurations of running can be taken for granted, however. Nor are they without ambiguity and they are not mutually exclusive. For example, fitness and achievement running can be (at least in part) fun. And they can also lead to careers in achievement running.[8] However, Eichberg's ideal types form a convenient starting point for a consideration of ways of running. In this chapter I also want to introduce the nexus between running, the body and space.

Fun, Frolic and Freedom

Tuan notes how the human body is unique among animals 'in that it easily maintains its upright position. Upright man [sic] is ready to act. Space opens out before him.'[9]

Children appear to run in a playful way but, even so, they have learned to run. They are not *born* walking or running. If, as anthropologist Tim Ingold forcefully observes, children deprived of contact with older caregivers will not learn to walk, how much more important it is to have supervised learning in absorbing the culture of running?[10] By the age of 2 or 3 years, most children can run. Perhaps they have tried, literally, to run before they can walk. Most of us can surely recognize young children frolicking at play. Tuan notes that for children 'life is joyous in its vitality, and vitality is motion when time is forgotten'.[11] This lack of concern for time seems to be an important distinction between the play mode of running and the other modes discussed below. As I will show, time is central to serious running, be it in the welfare or achievement form.

Consider four representations of playful running. First, the much-quoted reminiscences of Roger Bannister, the first runner known to have run faster than four minutes for the mile, reveal graphically the delight, vitality and élan found by children through the joy of running:

> I can remember the moment when I stood barefoot on firm dry sand by the sea. The air had a special quality as if it had a life of its own. The sound of the breakers on the shore shut out all others. I looked up at the clouds, like great white-sailed galleons, chasing proudly inland. I looked down at the regular ripples on the sand, and could not absorb so much beauty. I was taken aback – each of the myriad particles of sand was perfect in its way. I looked more closely, hoping perhaps that my eyes might detect some flaw. But for once there was nothing to detract from all this beauty.

In this supreme moment I leapt in sheer joy. I was startled, and frightened, by the tremendous excitement that so few steps could create. I glanced round uneasily to see if anyone was watching. A few more steps – self-consciously now and firmly gripping the original excitement. The earth seemed almost to move with me. I was running now, and a fresh rhythm entered my body. No longer conscious of my movement I discovered a new unity with nature. I had found a new source of power I never dreamt existed.[12]

Central to Bannister's experience of joyful running was a place – the beach. There is more than a suggestion that the place mattered. The beach is not artificially enclosed; it has a distinctive texture; Bannister's run had no prescribed beginning or end. He started and finished when he felt like it. For the runner whose running is freedom, *enough is enough*. Bannister's frolics took place on, what might conventionally be termed, a natural landscape. No one made him run; it appeared to be spontaneous. He did not time his run; there was no track, except for the marks left by his feet in the sand.

Secondly, a sense of frolic and gambol is also represented in the work of the Danish painter Jens Ferdinand Willumsen, as shown in his image of boys running on the Jutland beach at Skagen Strand (Figure 1.1). They are naked, unencumbered by clothing, exuberant and free. They are not constrained. The runners move according to the meaning of the Old English word *plegan*

Figure 1.1 'Sun and youth' by Jens Ferdinand Willumsen (1860–1942) (Gothenburg Museum of Art).

– 'to move with lively, irregular, and capricious motion, to spring, to fly, to dart to and fro, to gambol, frisk, flutter, flit, sparkle – as in the play of light upon water'.[13] The three boys in the centre of the painting are delivered into *jouissance*, 'the mindless play of the happy sand boy',[14] or Roger Callois's *paida*, that is, play at its most childlike.[15] For these youngsters, it seems that the joy of movement has priority over winning. They enjoy a sense of spaciousness associated with being free.[16] By contrast, the infants to their left are constrained by their inability to do anything other than crawl; to their right is another child, also restricted, physically, by an elder.

Playful running does not *require* a particular site at which it must take place. No rules govern where playful running can occur. Surely Huizinga was wrong to state that playfulness needs special sites that are spatially limited.[17] On the contrary, children appear to run in each and every milieu, natural or humanly constructed. A third impression by the New Zealand coach Arthur Lydiard avers that children should *play* at athletics. He alluded to boys 'who like nothing better than to run in packs over hills and valleys, jumping creeks and fences, enjoying fresh air and sunshine in a sport that recognizes *none of the confines of the measured field*'.[18] Such running may appear reckless but through learning such recklessness becomes converted into sensory experiences. Novelist Mark Helprin describes boyhood running thus: 'As I became more and more capable I ran faster, I took longer strides, and I sailed higher and higher over the obstructions in my way.' Yet 'Sometimes I frightened myself when my limbs, knowing better than I both the path and what they could do, stretched longer and pushed harder than my intent. Sometimes, it seemed, I was suspended in the air so long that I flew … I would dream at night of leaving the path and never alighting.'[19]

My fourth example draws on the poem 'The Song of the Ungirt Runners' by Charles Hamilton Sorley (1895–1915). As a schoolboy at Marlborough College, Sorley was known to dislike team sports and much preferred to go on long runs over the Downs in rain and wind. His poem (Figure 1.2) alludes to a natural body running in a natural landscape – the wild tempest, rising winds and 'rain on our lips'. Unencumbered by clothing the 'ungirt runners' move through 'the great wide air', 'the big bare sky' and 'the broad bright land'. The playfulness of such body culture is implied by Sorley's words: 'we run without a cause' and 'because we like it'. The poem evokes a feeling of freedom *with* nature.

Bannister's writing, Willumsen's image, Lydiard's idyllic invocation and Sorley's poem are reminiscent of Tuan's summing up of *The Good Life*: 'Consider those moments which seem to have only a sensual or an emotional-aesthetic character: for instance running barefoot on the sand as a child';[20] or, the feeling that, among children, there is a 'common delight in bodily movement – a biological exuberance'.[21] I cannot accept that there is anything serious in play though this is not to say that it is of no educational value.

We swing ungirded hips,

And lightened are our eyes,

The rain is on our lips,

We do not run for prize.

We know not whom we trust

Nor whitherward we fare,

But we run because we must

    Through the great wide air.

The waters of the seas

Are troubled as by storm.

The tempest strips the trees

And does not leave them warm.

Does the tearing tempest pause?

Do the tree-tops ask it why?

So we run without a cause

    'Neath the big bare sky.

The rain is on our lips,

We do not run for prize.

But the storm the water whips

And the wave howls to the skies.

The winds arise and strike it

And scatter it like sand,

And we run because we like it

Through the broad bright land.

Figure 1.2 'The Song of the Ungirt Runners' by C.H. Sorley (1895–1915)

Such behaviour rarely continues into the adult years. Before the end of their teenage years, for girls and boys growing self-consciousness seems to induce unease about running uninhibitedly.[22] 'To feel self-conscious about movement', writes Tuan, 'is to risk awkwardness, insincerity (or not least the appearance of it) and immobilization'.[23] It has been argued that 'civilised man, also, is conscious of self, and no more so than the runner'.[24] To run like a child when one is an adult is to appear foolish and out of place. But can such spontaneous running, with the childish exuberance displayed by Willumsen's boys, be (re)captured in adulthood? As we grow older, there may still be time for play but, as Tuan poignantly puts it, 'under restrained circumstances with a sort of lid placed on the élan of imagination'.[25] It is not a case of children losing the knack when they reach the age of 7 or 8; they simply prefer not to exercise it.[26] However, it is not only a preference. By coincidence (or not) it is at this point in their lives that running becomes part of the compulsory school curriculum where freedom is replaced by Physical Education (see below).

Nineteenth-century 'alternative living' and a 'culture of nakedness' may have begun to approach the uninhibited playfulness of children. A goal of such movements was to establish – or re-establish – 'an honest, unembarrassed relationship with one's own body'.[27] Naked running was far from unknown among nudist movements that continued into the 1920s and was later adopted by Nazi ideology with its anti-urban bias. It is exemplified, to some extent, by some of the images at the start of part two of Leni Reifenstahl's *Olympia*. As Taylor Downing describes it,

> … we see the outline of joggers running beside a lake. Through the morning mist the shape of men running in a line forms more clearly … The runners cross a bridge and disappear into the woodlands. Naked, they run from the lake into a sauna. The steam of the sauna replaces the dawn mist … The men massage each other, and beat each other with birch twigs … The naked men dive into the lake. Others sit on the wooden balcony. Man and nature in harmony.[28]

This is not the language of achievement sports, even if the athletes, who are seemingly transcending time and space, may have been meant to represent recuperating Olympic runners who would later be transformed from an 'eternal dawn' into uniformed representatives of a variety of nation states.[29]

During the 1960s and 1970s, counter-cultural movements in the United States promoted a sort of zen of running or, put more mundanely, the jogging revolution. Fred Rohé sees his running as a 'dance of joy' but, he continues: 'if the dance of the run/isn't fun/then discover another dance/because without fun/the good of the run/is undone/and a suffering runner/always quits/sooner or later/you will find your dancing run/doesn't tire you but *energizes* you.'[30] He talks of gaining spring in your stride, of his running as dancing even feeling like flying, being free in the air before touching down for the next stride. Rohé's opposite of fun is suffering, an important distinction for those who see serious running as pain and suffering.

On the face of it, Rohé's evocation of the dance of running seems similar to Bannister's poetic reminiscences. However, the zen of running, like 'flow' in running, does not take place spontaneously and unselfconsciously but is planned. 'Flow', for example, is described as the key to optimal experiences and performances.[31] It equips people for something other than a productive frolic or gambol. It has an objective and a meaning beyond that of the participants themselves and is applicable to a wide range of activities beyond running. 'Runners high', to which I return later in this book, is (I suggest) something different.

Fitness Running

When and how are children coerced into running? Sometimes perhaps by pushy parents who wish to see their offspring beat others, even on the most playful of occasions. Sometimes, the schoolteacher may be required to make children, from the ages of 4 or 5, run as part of the Physical Education curriculum. Compulsory running was widespread in nineteenth-century English private schools. As part of this burst of athleticism, boys at Loretto College, for example, had to experience the compulsory run, 'grind' or 'sweat'.[32] Later, this kind of running was deplored by the English coach F.A.M. Webster as 'one of the greatest evils of English school athletics … little short of cruelty and produces lasting harm'.[33] The inculcation of fitness through running was thought to be imbricated with an introduction – a rite of passage, almost – to manliness. Baron Pierre de Coubertin, widely regarded as the founder of the modern Olympic Games, observed that, 'No sooner has the young Englishman started to run by himself than he already knows he is a man, and that the tears his sister is allowed to shed are shameful for him'.[34] Rudyard Kipling put it explicitly:

> If you can fill the unforgiving minute
> With sixty seconds worth of distance run,
> Yours is the earth and everything that's in it,
> And – which is more – you'll be a man, my son.[35]

Today, running may form part of the exercise that reduces the amount of time which young children are said to waste. But the Physical Education curriculum often draws a fine line between educational objectives and the training of budding athletes. I will return to this later and here focus on fitness running, mainly with adults in mind.

Time is taken up by work, not play. When adults run it tends to be for reasons concerning their welfare – to keep fit, to enjoy the open air, to escape a shower of rain, or to catch a waiting train or bus. Running as a basis for reproducing a fit workforce or a trim body occurs in a variety of contexts though all display a tendency to abide by quantitative measures and records. In the military, running in uniform and with weapons in hand, but also in unison, creates bonding as well as fitness.

Few would deny that the kinds of frolicsome running described in the previous section assist the fitness and health of the human body. However, the self-consciousness in running to obtain better health is absent in play where spontaneity is the key. Running has long formed part of the fitness movement. Elspeth Huxley, in her biography of Lord Delamere, recalls that in the early years of the twentieth century, Sir Percy Girouard, the governor of British East Africa from 1910–12, took early morning runs around the outskirts of Nairobi dressed in shorts and sweater.[36] During the inter-war period the notion of the 'open-air body' was championed in much of Europe and North America as part of a discipline of fitness with the nation's health, as much as the individual's, in mind. Running, like walking, provided communion with the earth, being at one with the land.[37] However, for much of the twentieth century, public displays of running for fitness were not encouraged and were looked upon as being somewhat bohemian and subject to ridicule. Adults seen running through streets or over open country tended to be serious runners taking part in organized events such as road or cross-county races. Walking was considered much more appropriate as a form of keeping fit, something that was also believed by many serious athletes. As part of his training the great Finnish runner Paavo Nurmi enjoyed brisk walks with his colleagues, a training strategy that he was later to regret having undertaken. With hindsight he wished he had concentrated more on speed.[38]

Welfare running, which was central to the fitness movement that has swept much of the western world since the 1970s, may overlap with the zen of running, as championed by Rohé and others. Running for fun and fitness can also be readily co-opted by the world of commerce – and the world of sport. Looking good soon takes on a meaning dominated by cosmetics and clothes styles; and jogging could all too easily be transformed into an activity dominated by the stop-watch, even transformed into road racing. In other words it could become sportized. Fitness training does not require speed but sportization encourages records and hence a self-consciousness about time – 'an endless, aimless, illusionless performance'.[39]

Jogging and fitness running require *getting* people to run rather than taking pleasure in movement or simply enjoying themselves. According to postmodernist Jean Baudrillard, jogging is not to run but to *make* one's body run. He is adamant that jogging has nothing to do with sport but more with 'an endless functioning' rather than physical exertion.[40] The recreational motorist or the hot-rodder can enjoy an abstract, less tangible, world of speed, detached from the body.[41] The recreational runner, on the other hand, is said by Milan Kundera to be 'always present in his body, forever required to think about his blisters, his exhaustion; when he runs he feels his weight, his age, more conscious than ever of himself and of his time of life'.[42]

Fitness running can also be found as part of the aerobic training that takes running indoors and is accommodated on treadmills in fitness studios, often in sombre, concrete buildings. Here, a simulation of running appears better than the real thing. Commercialization and government policies have led to the development of 'fitness centres' and 'aerobic studios' which are extensions of the school gymnasium. Such adult-focused centres, however, are inhabited by people who have not only often used their automobiles to get them there but are consigned to personal spaces soon after locking their cars. Such training sites are often private (in more ways than one) and commodification is again central to this form of running. In such places running often becomes mechanized, planned, quantified and routine. Here the human body is made to become an extension of the machine. Here is a technological version of 'running on the spot', a traditional recipe of physical education. Quantification is important in fitness running. Pulse rate and blood pressure are monitored; body size is measured. And, at the same time, looking good is at least as important, it seems, as keeping fit. Such fitness regimes can also connote individuals mobilizing themselves for a world of work and commerce.[43]

Running for fitness is, however, far from being unambiguous. In a risk society, the dangers to our health resulting from allegedly health-promoting activities are difficult to predict. As sociologist Chris Shilling points out:

> Having taken up running over several years in the belief that it will make me fitter and healthier, I then learn that the wear and tear of the exercise has permanently damaged my hips. I then adopt a low fat diet in order to safeguard my health, but hear that some of the additives used in margarine may be a contributory factor to heart disease.[44]

Health-related 'body projects', such as running and jogging, are far from lacking in problems and obstacles.

Achievement Running: The Upright Human Body, Space and Time

Children in the UK are statutorily required to run and race at an early age. Running features prominently in an English Physical Education curriculum. It states that notions of competition should be inculcated from the age of 5; from 7 to 11 years of age students should be taught 'to develop and refine basic techniques of running, e.g. over short distances, over longer distances, in relays...' They must be taught 'to measure, compare and improve their own performances'. In later years they learn to 'apply the techniques, skills and competition rules' specific to at least one running event. They should learn the effects of taking part in aerobic and anaerobic events and to apply the 'relevant mechanical principles underpinning performance. They should take part in competitions and, again, refine their performances. By the age of 16 they should all learn how to 'plan, carry out and evaluate an effective personal training schedule' for a selected event or events.[45] There is no choice. These edicts are enshrined in a state curriculum, reflecting a paternalism that seeks a stake in children's bodies.

The authors of the (English) national curriculum for primary and secondary schools, represented above, presumably saw running as a contribution to physical education, that is, the paternalistic enforcement of running in the interest of young peoples' fitness and health. However, it can equally be seen as an initiation into serious running in the achievement mould. This is a more malign reading. As Jean-Marie Brohm noted, 'a child who practices sport is no longer playing but is taking his (sic) place in a world of serious matters'.[46] Worse, according to Berthold Brecht, was the fact that 'real sport begins when it's long past being good for your health'.[47] For some, running becomes work and 'working always breaks down workers' health'.[48] Learning running technique, maintaining personal records, seeking personal best performances and taking part in competitions, as stated in the Physical Education *National Curriculum* for England, all resonate strongly with achievement running. Indeed, the former sports-loving prime minister John Major seemed to believe that the source of future Olympic gold medals lay in the early initiation to serious running in the nation's primary schools.[49] In doing so physical education came to be seen as the base of a hierarchical structure that has elite competitive sports at the top, something that has become common well beyond the UK.[50] However, despite the prescriptions of school curricula, most children do not proceed to take part in serious running in post-school life and, instead, go on to lead 'normal lives'.

Serious running does not only colonize the bodies of youngsters. The elderly are also urged to participate in 'masters' or 'veterans' races. Associated with such events are the statistics, ranking lists and records characterized by racing per se. Sportized running also provides opportunities for the disabled (as conventionally defined), the apogee of which is the Paralympics. For people with learning and physical difficulties, engagement in serious, achievement-oriented sports is justified by modern society as 'triumph over adversity', the generation of self-esteem, or the satisfaction of 'equal opportunities'. Tuan, however, sees such activities as 'unintentionally cruel'. Watching a square dance performed by paraplegics in their wheelchairs, he felt that they looked ridiculous.[51] It does not seem to have dawned on him that to run 25 laps of the 400-metre track by any athlete can be read as equally ridiculous.

Achievement running is work-like. Sometimes athletes earn their livings from running. In one of his earlier writings, Tuan notes that the space of work is essentially directed.[52] A project – work or a race – has a beginning and an end. Its logic is characterized by the spatial metaphor, 'linear'. Physical work – the race included – requires the physical organization of space. A manufacturing process – making a car or making a race – starts here (now) and ends there (then). The space is historical and directed. Tuan is explicit about sport space, pointing out the elongated (start and finish) space of the work line. The 100 metres sprint is the paradigm. However, he also recognizes that the shape of racetracks is oval. The starting and finishing lines are clearly marked, but in racing the destination itself has no inherent significance; it can indeed be identical with the starting point: 'What is important is speed – speed in directed space.'[53]

Speed is widely regarded as being central to achievement running. From the late nineteenth century, the main aim of racing has been to achieve ever-faster times, suggests Henning Eichberg; Kurt Weis avers that in sport, speed is the consuming element with everything else being secondary to it; Otto Penz likewise states that time and speed seem to be 'the dominant principles which shape the modern form of sport'.[54] 'And in a race', observes Paul Weiss, 'an effort is made either to reduce the amount of time that is used, or to increase the amount of space that is traversed.'[55] Attempts to establish the longest distance that can be run in a given time have declined in attractiveness and importance. The record for how far can be covered in one hour is still recognized by the International Association of Athletic Federations (IAAF) but is rarely contested these days. Perhaps our interest in speed is greater than it is in distance. In an age of instant gratification, most emphasis in track meets is placed on sprint events. Paradoxically, the only way such races can be judged or appreciated is by slowing them down, thanks to slow motion and photo-finish technology. Fewer 10,000-metre track races take place today than in yesteryear. However, as Weiss reminds us, a race does not tell us the speed that is possible but the speed that is possible 'under such and such antecedently defined conditions and commonly accepted rules'.[56] Such conditions have resulted in sprinters such as Carl Lewis having lost 100 metres races that he had actually run faster than his opponents. This is explained by the fact that Lewis's reaction time ('the time it takes for the starting signal to translate through eardrum, brain, nerves, muscles') was

relatively slow – 'on the order of 140 milliseconds, compared with 115
to 120 milliseconds for the faster starters'.[57] Additionally, the physiologist
A.V. Hill noted that there were different qualities of speed, alluding to the
distribution of speed over space. Assuming that fatigue should be minimized,
the 'best speed' for a runner wishing to run a given distance in a given time
would be when it is the same throughout the race.[58] Paavo Nurmi (to whom
I will allude later) was widely cited as a practitioner of such even-paced
running, though it is possible that a risk-taking athlete might be willing to
maximize fatigue in order to break a record.

The sports-worker may experience the sensation of speed during a race.
But victory, a particular performance, or the defeat of a competitor is of
greater importance than sensory experiences; the athlete 'is occupied with
the impersonal and the distant'.[59] However, recreational running in the forest
and meadow or on the beach encourages the sensation of speed itself, in a
world in which meaning is the sole property of the runner him- or herself.

In *Space and Place*, Tuan provides an enticing diagram (Figure 1.3)
that unintentionally presents a framework for a geographical exploration
of sports. It is around this diagram that, in this and the following chapter,
I explore the achievement configuration of running. The vertical axis in
Figure 1.3 reaches from low to high. Excellence, in running and elsewhere,

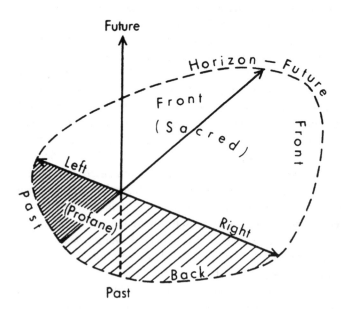

Figure 1.3 'Upright human body, space and time. Space projected from the
body is biased toward front and tight. The future is ahead and "up". The
past is behind and "below"' (Tuan, *Space and Place*, p.35).

is elevated. As Tuan notes, 'superior' derives from the Latin meaning 'higher'; 'excel' is another Latin word for 'high'.[60] Athletic status is designated 'high' and 'low'; being high in the ranking lists is lauded, being low is denigrated. Sports such as achievement running are organized hierarchically. At the top are the global extravaganzas, the Olympics and World Championships; at the bottom are the lowly local competitions.

Next, consider front space. It is primarily visual; it is perceived as the future. It is sacred space, towards the horizon, yet to be reached. Back space is in the past, the profane.[61] The relevance of the frontal space to running is that in human space (geography) humankind has constantly sought the horizon and the world beyond it.[62] In achievement sports (unlike play) athletes are thought to constantly seek the record through the generation of greater speed. The record, like frontal space, is sacred, something to be worshipped, something to be achieved (like the horizon). The record is about conquering distance and compressing space by time. Of course, time cannot act to overcome space; it is processes and events that do so, undertaken by human beings.[63] But once the record is found, like the horizon, a new one appears. As early as the 1920s the English newspaper *The Athletic News* stated that theoretically the four-minute mile was possible.[64] Opposition to this view continued into the 1930s but those who believed that the four-minute mile was impossible were proved wrong. Their ideas of a fixed limit rather than an ever-receding horizon were confounded when it was finally achieved in 1954. Today it is commonplace and a time of four minutes is considered a modest performance, having been achieved by schoolboys and men beyond their fortieth year.

Eichberg sees the history of running as a 'one way street'.[65] By this he means that since the nineteenth century nothing has happened to change the fundamental direction taken by serious running. He sees running being dominated by the 'production of results' and the 'prevalence of speed'.[66] Indeed, in the Olympic triad, *citius-altius-fortius*, the time factor is given priority. At a global scale this has certainly been the case, track racing becoming a 'pure history of records'.[67] A glimpse at the difference between world records in 1900 and 2002 illustrate the apparent validity of both Eichberg's notion of the recent history of track racing being 'the history of records and of movement techniques that help improve performances' and the centrality of speed and time-space compression, alluded to earlier.[68] In 1900 the best recorded 100 metres time for men was 10.8 seconds; in 2002 it was 9.79 seconds. Respective times for the 10,000 metres are 31 minutes 40 seconds and 26 minutes 22.75 seconds.[69]

Athletes and scientists each seek record performances, denying athletic limits as much as the horizon. The star runner has to keep returning to another, and more demanding, performance. Athletes seem to find it necessary to instil a sense of 'constant lack, of recurring incompletion', Juha Heikkala arguing that a 'limit cannot be set, because this would collapse the basic structural principle of high-performance sports, which is the constant enhancement of performance'.[70] Like pornography, the record seems to 'generate an appetite for more extreme versions of itself'.[71] However, in 1984 the sports scientist Ernst Jokl did predict (as others have done) the future records for the different track events, in this case for the year 2000 (Table 1.1).[72] When 2000 came, in several cases his predictions had been exceeded, records being set ahead of their time. This is well illustrated by the case of the women's 10,000 metres record achieved by the Chinese runner Wang Junxia, which was almost a minute faster than Jokl predicted. Even so, for the serious runner, where time is money, it seems that *enough is never enough*.[73] For many, of course, it is this tendency towards excess, this freedom to exaggerate, and the possibility of extreme exertion that makes serious sports attractive.

Table 1.1
PREDICTIONS OF RUNNING HORIZONS (JOKL)

Event	Jokl's Projection (1984)	Actual (2000)
Men, 100 metres	9.74s	9.79s
Men, 200 metres	18.96s	19.32s
Men, 400 metres	41.09s	43.18s
Men, 800 metres	1m 38.4s	1m 41.11s
Men, 1500 metres	3m 26.1s	3m 26.00s
Men, mile	3m 44.6s	3m 43.13s
Men, 3,000 m steeplechase	7m 52.4s	7m 55.72s
Men, 5,000 metres	12m 51.4s	12m 39.36s
Men, 10,000 metres	26m 34.8s	26m 22.70s
Women, 100 metres	10.56s	10.49s
Women, 200 metres	20.97s	21.34s
Women, 400 metres	47.1s	47.60s
Women, 800 metres	1m 49.5s	1m 53.28
Women, 1,500 metres	3m 46.1s	3m 50.46s
Women, 5,000 metres	14m 32.2s	14m 28.09s
Women, 10,000 metres	30m 29.6s	29m 31.78s

The time-space compression witnessed in the overall acceleration of athletic performance on the running track parallels, at a different scale, the compression going on in global time-space.[74] Such changes are often thought to be the result of new technologies. In running, these technologies include the synthetic running track, starting blocks, athletic footwear and clothing, medicine and pharmacology. The Australian miler John Landy felt sure that the reason why he never achieved the four-minute mile in Australia was because of the poor quality of Antipodean running tracks.[75] However, the technological advances that have, in part at least, improved performances and results are certainly ambiguous. For a start, the use of technological aids raises the question about who 'owns' the improved performances. Pierre de Coubertin recognized this. In 1936 he foresaw track shoes and tracks 'with springs that would somehow throw the runner forward with each step'. Such advances, and those noted above, would have the effect of making movement easier but 'some of the athletic effort would then be done by the equipment the athlete is using'. Hence, 'the speed achieved in this way will not be entirely his own'.[76] Coubertin's observation also recognizes the profoundly technologized quality of the sportized body and that this is nothing particularly new.

Additionally, the assumption that such technological 'developments' necessarily result in time-space compression can be viewed as a form of technological determinism. Jeremy Stein notes that the 'danger here is to assume and exaggerate the consequences of technology'. He poses the question: 'Are new technologies always faster and more efficient than earlier ones?'[77] The consideration of *only* technological improvements ignores the social processes in which technology is embedded. For example, improvements in running records (that is, faster times) may have resulted from the fact that more people have been taking up running over time. Concomitantly, if fewer people took part, time-space compression might be replaced by time-space expansion (that is, slowing down).

I will return to the idea of time-space compression later but for the moment consider what would happen if world records did stop being improved upon? Declining public interest might set in and the sport might die out through lack of interest. Equally possible, however, is that times will be recorded in finer and finer increments of a second. Should the 100 metres record ever become stuck for many years at 9.66 seconds, with several athletes achieving this time, the event will be timed to one-thousandth of a second and a 9.659 result will soon appear as a new record. When timing to a thousandth of a second presents the same problem, the sport will adopt measurement to the fourth decimal point. There is, in theory, no limit to the speed that can be run.

Alternatively, it could be recognized that the shorter the distance raced, the more demanding the minima required to break a record. Sprinters suffer discrimination because they are asked to improve the 100 metres record by at least 0.10 per cent whereas 10,000 metres runners need only 0.00062 per cent. The logical outcome of this is that records should be set in percentages rather than seconds.[78] A less likely scenario is one in which performance gains precedence over result. But how, asks James McNeish, in the voice of 1936 Olympic 1,500 metres champion Jack Lovelock, could one 'perform a race' in a manner never to be improved upon? 'Perfection might apply to something like gymnastics, or a score in marksmanship, or parachuting where you might hit a target dead on. It could [even] apply to a short story' but to apply it to running 'was silly'.[79]

How fast could I have run? Many runners ask this question when reviewing their personal records. Marty Liquori observes that the 'runner is often vexed by the visceral feeling that he has not yet done his best, and the thought prods him towards seeking that one race where he extends himself to the fullest degree possible and achieves the maximum'.[80] Had, in 1956, Gordon Pirie, my boyhood hero, run on a synthetic track at, say, Monaco on a warm, late summer evening, rather than on saturated cinder track on a rainy night in Bergen, Norway, how much faster than the world record breaking time of 13 minutes 36.8 seconds would he have run? Some would say at least 10 seconds. But we will never know and, as I implied earlier, it is dangerous to suggest that a single factor like the weather (or technology) is anything but one of many determinants of athletic performance. The Finnish running hero Paavo Nurmi, thought he could run around 1 minute 51 seconds for the 800 metres when his best time was 1 minute 56.3 seconds. For each of the middle- and long-distance events that he contested, Nurmi claimed in 1926 that he could potentially make substantial improvements in events from 800 metres to the marathon, though he never achieved any of them (see Table 1.2).

Table 1.2
PAAVO NURMI: BEST PERFORMANCES AND
SELF-PREDICTIONS

Event	Best time	Predicted best time
800 metres	1m 56.3s	1m 51s–1m 51.5s
1,500 metres	3m 52.6s	3m 46s–3m 47s
1 mile	4m 10.4s	4m 6s–4m 7s
3,000 metres	8m 28.6s	8m 17s–8m 18s
5,000 metres	14m 28.6s	14m 15s
10,000 metres	30m 06.2s	29m 40s

Sources: Antero Raevuori, *Paavo Nurmi: Juoksijain Kuningas* (Poorvo: Werner Söderström, 1997), p.166.

What do the statistics that surround achievement running mean? They define achievement and progress – progress towards the record. They are also said to serve as a universal athletic currency, enabling unambiguous comparisons to be made between places and regions. The cold statistic, shorn of any context, can reveal apparent differences in the performances of human groups. In the 1950s it was shown that whereas the 'Caucasian'/'white' best performance for 3 miles was 13 minutes 14.8 seconds by the Hungarian

Sándor Iharos, that for the 'negriform'/'black' was 13 minutes 45.0 seconds by the Kenyan, Nyandika Maiyoro.[81] Apart from the assumption that people can be categorized into 'racial groups', this is, I think, a malign form of statistical application, an application of pseudo-objectivity. Such a comparison is spurious, not solely because of its racialized language. The statistics do not compare like with like. Iharos had half-a-century of western body culture behind him and a scientific coach in Mihily Igloi. He ran with other brilliant state-aided Hungarians – Istvan Rózavölgyi and Lázsló Tabori – and ran on one of the best running tracks in the world at the Népstadion in Budapest. Maiyoro, on the other hand, came from a nation that had not taken part in the Olympic Games until 1956 and lacked the opportunities to train and compete that were then available to Europeans. But decontextualized statistics, ignoring history, culture and milieu, confirmed – indeed, 'proved' – the prevailing view that at distances beyond 400 metres the black runner was inferior.

Achievement running is a world of numbers, ranks, hierarchy, records and a sense of certainty. The Swedish geographer Gunnar Olsson observed that 'those who race are different from other people. .... They have left their hearts at home, for otherwise they cannot be objective. They feed on a diet of certainty and get upset by ambiguity.'[82] With these words Olsson sums up achievement running. It is a serious business. The record provides certainty and security – 'safety in numbers'. The statistic, the rank, the record, identifies the runner as a number – a 10-second man, a 15-minute woman, decontextualizing the performance and dehumanizing the runners. Athletes become 'statistical persons'.[83] The measured time, to a tenth or hundredth of a second, appears definitive and unambiguous. Tuan avers that 'for children *and athletes* life is joyous in its vitality, and vitality is motion during which time is forgotten, space becomes freedom, self and world unite'.[84] However, in the world of serious running, time is far from forgotten: it is a central and permanent concern. And for the athlete space can be a constraint rather than freedom; space always has to be overcome. The confinements of the running track, of the starting and finishing lines, of the lane boundaries, are always present.

Toward Slowness

Although taken for granted today, and central to achievement sports, the record – which implies an increase in speed – has not been without its critics. The late-nineteenth-century observers of early-modern running, Montague Shearman and Pierre de Coubertin, were upset by the record mania of their day. The former was 'heretical enough to believe that the worshipping of records is idolatrous, and inconsistent with the creed of the true sportsman'.[85] In an article in *Figaro* in 1903, the latter felt likewise.[86] Some of their observations resonate with the current situation in sports. Shearman deplored records that were made with the help of pacemakers, or a high-class athlete who competed against modest opponents. Races, he felt, should be between athletes of equal ability with the emphasis placed on performance rather than result. 'The sooner, therefore, that athletes learn that time is a test of speed but nothing else, the better for the sport. The race is not always to the speediest, and to possess speed without pluck or judgment is to have very little title to genuine merit', he concludes.[87] Shearman's de-emphasis on records and speed sounds strange in the twenty-first century but it is not without support, particularly from philosophers such as Sigmund Loland who pleads for greater moderation and more subjective, qualitative progress in sports.[88]

The notion of *slowness* that Loland implies in his advocacy of moderation has perhaps failed to gain the attention that it deserves from sports (and social) researchers.[89] However, the novelist Kundera asks:

> Why has the pleasure of slowness disappeared? Ah, where have they gone, the amblers of yesteryear? Where have they gone, those loafing heroes of folk song, those vagabonds who roam from one mill to another and bed down under the stars? Have they vanished along with footpaths, with grasslands and clearings, with nature?[90]

In these words Kundera nostalgically bemoans the seeming demise of a slower pace of life in general. But in a world predicated on speed, slowness, even in athletic victory, is not generally respected. Even an amateur, such as the English track and field coach F.A.M. Webster, felt that 'there is more pleasure to be derived from beating one's personal record than from winning a championship with a mediocre performance'.[91] The Australian world mile record holder John Landy repeated this sentiment some decades later. He said: 'I would rather be beaten in 3.58 than win in 4.10. There's no point in running a 4.10 mile.'[92] In an environment where speed is considered worthier than victory, the old adage 'slow and steady wins the race' carries little weight.

Certainly, respect for slowness was absent at the Goodwill Games of 2001, held in Brisbane, Australia. At this event, two 5,000 metres races were held, one for women and another for men. The women's race was won in a faster time (15 minutes 12.22 seconds) than the men's (15 minutes 26.10 seconds), an outcome that was generally deplored. The reporter for *The Guardian* newspaper went so far as to declare that the slowness of the men's race 'went beyond farce and brought the sport into disrepute'. The crowed issued 'boos and catcalls' and the athletes ran 'at little better than a jog with no pacemaker to stir things up'.[93] The runners ran the first 11 laps at a 'funereal' pace but the winner, Paul Bitok, covered the last 400 metres in 51 seconds, winning the US$20,000 prize money. Slowness was seen in an even more deplorable light in 1954 when a Soviet middle-distance runner, Vladimir Okorokov, competing in the national 1,500 metres championship, recorded a time of 3 minutes 49.8 in his heat but (only) 3 minutes 54.6 in winning the final. His relative slowness (an effective strategy to achieve victory) resulted in him being denied his national title and prize. An official pronouncement stated: 'Instead of running to the best of his possibilities, he let others set the pace and just forged ahead in the last few yards to win a cheap victory.'[94] These stories, and the responses to them, reveal the significance of both speed and the result in achievement running. Performances, tactical though they might have been, and with exciting sprint finishes, are felt to be devalued if they are characterized by overall slowness. To race is not enough. For athletes to run slowly is to transgress the norms of modern running.

Despite the widespread denigration of slowness in serious running, there may be more of it around than there seems at first sight. Acceleration is a relative concept; there cannot be a speeding-up without also a slowing-down. It is never simply a matter of speed but of speed and slowness.[95] Roger Bannister's 3 minutes 59.4 seconds for the mile made previous runners, such as Gunder Hägg, Arne Andersson and Sydney Wooderson, look much slower than they had previously appeared. In some countries it appears that slowness has replaced acceleration in athletic performance. This has occurred in absolute as well as relative terms. In such countries athletes are running slower than previously and some national records have stopped being improved upon. Put another way, in some places (for the time being, at least) the perfect race seems to have been run. For example, the British 800 metres record has not been improved upon since 1981; nor the 5,000 metres since 1982. Today's performances are profane in comparison with the apparently sacred records of Sebastian Coe and David Moorcroft. There are more dramatic cases: the Australian 800 metres record was set in 1968, that for New Zealand in 1962. The 1,500 metres record for Estonia was run in 1966, that for Finland in 1972. The Egyptian 5,000 metres record was established in 1971, while that for Hungary was in 1968.

Another way of looking at the national differences in time-shrinkage is to consider the year in which a current national record would have broken the world record. For example, the 5,000 metres record for Afghanistan, set in 1991, would have improved on the world's best ever performance as it stood in 1899. Respective dates for the records of Albania, set in 1990, is 1932, Venezuela, set in 1987, is 1955, and India, set in 1992, is 1965. These are a small sample of such records in nations where time has stood still.[96] In some places, if the average performances of runners over a particular distance are examined, average times are seen to be getting slower. While in global terms the average time of top runners is improving dramatically, in individual nations it is getting slower. For example, the graph depicting the time of the tenth fastest 5,000 metres runner in the UK, plotted against the years 1970–2001, depicts a U-shaped pattern. The slowest times are found in the early 1970s and the late 1990s. Perhaps progress does not seem inevitable and the world is full of 'old time', as the geographer Edward Ullman put it.[97] Where changes in speed are concerned, the national is not necessarily a reduced mirror image of the global. Accompanying the global improvement in speed is a sense, in some countries, of running getting slower. Time-space compression possesses uneven geographies.

Where a slowing down has occurred, it may be the result of a 'declining significance of industrial work as a paradigm of human activity and modernity'.[98] Running may have become too fast and, as a result, involve too much risk. In some countries running as a work-like activity may no longer be attractive to many people. They may have been emancipated from the constraints of its tradition. In world terms, time-space compression in running (and other kinds of movement, human or otherwise) was traditionally regarded as a metropolitan or 'western' phenomenon. For much of the twentieth century this was almost overwhelmingly the case, simply because about three-quarters of the world's population had not been exposed, for any length of time, to running in its modern form. To take one typical example, in 1936 the fastest recorded mile run by a Kenyan was thought to be 4 minutes 38.5 seconds by Kumunya.[99] The world record at the time, however, set by the American Glenn Cunningham, was 4 minutes 6.8 seconds. Time-space was much more compressed in the USA than in Kenya. At the time of writing, however, it is African middle-distance runners who are compressing time-space faster than those in global metropolises. The Europeans and Americans have been squeezed out. In 2001, 27 of the 100 fastest 1,500 metres runners in the world came from Kenya (39 from Africa); in the 5,000 metres the figures were 44 from Kenya (60 from Africa). In these, and other middle- and long-distance events, world records are held by Africans. However, the geography of 'production' of world-class African runners is itself very uneven, the best runners coming from a very small number of African nations.[100] Again, I stress that the human ability to annihilate space by time has occurred much more unevenly – both between and within continents – than is often suggested.

Records Beyond Quantification

How else might the record be read? Quantification and the record are two characteristics of serious running which are less evident in play and fitness running, though far from absent in the latter. Sports records might be called 'anaesthetic' because they are objective, bare, cold statistics devoid of any feeling or sensory pleasure; they reduce performances to results, a moving human body to a number.[101] In seeking different kinds of records of achievement running, I now return to Figure 1.3. The past and back-space are described as profane. In sport they are best described as nostalgia but stand in the same relationship to the record as does sacred to profane. Nostalgia is a major phenomenon in sports.[102] It presents a human(e) characteristic of achievement sports that lies next to the scientific qualities found in statistics and records. It is a world of past achievements, glories, golden ages and heroes. Biographies of past stars provide evidence of such affection for past deeds. Sports museums and halls of fame generate a sense of nostalgia coupled with religion. Halls of fame, such as the United States track and field hall of fame in Indianapolis or the national distance running hall of fame in Utica, New York, combine being both a museum and a shrine, dedicated to praising athletic heroes and displaying various quasi-religious relics or memorabilia of the past. It has been suggested that 'the ultimate *raison d'être* for a sports hall of fame, like the ancient Greek sanctuary, is the glorification of the sporting heritage'.[103] Heroic figures of yesteryear are also immortalized as statues and in other iconic forms. All these records differ from those of quantification, but records they are, subjective, aestheticized in writing, painting and sculpture.

In Finland, running put the country on the world map in the years following its political independence. The great distance runners Hannes Kolehmainen and Paavo Nurmi were each commemorated as statues in their respective hometowns of Kuopio (Figure 1.4) and Turku. Two other statues of Nurmi exist, one of which is near the Olympic Stadium in Helsinki.[104] Likewise, a statue of Grete Waitz can be found next to the Bislett Stadium in Oslo, in recognition of her remarkable contribution to women's distance running in the 1980s (Figure 1.5). Furthermore, Nurmi and Waitz have each appeared on postage stamps of their respective nations, with Nurmi even appearing on the old Finnish 10 mark banknote. These are sure signs of national affection and heroism. After Jean Sibelius, Nurmi is arguably the most well-known person in his nation's history. Because of the identification of Kolehmainen and Nurmi with Finland's nationhood, their statues cannot be regarded as politically innocent: they are 'potent symbols of values', their 'moral messages can be eloquent expressions of human ideals'.[105] They are physical manifestations of a national achievement ideology. Other track athletes have been recorded in statues. In Addis Ababa, Abebe Bikila, the two-time Olympic marathon winner from Ethiopia, is memorialized while his successor, Haile Gebriselasse, is represented in huge murals, and in Kingston, Jamaica a composite statue commemorates the 1952 Olympic 1,600 metres relay victory of the Jamaican team – Herb Mackenly, Arthur Wint, Leslie Laing and George Rhoden. I cannot speak for the statues in Ethiopia and Jamaica

Figure 1.4 Hannes Kolehmainen, Kuopio, Finland

Figure 1.5 Grete Waitz, Oslo, Norway

but in the cases of Waitz, Kolehmainen and Nurmi there is no evidence of any graffiti, no video surveillance, and no barriers enclosing them.[106] The absence of such enclosure and surveillance tells us that the athletes are still respected, loved and live on in peoples' heroic histories. Such statues are not, therefore, 'isolated icons or disembodied texts but part of the material and ideological fabric'[107] of achievement running and a form of popular nationalism.

Somewhat more mundane examples exist of such memorials, though their modesty in no ways suggests a lessening of significance. Near the entry to the University of Iowa track and field stadium, abutting the nondescript strip where Iowa City meets Coralville, there is a small plaque, set in a wall. It records the achievements of the former university track coach Francis X. Cretzmeyer. At the time of Cretzmeyer's appointment as coach, it was widely felt that black athletes had 'great speed but little stamina'.[108] During his time at Iowa he recruited two black athletes who were to become Olympic-class distance runners. He also recruited them to the last place in the United States most track enthusiasts would have expected – Iowa, the American heartland. One of the runners was Ted Wheeler, the other Charles 'Deacon' Jones. Only track *aficionados* today know their names, but in the late 1950s Wheeler was one of the best milers in the USA. He competed on the US Olympic team in 1956 and became track coach of his *alma mater*. Jones was a NCAA cross-country champion and an Olympic steeplechaser in 1956 and 1960. But the memorial draws attention to 'Cretz' who, through his avoidance of conventional wisdom, nurtured two black athletes who transgressed the norms of 1950s middle-distance running. As successful distance runners they were simply out of place.

In downtown Coos Bay, Oregon, next to the Chamber of Commerce Visitor Information Center, is the Steve Prefontaine Memorial, a plaque in memory of one of America's great runners, who was born in the small town of Coos Bay. In many ways it is unremarkable, an embossed head, details of birth and death, a list of quantified results.[109] On Skyline Boulevard in Eugene, Oregon, the following sign has been painted in white on a roadside rock face: 'PRE R.I.P. 5-30-75'. It is the handcrafted memorial at the site of Prefontaine's death and has been maintained for over 20 years. Other such etchings exist there (Figure 1.6). It has become known as 'Pre's Rock'.[110] Many runners visit the site every year, making a pilgrimage, leaving bouquets of flowers, gifts and mementos of their races, shoes, hats, student ID cards, poems, race medals, ribbons, numbers, handkerchiefs and so forth. The site is a roadside shrine to the memory of Prefontaine.[111] In many ways, it is more powerful than the memorial.

A cult figure among North American track fans, 'Pre' was a precocious running talent. He was killed in a car crash on Skyline Boulevard in 1975 while he was still a rising star. As a University of Oregon student he was

Figure 1.6 'The crash site became an instant memorial' (Photograph by
Don Chadez, reproduced with permission)

already a state hero with a fan base throughout the United States. He held
every US track record from 2,000 to 10,000 metres and from 2 miles to
6 miles at the time of his death in 1975. I will have more to say about
Prefontaine later, but at this stage I simply want to comment on the act of
leaving artefacts at the site of his death. It has been suggested that where
'people leave objects in the face of death', presence is paired with absence.[112]
What do the artefacts symbolize? Gifts of beauty and culture in the face of
death? The gifts left by pilgrims suggest reciprocity, something to exchange
for the experience of a holy place.

  What more can be read into such athletic icons? First, they stand in praise
of great athletes, not fitness fanatics or children who unselfconsciously enjoy
the bodily sensations of freedom. They are about heroes, heroic because
of quantified performance, or more precisely, quantified results – since in
serious running results take precedence over performance.[113] Sometimes,
these statues of athletes are almost like idols and sometimes those they represent were once living idols, providing reassurance and comfort to some
people.[114] They evoke nostalgia, a world of performances that today appear
ordinary, mundane, routine, poor – like the four minute mile. In this sense,
the world that such statuary evokes *is* a world of the profane – a world of
going down and out of the ranking lists – to be mocked and abused were the
statues and shrines not there to remind us of these athletes' glorious pasts.

The time you won your town the race
We chaired you through the market-place;
Man and boy stood cheering by,
And home we brought you shoulder-high.

To-day, the road all runners come,
Shoulder-high we bring you home,
And set you at your threshold down,
Townsman of a stiller town.

Smart lad, to slip betimes away
From fields where glory does not stay,
And early though the laurel grows
It withers quicker than the rose.

Eyes the shady night has shut
Cannot see the record cut,
And silence sounds no worse than cheers
After earth has stopped the ears:

Now you will not swell the rout
Of lads that wore their honours out,
Runners whom renown outran
And the name died before the man.

So set, before the echoes fade,
The fleet foot on the sill of shade,
And hold to the low lintel up
The still-defended challenge-cup.

And round that early-laurelled head
Will flock to gaze the strengthless dead,
And find unwithered on its curls
The garland briefer than a girl's.

Figure 1.7 'To an Athlete Dying Young' by A.E. Housman

In 1956, Ted Wheeler's mile time of 4 minutes 4.7 seconds was the fastest ever by a black athlete. Today the equivalent time is about 20 seconds faster (assuming that one can meaningfully operationalize the term 'black athlete' in this way). Paavo Nurmi, the 'flying Finn' of the 1920s and 1930s, today lies low in the ranks of the Finnish all-time ranking lists. Nurmi is said to have told his son Matti that he would never be a great runner, to which his son replied, 'I'll beat your times though' – a poignant tale about 'progress', speed and sports.[115] Results (and the training that produced them) that were once adequate are now obsolete. There is no public esteem in matching past records. And all record holders are eventually displaced.

The story about Nurmi recalls a poem by A.E. Housman titled 'To an Athlete Dying Young' (see Figure 1.7). It is a story of a young athlete who dies following a popular victory. In an insightful analysis, Allen Guttmann reads the poem as failure being success. This is because the athlete's death (he 'slips betimes away') spares him the metaphorical death that awaits him when he reaches his peak and begins to decline, seeing (as Nurmi did) modest athletes bettering his times ('glory does not stay'). At his 'threshold' (that is, grave), he will never experience defeat, never witness his record being eroded, and will never be ignored by those who had once idolized him.[116]

In seeking to humanize and moderate running, it may be salutary to re-evaluate the notion of the record. A recognition of the distinction between the two kinds of record, anaesthetic and aesthetic, may, building on Loland's idea of moderation, mark a start in this direction.

Other Runnings

Several examples of other kinds of runners who seek achievement are less familiar to most athletic fans. Basically, for many elite athletes, running is work. It is also work-like for many other runners whose results are much more modest than those of the stars. In past times other runners earned their living through their running. Preston, the flying butcher from Leeds in England, won more money from his running than he earned in his shop. In 1688 he beat the King's favourite runner.[117] The courier was a major carrier of information, widely employed before the age of mechanized transport. Runners were employed in the colonies as well as at home. In Kenya, for example, the district commissioners used runners as messengers and it was recorded that commissioner St John Orde Browne's favourite runner covered 92 miles in 28 hours, having to contend with fairly hilly country, darkness and the risk of wild animals.[118] The European urge to quantify and record was not restricted to the running tracks of Oxford and Cambridge.

Running as an occupation, as a transport medium, declined with the growth of mechanical transport. Professional running today is part of the entertainment industry. Elite track and road runners run for their living, if not their life. Prize money can be substantial. Stars such as sprinter Maurice Greene have earned $100,000 for a single 100 metres race.[119] Additional income can be made from advertising and by athletes giving their names to merchandise of various kinds. In a different age this was impossible, contravening as it did the amateur code. While professional footballers and cricketers could help sell hair cream or jock straps, runners were forbidden from supplementing their income in such ways.

Track runners can also earn money from their role as pacemakers. Chronobiologists define a pacemaker as 'an entity adopted or influencing rhythmic activity'.[120] As evidenced earlier by Shearman, human pacemakers in running have long been deplored. Pacemakers are human hares, 'deluxe hares' in 'cuckoo-clock racing', in the words of James McNeish[121] – purchased or paid to run ahead of the field and to set a record pace or regulate the other runners' sense of time. They rarely complete the race and drop out when their task is finished. It seems to me that they are, to some extent, dehumanised when paid (good money, it is true) to work in this way. However, it is not always quite so simple and the mechanical human pacemaker can, on occasions, turn out to be a hero who upsets the script. In 1981, the American miler Tom Byers was chosen for the task of pacemaker in a 1,500 metres race in Oslo, which included the world record holder for the mile, Steve Ovett. Byers opened up a large gap on the field. At 800 metres he was 40 metres ahead of the next runner. Towards the final stages of the race he felt that he was so far ahead that he could win – which he proceeded to do. The runner that no-one had expected to even finish had assumed the role of victor. Gebauer notes that what athletes seek in competition is their *chance* – 'the fortuitous accrual of positive opportunity'. Byers may have threatened 'the meritorious aspect of achievement'[122] – an outsider nullifying the expected result – but Ovett couldn't avoid smiling as he finished in second place.

Tuan poses the question: 'Is there a ladder of aspiration or pretension, at one end of which are the exuberantly or crassly playful and at the other the deeply serious and real?'[123] My answer would be that running and racing respectively represent each end of the ladder. Today, achievement running is less about health and happiness or fun and fitness than about seeking the result or the record. Indeed, it seems that serious running, when aided by pharmaceutical aids of various kinds or by excessive 'training', can be dangerous and injurious to health. Sports medicine and the associated practitioners of medicine and surgery have forged an occupation and an industry dependent on athletic injuries. Yet it is almost impossible to conceive of even the most paternalistic of governments intervening to ban serious sports and hence prevent sports' injuries.

Caillois regarded serious sport as the highest form of play, using the term *agon* to describe it.[124] It lies at the polar extreme in relation to *paida*. But can playfulness and improvisation continue to exist in serious running, a 'cult of achievement' or 'meritocracy in action'?[125] This depends on time, space and the strength of the competition. All other things being equal, the shorter the distance that is raced, the less time there is for a mistake or playfulness. By distracting concentration from the finish line, the 100 metres sprinter runs the risk of losing. In this event, the paradigm of achievement sports, there is no time or space for improvisation.[126] It is a race that involves pure speed with hardly any time for tactics. But in a 10,000 metres track race, it is possible to stumble or fall over, yet still win the race, something that would be almost impossible in the 100 metres. The Finn Lasse Viren demonstrated that it was possible to crash to the ground and still emerge victorious in the 1972 Olympic 10,000 metres final. He recalled, 'I got up instinctively, but at no time did I think that I had lost the race'.[127] And if a winner is sufficiently far ahead of the rest of the field, he can playfully gesture to the crowd and display pride and exhilaration in his victory. Sometimes such behaviour is construed as arrogance but for victorious athletes it is a way of showing a less serious face (a human face) to the world around them.

In this chapter I have considered three configurations of running. It could be argued that society should pay more attention to frolic and fitness and less to achievement sports. Which of these configurations should be privileged and valued in society is, to some extent, an ethical question. It is one I will return to in the final chapter.

2

Running Ways

Human power over nature seems inescapable. The construction of places for running (tracks, stadiums and arenas, for example) readily leads to a view that achievement sport is anti-nature. Such a view might be expected, particularly from deep ecologists.[1] After all, topographies are levelled and fields and forests are destroyed and replaced by concrete bowls and synthetic surfaces. Two of Tuan's books, *Dominance and Affection* and *Segmented Worlds and Self*, can inform a reading of running's physical milieu. The former tells how human power and design, expended on improving the 'productivity' of the landscape of running, is a form of power, but power that is ambivalent. The latter points to the ways in which running places have become increasingly broken down into segments or geometries, in so doing individualizing the athlete. Bodily movement takes place in time and space. It also requires spaces and places. Although serious running takes place on roads (for example, the marathon), fields (cross country and fell running) and in forests (orienteering), it is the track that accommodates the most well-known varieties, from sprinting to middle-distance races up to 10 kilometres. It is the red oval surrounded by the concrete bowl that forms the focal point of the Olympics.

The running track and the races that take place upon it exemplify what cultural geographer Philip Wagner recognized as the spatiality of sport – struggles over space, possessing 'elaborate spatial strictures', where 'the infractions and the measurement of spatial progress [...] are of great importance'. Sports, Wagner added, are 'dramas acted out within minutely prescribed spatial frames', requiring 'exactly specified and formalized environments, for in most cases the contest explicitly concerns dominance of territory or mastery of distance'.[2] In Figure 1.3 frontal space is presented as a plane surface with no physical features. This can be read as being akin to Wagner's 'spatial frame' or 'formalized environment' on which movement in a forward direction proceeds towards the horizon. This is not the milieu of playful running but rather that of achievement running. The norms of achievement running suggest the need for a formal space; informal places will not do. For speed to be maximized, the track must be smooth and level. For a record to be meaningful, all running tracks should be the same. Such sameness is devoid of topographic difference and *genius loci*.[3]

In this chapter I argue that a 'placeless' plane can be read as the ideal site for achievement running. I want to start by outlining why such a normative model of the running track might be expected to have emerged over historic time – a model of running along Eichberg's 'one way street'.[4] I do this by outlining the evolution of the modern running track, from being an unspecialized, unsegmented and non-territorialized place, to becoming close to an isotropic plane surface, as placeless as the plane in Tuan's diagram (Figure 1.3). I proceed to look at the arena as a Tuanian 'garden' and consider the extent to which the garden metaphor provides insights into sport and the environment – and whether an alternative metaphor is, these days, more appropriate. I then outline the place of spectators in foot-racing. What do they see, why do they attend and what effects might they have on athletes?

The Norms of Achievement Running

Serious running, I suggest, has two norms. One is the seeking of the record, be it personal, school, stadium, regional, national or global. All runners cannot be winners but they can all set records. The other norm is 'fair play' or the absence of unfair advantage. These are the widely held ideals of modern sport.[5] They do not apply to running as play or as a form of finding fitness and health. Upon these norms can be built a model of what running space ought to be. Note that this is a normative model, a model of what 'ought to be' rather than 'what is'.[6] The philosopher Paul Weiss writes that

> Ideally a normal set of conditions for a race is one in which there are no turns, no wind, no interference, no interval between starting signal and start, and no irregularities to the track – in short, no deviations from a standard situation.[7]

This is, more or less, one view of what geography is: 'A homogeneous space which becomes an order of knowledge through universal indexical measure of the land.'[8]

Such an 'environmental-less' space (Weiss's 'standard situation') approximates to geographer Edward Relph's idea of 'placelessness' or anthropologist Marc Augé's notion of a 'non-place'.[9] Placelessness is both a form of, and an attitude to, the cultural landscape. A practical demonstration of placelessness would be the 'technocratic gesture' of 'bulldozing of an irregular topography into a flat site',[10] as has happened in the construction of many sports sites. Many modern landscapes are characterized by placelessness and sameness:

Suburbia, shopping malls, international airports, factory farms and fast food outlets. However, it is not *necessary* for the functioning of, for example, McDonald's restaurants for each to be the same. In the production of athletic performances and records, on the other hand, it *is* necessary for the spatial and environmental parameters of the immediate physical environment to be as identical as humanly possible. The sites of track running are internationally standardized of necessity. For records to be meaningful, this is a logical requirement. Track is one of the most placeless of sports and in few, if any, other areas of life is there so much pressure for one place to be the same – exactly the same – as any other of its kind. This is because global sport can only exist when everyone knows the same rules. It might be more amusing for spectators if athletes did not know what height the hurdles would be before a race, or if the hurdles were spaced at random rather than in strict order. There might be more laughter if there were no zones in the 4 x 100 metres relay. It might be more fun if runners did not know when the last lap was going to be called. But sport is a serious business and achievement running occupies serious spaces.

Does the history of the running track display a trajectory towards the model outlined above, that is, towards a plane surface or a non-place? Consider the word 'track'. According to *The Shorter Oxford Dictionary* a track was, in pre-modern times, a mark made by the passage of a wheel, footprints or a rough, unmade road. Its current sportized definition – a course prepared or laid out for racing – dates from the late nineteenth century. Clearly, the early meaning implies that a track could be made on a field; the two were not separated (as in track *and* field), geometricized or segmented. In pre-modernity a track connotes a winding way, irregular and rural. Clearly, in its modern context, the running track is something quite different. A single or conventional *meaning* is not immediately present in the word 'track'.

Specially designated spaces for foot-racing are not a modern innovation. Ancient Greek athletics took place in stadiums, some of which were probably constructed with an express concern for sport-like activities, including running. And distinctly 'modern' characteristics characterized Greek foot-racing. For example, the use of a of a starting gate (*husplex*) – never generally accepted in modern track running – aided the prevention of false starts. However, in contrast to modern running tracks, the Greek arenas contained courses of varying lengths.[11] As Allen Guttmann points out, 'the Greeks, and certainly the Romans, were sophisticated enough to have standardized these distances, but they chose not to'.[12] Nineteenth-century native-American foot-races also often took place on specially designated tracks. A large number of kinds of foot-racing existed among native American peoples, rich descriptions of which have been provided by the early twentieth century anthropologist Stewart Culin.[13] In several cases, tracks were specially prepared for racing, though no indication of standardization is found. Some were used for racing purposes only.[14]

Foot-racing in England, widely regarded as the home of modern sport, was held in a variety of spaces and places in medieval and early modern times. Commons, city streets and fields were used for a variety of racing events, many having a carnivalistic flavour. If Montague Shearman, the nineteenth-century chronicler of running and other athletic sports, is to be believed, races took place between such conventionally non-athletic groups as fat men racing against a jockey riding a man, and a man on stilts versus a man running. There was also a 'cripples' race[15] (a bizarre precursor of the para-lympics?). The inclusion of such people should not be seen as either acts of generosity, equality or therapy, but as entertainment. The same applies to the prostitutes' races held in sixteenth century Switzerland. In this latter case, it may have been entertainment laced with punishment.

From the mid nineteenth century the varied forms of running outlined above became dominated by comparisons between results. Regular athletic meetings began in the 1840s, associated with the widespread interest in pedestrianism. Organized meets were held at the Royal Military Academy in London in 1849. But to make meaningful comparisons between events a bureaucracy was needed to administer meetings and draw up a set of rules. In the case of running, the Amateur Athletic Association (AAA) was established by a group of upper-class gentlemen at the Randolph Hotel, Oxford, in 1880. The location was significant. Not only had the first athletic club been founded at Exeter College, Oxford in 1850, but also the elite constituency of the university was reflected in the social class composition of the men that founded the new organization, and those who were admitted as members of the newly founded association. Professionals – the mainstay of the pedestrian era where the norm was gambling rather than fair play – were excluded. Much running had traditionally been over long distances and the road had been the prime site for events upon which huge stakes were wagered. With the demise of professionalism and the rise of the gentleman amateur, the distances raced became standardized and performances measured and recorded. The running track became a new element of the sports landscape.[16]

Gardens of Running: Dominance and Affection

In the decades that followed the formation of the AAA, the running track underwent three important changes. These were artificialization, standard-ization and segmentation. The conversion of, what might loosely be called, 'nature' into 'culture' is informed, I think, by applying Tuan's ideas in *Dominance and Affection*. In this somewhat depressing work, he approaches the landscape as a reflection of human power over nature. Sport, like civiliza-tion itself, 'could only emerge through a mastery of nature'.[17] The seemingly inescapable fact of human power over nature reflects the view that the world and its bounty were created for humankind and that all other biological species were to be subordinated to human wishes and needs. This, noted Tuan, 'made it possible to exploit nature in a mood of indifference to the feeling of natural objects'.[18]

Tuan's ideas are relevant, I think, to the milieu of running. At a basic level, the domination of nature results from the need for survival. Once the necessity for food and other basic requirements have been satisfied, less necessary facilities of various kinds can be constructed on the natural landscape. Facilities for running, therefore, are forms of domination which do not seem to come from a hatred of nature but from a desire to civilize it.[19] Even so, 'whether we use plants and animals for economic, playful or aesthetic ends, we *use* them; we do not attend to them for their own good except in fables'.[20] This seems rather harsh and Tuan also notes that domination may assume 'playful' forms[21] and that the dominated are often treated with affection. This illustrates the ambivalent nature of power and the relationship between dominance, on the one hand, and affection on the other, though throughout *Dominance and Affection* Tuan stresses that dominance is not the opposite of affection but that affection is dominance with a human face. 'Dominance may be cruel and exploitive, with no hint of affection in it. What is produced is the victim. On the other hand dominance may be combined with affection, and what it produces is the pet', or garden.[22] The sportscape or athlete to which we show affection is the athletic analogue of, respectively, the garden and the pet. As Tuan notes, 'affection mitigates domination, making it softer and more acceptable, but affection itself is only possible in relationships of inequality'.[23] Put another way, even if we appear kind to nature, we still exert power and domination over it. The moderation of dominance by affection is most graphically illustrated in the case of the human construction of the garden. Here nature is undoubtedly controlled and exploited but, at the same time, is shown care and affection.

In England, the venue for many track races during the nineteenth century was the cricket ground, long an example of the comfortable co-existence of dominance and affection. The groundsman emerged from the job of gardener and combined an obvious dominance of nature with tender, loving care. Shearman stressed that the best grass tracks were in no way inferior to the best of those with a cinder surface and that in longer races 'a grass course may suit some athletes better than cinders, there being less concussion at each stride'.[24] Until 1866 the Oxford and Cambridge University sports, one of the main amateur meetings of the time, were run on grass courses, at Christchurch cricket ground at Oxford or at the Fenner's ground at Cambridge. In 1867, however, the event was moved to London and utilized the cinder track at Beaufort House.[25] Such facilities were far from widespread. A.R. Downer, a well-known British sprinter during the late decades of the nineteenth century, recalled a typical site on the Scottish professional circuit: 'a rough stubble field, and a "track" staked off theorem of about 200 yards to the lap, with square corners, and the going like a switchback railway.'[26] Nature needed to be improved upon.

Apart from the unevenness of the micro-topography, why should the natural surface of grass give way to the manufactured cinder surface? Why, in other words, should the land used for running become a specialized, permanent facility – the running track – rather than the multi-functional facility of the grass field? And did the change from grass to cinder, and thence to a synthetic surface, reveal sport as anti-nature? Grass tracks were often uneven and distances were sometimes difficult to confirm, the white markings rapidly disappearing and lacking any permanence. They lacked the fixed exactitude of modern sports space. The correcting of nature, writes Ingo Pyker, 'is justified according to the requirements of sport, confirmed by the general ideology of growth and progress'.[27] Natural grass, even with the application of 'turf science', cannot support sufficient training or competition for athletes under all physical conditions. Given the vulnerability of natural vegetation cover, progress in the output of record performances is also likely to be retarded. Even so, from the 1920s to the 1950s many major track meets were held on grass courses. In 1950 the Empire Games track events were held at Auckland, New Zealand, on a grass circuit. Separate records were unofficially maintained for grass tracks, implying that they were inferior to those made of cinder. In 1954, the British athlete Gordon Pirie was proud enough to announce that he had set a world grass track record of 4 minutes 5.2 seconds for the mile.[28] Yet as late as 1962, world records for the men's mile and the women's 800 metres were set on grass tracks at Wanganui, New Zealand, and Perth, Australia, respectively.

The first purpose-built running track in England was sited at Lord's Cricket Ground in London in 1837 – a narrow path designed for two-man races – but faced with gravel and *measured by surveyors*.[29] The composition of non-grass tracks varied considerably. They were neither standardized in terms of the materials making up their construction, nor in their size. In Reykjavik, Iceland, the track was made of volcanic lava; the 15 cm surface of the track used for the Stockholm Olympics in 1912 was mixed (as in concrete) from slag (from locomotives and a local electricity works), mould mixed with sand, mortar and marl.[30] Other tracks had a large clay content, but whatever the composition they were tended by skilled artisans who doubled as groundsmen. In tending the track, they needed to water it, exclude the colonization of weeds and grass, and regularly inscribe the geometric markings. They combined the skills of horticulture and geometry. Their reputations were often highly regarded and the hand of a human being was still reflected in the track. The running track had become a clearly defined and marked place. Running tracks assumed what Tuan terms 'a high degree of integrity', meaning that they became reserved for special functions (training and racing), and any departure from the accepted practice was discouraged.[31] The cinder running track was a facility that could be used for little but running.

Changes in track surfaces aimed to improve the output of races. But speed could be increased with another technological development: starting blocks. They were invented in 1927 and first used in Chicago in 1929. The scientific essence of achievement sport was reflected in research that concluded that, from the use of starting blocks, an average sprinter could gain 34/1000 of a second (that is, about 30 centimetres in distance) in a 100 yards race.[32] For several years, however, starting blocks were perceived as unfair aids to racing and were not widely used. George Simpson's 100 yards time of 9.4 seconds was disallowed because of the use of blocks. In the 1936 Olympics, sprinters still had to use small trowels to dig holes in the track to improve their starts. The International Association of Athletics Federations (IAAF) did not sanction blocks until 1948 when they were used for the first time in the Olympics. Today they are a compulsory part of the sprinter's micro-environment.

The history of the direction in which athletes run their circuits around the track is blurred and seems to be lacking in any fully satisfactory explanation. In England the majority of late nineteenth-century track races were run clockwise, though today the anti-clockwise direction is universal.[33] It seems likely that it was the slope, especially in the shorter events, which influenced the direction run in the early modern years of track racing. The standardization towards a general anti-clockwise rule came quite late and photographs from the 1930s show athletes running in a clockwise direction. For a time the two coexisted without any 'legal' requirement, but standardization eventually prevailed.

The synthetic track was developed in the 1970s for the same reason as the cinder track. Further refinement of the running surface allowed the intensification of training, the track being useable in all conditions. It required no tending, severing any link with the traditions of gardening. The gardener had given way to the scientist, an expert in synthetic chemistry. Additionally, output – the record – could be increased further with a milieu that placed even greater emphasis on speed. The synthetic track has been said to increase the speed of an athlete by as much as one second per lap. It was also easier to impose internationally comparable standards with a prescribed synthetic surface than in case of grass or cinders.

I now return to matters Tuanian. What are we to make of the tendency towards artifice in the landscape of the athletic arena? Until the 1960s, I suggest, the running track could be read as being analogous to a garden. As Tuan notes, it was dominance mixed with affection.[34] The tending of the grass track required the dominance of the groundsman, tempered, however, by affection – dominance with a human face. The sensitive autobiography of W.R. Loader refers to the 'pampered turf' on which he raced during the

1930s.[35] 'Pampered' is a word often used to refer to the treatment of pets or infants. Roger Bannister talked of visiting Iffley Road running track at Oxford, deserted except 'for a groundsman, who stooped low, coaxing out [even] the daisies as though they were his pet treasures'.[36] Nature was tamed, to be sure, but nurtured like a pet rather than destroyed.

Returning to Tuan's model (Figure 1.3), if I superimpose on the front space some lines representing a 400 metres track, I have a map or plan of the plane surface over which runners race – an approximation to pure space, well exemplified by the sanitized and synthetic track. The track is, of course, planned. Like urban planning, the track is planned to make the world of sport better, fairer and more efficient. But despite the apparently beneficent aims, this is a form of domination and it is possible that what might appear as humane can also be read as crude and inhuman, when used in particular ways.[37]

It is possible to 'contrast space with place by noting that space refers [etymologically] to something that allows spreading or progressing, something that yields to an expansionist effort, allowing *speed*, and makes it possible to achieve expansive feeling and hope. In contrast to this, place refers to a site of inhibiting'.[38] The space beyond the starting line lacks friction; the place behind the starting line is enclosed and peopled. The synthetic track can be seen as an attempt to close the gap between practice and theory – the practice of the lived world with the theory (the 'ought to be') of the optimal athletic space. With the synthetic track the metaphor of the garden gives way to that of the motorway. Henning Eichberg reveals that the original model for the *autobahn* was the racing track.[39] Today, it seems to be the other way round; for advertising purposes the Peugeot car company used the synthetic running track as a metaphor for swift movement through the countryside, dominating and colonizing it (see Figure 2.1). In the words of Zygmunt Bauman, such a route has 'the impersonal elegance of a cartographic grid', possessing 'the supra-partisan nature of spatial modernization and the absence of any link between its principals and political ideologies' and 'standardization and prefabrication'.[40] He is talking about the modern city but his words apply equally to the geometric and compositional perfection of the late-modern running track.

Ronald Rees has described how 'landscape' has become increasingly interiorized over time, first, through interiors being decorated with flowers, to tapestries with woven scenes, Chinese wallpapers full of rural life, to twentieth-century winter gardens, conservatories and wardian cases.[41] Running too has become interiorized as further attempts are made to eliminate the effects of the natural environment. Wind, rain and temperature can be controlled. The interiorization of the running track takes us closer to Weiss's ideal type and to Tuan's segmented and dominated worlds. Although the environment cannot be totally eliminated indoors, it is, to varying degrees, neutralized or under human control.

Figure 2.1 The Track as a Metaphor for the Motorway

The first indoor track meet is said to have taken place in 1861 in Cincinnati, Ohio, and gas-lit events took place in London, England, a year later.[42] Indoor track meets are a significant part of the modern athletic calendar. In some ways, such events approach the atmosphere of the theatre or circus, bringing spectators closer to the action in the more confined space where tracks generally have a circumference of only 200 metres. Current developments in sports architecture, however, suggest that the 400-metre track will soon be accommodated in larger indoor spaces, in arenas often having retractable roofs. Here, an element of 'nature' is an option, but only to an extent, and can be eliminated at the press of a button. The retractable roof results in a liminal space – betwixt and between the indoors and out. The Skydome in Toronto has already featured at least one race, a novelty event between Olympic champions Donovan Bailey and Michael Johnson over 150 metres.

Madison Square Garden in New York is a long-standing venue for indoor track racing where many famous athletes, from Paavo Nurmi to modern racing legends, have competed. The 'Garden' has no grass, no lakes or saplings. The lingering use of the word 'garden' in a totally non-horticultural setting reminds us of what has existed and what it has become. Sports *parks* and *gardens* are therefore spaces whose instability and ambiguity are clearly evident through the words themselves. The relative sterility of the indoor arena may lead us to assume that indoor results are faster than those set out of doors. On the other hand, more races take place out of doors and the bends of the outdoor tracks are less sharp than those indoors. The McWhirter twins, chroniclers of track and field in the early 1950s, supported 'the view that indoor conditions flatter performance over longer distances', citing the example of a dozen Americans who had bettered 9 minutes for 2 miles indoors whereas only one had done so out of doors.[43]

Anti-urbanists have not been absent from the critique of such developments – if that is the right word – described above. Lewis Carroll had opposed even the establishment of lawn tennis courts in the University Parks at Oxford. By the mid-1930s Nazi ideology, which incorporated a strong 'back to nature' element, predicted the end of such monstrosities as huge arenas and dimly lit halls for body cultural practices. Running tracks, it was argued, should be torn up and the spaces returned to nature. This apparent reclamation of nature reflected Volkish daydreams:

> Gradually, then, the symbols of our asphalt culture that have penetrated physical culture will disappear: the cement stadium, the cinder track, the measuring tape, the stopwatch, well-tended lawns, and running shoes which have served to intensify the pursuit of 'sheer performance'. In their place will be the simple meadow, untrammelled nature.[44]

This was put into practice by Nazi college students who, in opposition to the 1936 Olympics, ripped up the cinder track at the *Deutschen Stadion* and replanted it with young oak trees.[45] However, six weeks after the students had planted their saplings, they were torn out and the cinder track reverted to its sportized form as the Berlin Olympics, with their propaganda value, loomed on the political and sporting horizons. In any case, given the trajectory that modern sport was taking, 'it would be difficult to formulate a less accurate vision of sport's destiny in the modern world' than the comments of the romantic discontents.[46]

Although the 1896 Olympics at Athens were held in a stadium built with sport in mind, those of 1900 were not. At the Paris Games, the track and field events were held in the Bois de Boulogne, reflecting the low-key status of the event. However, all subsequent Games were stadium-based. There was to be a place for everything, with everything in its place. The standardization of racing-space reflects the placelessness of the modern stadium – or more accurately, of the modern track. Standardization has also occurred in the distances over which races are held. Shearman's concern with record mania in the 1880s was that there were too many records because there were too many distances to be run. Gradually, the number of distances contested have been reduced and standardized. The steeplechase was run over a distance of 2,400 metres in the 1900 and 1904 Olympics. In 1908 it was extended to 3,200 metres and only thereafter standardized to 3,000 metres. The steeplechase remained an anomalous event and it was not until 1954 that the IAAF introduced rules that regulated, for example, the number of hurdles required for the event. Even today, the geography of the steeplechase has not been fully rationalized. Tracks vary from place to place with regard to the siting of the water jump, some being inside but others outside the 400-metre circuit.

Accompanying the standardization of the distances run has been the standardization of the size and shape of the track. Some straight 400-metre tracks existed at the start of the present century and 200-metre straightways were quite common until the 1960s. In 1976 the IAAF congress approved a recommendation by its technical committee to discontinue 200 metre (and 220 yards) performances on straight tracks from the world record schedule, as part of a strategy of standardization. The 1896 Olympic track was U-shaped, resembling a theatre extended at each end. The track had a narrow radius with right angles at one end of the arena. The grass oval for the Paris Games of 1900 measured 500 metres; at London's White City in 1908 it was one third of a mile (536.45 metres). On such a large track, the straights were very long, encouraging greater speed. The runners had to negotiate only one turn and the start of the 400 metres was opposite the end of the straight where the race finished. At the Stockholm Olympics of 1912, on the other hand, the track was 383 metres. The athletic events of the 1920 and 1924 Olympics took place on tracks measuring 500 metres. At the time this seemed a reasonable size and Shearman had stigmatized the Stamford Bridge track as being too small, amounting to *only* a quarter of a mile in circumference.[47] This perceived fault was remedied by constructing a long straight of 250 yards extending along one side. The first 250 yards of races over 440 yards were run along this course, hence reducing the number of turns and thus increasing the possibility of fast times. Writing in the 1880s, the sage Shearman propounded that:

> we are strongly of the opinion that [...] in every path there should be as much straight as possible and as little corner as possible, or, in other words, that the path should be quadrangular with rounded corners, not an oval with two sides flattened.[48]

Shearman's logic did not prevail and the oval route was to become the norm but, despite his aversion to records, his observations also reflect an enthusiasm for speed and fast times well before the *fin de siècle*.

Standardization and Segmentation

The Amsterdam track, constructed for the 1928 Olympics, measured 400 metres, and this became the norm. It is now the regulation distance for tracks on which official records can be set. It may be no accident that the standardization of size of tracks coincided with a period of growing commercialization of sports. Larger arenas would have provided less than satisfactory viewing positions for the increasing number of sport's spectators. From the 1890s onwards, a further move was to provide, literally, a level playing field. Shearman observed that at the Aston grounds, in Birmingham, 'there is a drop of over 6 feet in the 300 yard course, the part between the finish and the beginning of the quarter being a stiff up-hill'.[49] Until 1948 the Iffley Road track at Oxford was of three laps to the mile with a 'six foot rise and fall'.[50] Records would be meaningless in such environments, especially if downhill stretches were not compensated for by an uphill section of the course.[51]

A frequently recalled story from the late 1860s illustrates the spatial impurity of the running tracks of the time. In 1868, the quarter-mile championship of England was held at the Beaufort House grounds, London. The victor was Edward Colbeck but the story of his victory is worth recalling, best undertaken, perhaps, in the words of Montague Shearman:

> Coming along at a great pace, he led all the way round the ground, and was winning easily when a wandering sheep found its way upon the path and stopped still there, being presumably amazed at the remarkable performance which the runner was accomplishing. The athlete cannoned against the sheep, broke its leg, and then went on and finished his quarter in 50 2/5 seconds.[52]

This story reveals the porosity of the boundary between man and animal, culture and nature, athlete and spectator, in the context of early-modern running. The track was not a bounded space but a porous one. Likewise, though less dramatic, was the concern expressed by de Coubertin about the excessive number of people who had access to the track at the 1906 London Olympics.[53] In order to eliminate incidents such as Colbeck's accident with the sheep, the track's environment needed to be rationalized. This was done by separating the track from the spectators' area by a well-marked boundary, an act of territorialization.[54]

Rationalization also occurred through the segmentation of the track into clearly defined lanes and zones. Early sprint races beyond 100 metres were not held in lanes. Racing space was not segmented, illustrating the less spatially defined character of sport in those days. Although lanes were first used in the 400 metres in the Olympics of 1912, they were far from universally adopted in this event, even in the 1950s. Particular spaces had not yet been reserved for particular athletes and in such non-spatialized events body contact and interference were frequent. Britain lagged behind the USA and some countries in western Europe in having the 400 metres run entirely in lanes.

Guy Butler felt that the tendency for runners to dash off at the start to gain an inside position at the first corner added to the interest.[55] But fun was sacrificed for formality and today all track events up to and including 400 metres are run in lanes, as is the first 100 metres of the 800 metres, seeking to reduce human physical contact. In addition to lanes, various zones have also been added to the track. Specific marks indicate where hurdles must be placed, and zones have been drawn within which the baton must be passed from one runner to another in the relays. Here are applications of human territoriality, the clear marking of a segmented space for specific activities.[56] Robert Sack would see it as a form of territoriality – a reflection of human power.[57] Tuan would see segmentation or partitioning as the result of a long-term trend towards 'people's growing sense of self and their need for greater individual and group privacy', and takes the house and the theatre as examples.[58]

However, the markings on a plane surface reveal other aspects of the human experience of racing. Fear and spatial segmentation are related. As Tuan notes,

> Generally speaking, every human made boundary on the earth's surface – garden hedge, city wall, or 'radar fence' – is an attempt to keep inimical forces at bay. Boundaries are everywhere because threats are ubiquitous: the neighbor's dog, children with muddy shoes, strangers, the insane, alien armies, disease, wind and rain.[59]

It is partly because of fear that we enclose many of the spaces inside the sports stadium. After all, crowds are often perceived as fearsome and dangerous. If they are contained, fear is reduced. Sports organizers fear rain or snow. As a result they enclose arenas, increasingly placing retractable roofs above them. Athletes fear competitors (or sheep) interfering with them, so we segregate them into lanes.

Attention! Racing as Inattention

In racing's ideal type we rid ourselves of nature and replace it with synthetic surfaces and geometries. In this way, nature becomes simplified through a simulation of its reality without aesthetic distractions. In its pure form, racing is a world of unambiguous dualisms – there are winners and losers, we have success or failure, you are on the track team or off it, you are in your lane or outside it. Tuan has noted that:

> Few of us in social science can bear the attention of attending to social reality – its bewildering webs of exchange, its contradictions,

and its heavy burden. We prefer to act. Armed with questionnaires we go quickly into the field and collect data, worrying more whether the data are of a quality sufficient for statistical manipulation – whether they will generate enough graphs and tables to charm the referees of a journal – than whether they are of a quality for reading the heart of a problem.[60]

Nature is as difficult to understand as social reality. We enclose the sportized field with concrete and we make the horizon of the record our sole goal. To understand what we are doing needs too much attention. When we begin to understand it we become uneasy with what we have learned and seek consolation in numbers. How true this seems of the statistical gazetteers so loved by track fans. When my interest in the nature of nature, or of body-cultural experiences, wanes, I race around a 400-metre track to fit in as much effort as I can into as little time as possible. The stopwatch (and the camera, to which Tuan alludes), 'like all machines invites action and sharply narrows the range of experiences'.[61] To athletes the stopwatch 'is a source of psychological reassurance and not merely a recording instrument'.[62] The tendency in many track meets, and telecasts of them, is to place greater emphasis on speed events and less on those over longer distances. Sprints require less attention. It is a form of running for an age of zapping between different TV channels, an age of instant gratification.

It is difficult to get lost on a running track. Runners are aware of the layout and where they are in the overall distance to be run. Its spatial details are clearly demarcated. The start and finish are explicated. Indeed, the rules of sport insist that I must be behind the starting line before I start, that I must not wander into another athlete's lane or that I must not accept the baton outside the marked zone in a relay race. But it is all too easy to get lost in nature as I, and others, have found while running in forests. The world of achievement running, therefore, can be viewed as a symptom of inattention. Orienteering (see below), on the other hand, prioritises attention over speed. It may be possible to argue, therefore, that running is a much-impoverished form of locomotion compared with other forms of perambulation, including walking, when seeking to experience environmental quality.

Stadium, Topophilia and the Spectators' Gaze

The rather dystopian world of track running that I have painted in previous sections of this chapter exemplifies Tuan's notion of dominance. There appears little room for affection when nature is totally eliminated in the interests of a sport that occupies a world of anaesthesia. However, this is not necessarily the case.

The experiences of running do not leave any mark on the landscape and even a record, in quantitative terms (and in contrast to the statue or hall of fame), does not last. 'Work ends', writes Tuan, 'in things that last.'[63] Tuan likes to allude to the significance of durable artefacts in the good life. In the world of running and runners the most durable of artefacts may be the stadium, elevated in some places to an informal 'sacred place' or formally designated as a site of cultural interest and protection by municipal or national agencies. Tuan observes that 'architectural and technological imagination at its best have enabled people to experience a level of well-being and stimulation that they could not otherwise have known'.[64] Consider the cases of the running track and the stadium.

The running track is the site where athletic dramas (and dreams) are played out. It is also on the track that the most obviously mathematical and scientific training regimens are imposed upon athletes' bodies. The geometric character of the 400-metre track permits – indeed, encourages – a form of Taylorized training known as interval running as part of aerobic training. This highly regulated and formalized form of training is dealt with in the next chapter but at this point it can be noted that although highly work-like – a time-space routine – a number of such routines meet regularly in time and space.[65] At a running track, people who might not know each other become acquainted, even friends. So, although the training routine might be tedious, the interaction of many time-space routines – what Seamon calls 'space-ballet' – leads to 'space becoming place through interpersonal, spatio-temporal sharing'.[66] The stadium can be read as a meeting place. Enjoying a place – through meeting friends – generates a sense of topophilia. It would be unwise to imply that the aesthetic has been totally eliminated and that affection no longer exists.

Tuan defines topophilia as 'the affective bond between people and place or setting'.[67] It includes 'all of the human being's affective ties with the material environment'. Such ties may be aesthetic, tactile, or feelings 'toward a place because it is home, the locus of memories, and the means of gaining a livelihood'.[68] Topophilic sentiment can be obtained by runners and, because racing is often a public activity, by spectators. McNeish's subject, Jack Lovelock, is said to have 'loved that old Iffley Road track' at Oxford,[69] and different stadiums, large and small, have assumed the status of much-loved places for spectators and athletes. For the Cambridge graduate and sprinter W.R. Loader, Fenner's was a beautiful ground. It was an old ground, but it had

> seen a lot of men come and lot of men go. Deeds of note had been done here, by runners who were no less notable. On this elm-shaded enclosure, with its unorthodox 600-yards track on

which we ran right-hand inside, had performed giants of the
distant and not so distant past.[70]

For Loader, a love of place lies not solely in the physical environment but
in the memories of people who have performed there and stories associated
with them.

Stadiums are more than simply running tracks. They have aesthetic surroundings that contrast with the anaesthetic plane of the track itself. The
track is but part of the overall landscape ensemble of the arena.[71] Coubertin,
writing in the first decade of the twentieth century, deplored the Athens and
London stadiums as aesthetically displeasing. They were 'boring ellipses'.
The track at the Racing Club de Paris, on the other hand, was 'artfully designed
across shaded lawns', proving 'that we can achieve technical excellence
without sacrificing the beauty of the facility'.[72] He also admired the Olympic
Stadium at Stockholm – gothic, red brick, part castle, part manor house, part
stadium (see Figure 2.2). It was built for the 1912 Olympics and designed
by the Swedish architect Torben Grut. Although the original plan was to
construct a simple structure with Greek associations (recalling the Greek
origins of the Games), the final design was in the 'form of a medieval-wall
in rough hewn granite and handmade brick, and since its completion it has
not only been a symbol for Swedish sport and athletics but also one of the
foremost examples of Swedish National Romantic Architecture'.[73] The official
report of the Games' organizing committee noted:

> The stadium is a modern, constructive application of mediaeval
> brick-architecture, such as occurs in ancient Swedish city-walls,
> fortresses, monasteries and churches. Every part has sprung
> organically from its intended use; no extraneous motif-architecture
> being anywhere to be found. The building has been composed
> simply and plainly, just as a boat or a bridge is, but nobility in
> the material and proportion.[74]

With a capacity of 22,000 spectators it was smaller than stadiums that had
hosted the previous Games but Grut explained that his aim was 'to establish
harmonious relationships between man, nature and architecture',[75] clearly
akin to Tuan's idea of a garden where dominance is benign.

The Stockholm stadium has become a much-loved place, not only among
track and sports fans but also among the broader population of the Swedish
capital. The Bislett Stadium in Oslo does not possess many architectural
qualities but for middle-distance runners, and spectators and local people, it
also generates a sense of topophilia. At Bislett, a disproportionate number of
world track records have been set in the last 30 years. The attraction of Bislett

Figure 2.2 The Olympic Stadium, Stockholm (Photo by Micael Ekberg, reproduced by permission).

lies, in part, in the perception that there is something almost 'magical' about Nordic summer evenings. Others suggest that it the closeness of spectators to the athletes that assists in the production of good results. Which ever is the case, it is a much-loved place.

However, even the city is mortal and can all too easily be razed to the ground, and the same is true of stadiums. Like other places, stadiums are ultimately shaped by institutional forces ranging from local planning ordinances to the International Olympic Committee. The White City Stadium, built for the 1908 Olympics in west London, witnessed many great moments in the history of running. Many world records were broken there. I recall to this day being a spectator at the floodlit White City in 1957 when the Yorkshireman Derek Ibbotson broke the world record for the mile with a time of 3 minutes 57.2 seconds. A few years earlier I had watched, via grainy images on a black and white television screen, the epic race between Vladimir Kuts and Chris Chataway at the same stadium. The Oxford graduate, Chataway, prevailed over his Soviet adversary in a thrilling and world record-breaking 5,000 metres race, and won by a stride in 13 minutes 51.6 seconds. Such memories created an image of the White City as having a certain sacredness, even if on conventional architectural criteria it may have been lacking. Topophilia is not determined by architecture but from the experiences that may have been felt in a specific place, but neither its history – nor the memories it contained – failed to prevent the old stadium being razed in the early 1970s in order for more lucrative land uses to replace it.

What do spectators bring to stadiums such as these, and those of a more mundane character? Bounded space requires that spectators be spatially separated from those they are watching. The incursion of spectators (including sheep) on to the track contravenes the norms of sport; it is simply unfair to the competitors, even if it might provide more fun for the spectators. Hence interaction between performer and spectator is explicitly discouraged by the provision and visibility of dividing lines of various kinds. At the same time, however, the presence of spectators and athletes inevitably humanizes the arena and presents a tension between the ideal model of racing *space* and the existing situation of a *place* for running.

The spectators occupying the stadium can be read in several ways. Like the athletes they too are often occupying segmented spaces. But what is the object of their gaze? How are their senses stimulated by the presence of athletic bodies, being pushed to the limits of speed and endurance? What are spectators' attitudes to losers? Sigmund Loland suggests a threefold categorization of spectators: (i) connoisseurs, (ii) fans and (iii) supporters.[76] Spectators may be motivated to attend a track meet by a range of factors.[77] True, they might want to be entertained, to be excited by the struggle of great athletes, to be able to boast that 'I was there' when a great performance was achieved, or to witness a particular star who has agreed to perform in front of them. But what senses are being excited by spectatorship? Pierre, Baron de Coubertin, founder of the modern Olympics, felt that the main purpose of watching sports was educational. The ideal spectator was a resting sportsman in possession of a knowing gaze – Loland's connoisseur. The ideal spectator was a reflexive spectator, seeking personal meaning by watching others do what he or she had done also. Douglas Brown suggests that, for Coubertin, the ideal spectator should be an 'aesthetic subject: that is, one who experiences beauty, or pleasure, through their own participation in an event'. It took a sportsman to do this. Tuan also sees spectatorship as a skill that draws on knowledge and is far from passive.[78] Indeed, Coubertin thought that spectators, like athletes, should be selected or invited to attend, on the basis of their knowledge and involvement in sport.[79] 10,000 spectators would constitute the optimal crowd size.

Most of those who watch sport do not do so from a seat in a stadium. It is in their homes, watching television or reading magazines, books and newspapers, that the majority of the sporting public subject runners to their gaze. Such spectators consume running as entertainment and are, in Loland's terms, fans (though not necessarily fanatics). Fans may be gratified by the pleasure gained from gazing at the aesthetic qualities of the athletic body; witness the grace of a great sprinter or the economy of style of the long-distance runner. Witnessing an athlete's grace, skill and speed is likely to lead to envy, something deeply embedded in human nature. 'If only I could run as fast as him' is a thought that frequently recurs in the minds of the mediocre. Tuan regards envy as 'the sin we are most reluctant to acknowledge in ourselves because, unlike pride, it implies inferiority'.[80] Such an envious gaze may well contain, in some cases, a strong degree of erotic pleasure bordering on sexual voyeurism, given the skimpy and tight-fitting uniforms worn by modern athletes. In *The Front Runner*, the gay coach

> went to meets with a throbbing excitement that devoured me. Outdoors under the sky, or indoors in the smoky arenas, I devoured the sight of those other fine-looking young men. They were stretched out in full flight, gleaming with sweat as their muscles and tendons strained toward the unattainable. Now and then I'd see someone whom I found so attractive that he gave me that hurting, wanting feeling.[81]

It is also possible that pleasure could be obtained from seeing athletes in pain and suffering. The number of spectators at track meets or marathon races who display sadistic tendencies is simply not known but it is surely plausible that at least some do. Loader refers to the famous 5,000 metres race between Chataway and Kuts at the White City, London, in 1954. He observes that 'the physical agony both of the Russian trying to break away and the Briton refusing to let him, was *cruel*. It couldn't only be seen by the spectators. It could be *felt*.'[82] Kirsten Roessler has pointed out that spectators' enjoyment of watching a race can, on the other hand, be understood as an identification with the suffering person, a kind of catharsis, or as a 'voyeur' interested in other peoples' suffering.[83]

Perhaps spectators are happier to watch self-inflicted pain, being more acceptable and more entertaining, but in some track races, when only two runners may be left to contest the result, it becomes almost a case of one person torturing another. Drawing on Adam Phillips's remarkable book on the escapologist Harry Houdini, the modern runner, in his profession, exposes what spectators take pleasure in seeing being done to bodies – or what they want to see bodies doing to themselves. With the commercialization of running, spectators see what economics can do to biology. Athletes show spectators new ways in which the body may be tested, endangered, exploited or confined by time and space.[84]

The Swedish philosopher Torbjörn Tännsjö poses the question: Why do we admire those who excel in sports? The admiration of sports heroes – Olympic winners, world record breakers and so on – whether in the stadium or via press or electronic media, tends to resemble fascism. It is, he suggests, 'fascistoid'.[85] This is because the excellence of the athletes we admire is based on their competitive 'strength', a word used literally. The losers of a race are relatively weak and are therefore less valued (as in fascism, where weakness is met with contempt). This, Tännsjö continues, leads to contempt for losers and we like to see runners beaten (note the double meaning of beaten). Many of us like to see representatives of certain nations (or 'races') defeated by those of our own. Such spectators, he suggests, are most likely to be those who do not regard themselves as being good at running, or anything else in life. These may number more than we think. When athletes become representations of nations, wearing national uniforms, the chauvinism of some spectators – Loland's supporters – can turn them against athletes from particular nations. This suggests that spectators see runners as their representatives and hence attend some meets, indirectly at least, in order to display a form of nationalistic identity. The notion of spectators as supporters recalls Tuan's notion of topophilia, this time applied at a different level of scale, that of the nation. The claim that representational sport may play a major role in the bonding of collectivities is well documented.[86] National success in sport, be it through individuals or teams, is argued to foster a love of place. This is rarely known as topophilia: patriotism is often used instead though the latter tends to refer to one's birthplace, rather than any place for which affection might be felt. Patriotism may result from, but may also fuel, national success in sport. In *Topophilia*, Tuan suggests there are two forms of patriotism – local and imperial. The former rests on intimate knowledge and experience of place; the latter 'feeds on collective egotism and pride'.[87] He believes that the 'modern state is too large, its boundaries too arbitrary, its area too heterogeneous to command the kind of affection that arises out of experience and intimate knowledge'.[88] State-level topophilia all too easily gets perverted into collective egotism, jingoism and racism. Such malign sentiments are often reflected in sporting nationalism. Tuan's view recalls Coubertin's wish for nations, rather than countries, to be represented in the Olympic Games.[89] However, as Tuan suggests, even nations may be too large, and a city is about the upper size limit for which the term might reasonably be used – before topophilia becomes perverted into racism.

The Finishing Line

Does the future lie in the dystopian world of non-places or can alternative models be written? Certainly, the sportscape of track running does not seem to have reached its ultimate in terms of rationalization. The surrounding milieu of the stands, the flags, noise and smells all impose placefulness on what otherwise tends toward a sterile space, revealing that the arena has not yet approached ultimate rationalization. Even a 100-metre sprinter fails to run in an exact straight line. In middle- and long-distance races the distance covered exceeds that notionally attributed to the race because of the extra distance covered in overtaking or running away from the curb. Indeed, if the record became the ultimate objective of running, individuals would simply run time-trials against the clock. Despite the time-space fetish of achievement running, track measurements are allowed to vary. The track measurements are taken 30 cm outward from the kerb or, where no kerb exists, 20 cm from the line marking the inside of the track. Hence, running tracks do not measure exactly what they claim to be. In measuring a track, two independent measurements must be taken. These must not differ from each other by more than $0.0003 + L \times 0.01$ m, where L is the length in metres. This formula gives the highest permitted difference between two measurements for 100 metres of 4 cm. and for 400 metres of 13 cm. This has important implications for the timing of races since an improvement of a record by 0.001 of a second in say, a 10,000 metres race, will be meaningless if tracks vary by as much as a centimetre per lap – which they are likely to.

Curved tracks, even if they are of identical distances, do not provide athletes with equal opportunities. The geometry of the 200 metres of curve both enables and constrains. Athletes in the outer lanes run round more gentle curves than those on the inside. It has been shown that, as a result, in a 20 second 200 metres race the runner in the inside lane suffers a penalty of 0.07 seconds. For 400 metres the difference between the two innermost lanes is 0.02 seconds.[90] This is paradoxical in view of the demise of the 200 metres straight tracks of the pre-1960s. There remains, therefore, a considerable amount of irrationality in modern achievement sports. The flat 400-metre running track might more logically be replaced by a banked track, as used in indoor racing. This would increase speed in 200, 400, 800 metres races and during the closing stages of middle-distance races.[91]

Although attempts have been made to eliminate nature from the running arena, or at least, to take it into account, one perennial physical factor continues to provide problems for the rational athlete. Although temperature effects can be reduced, to some extent, by selecting the time of day at which meets are held, the question of wind strength is more problematic. The wind does not blow in straight lines so that even if a wind gauge is used to define wind speeds of more than 2.0 metres per second (the highest 'legal' wind speed allowable for records to be recognized), inconsistencies can occur. If several measurements were taken at different points along the track, they would not be equal and it is possible to establish that an occasional positive reading will be found among a general negative wind flow.[92] An anemometer placed at the 50-metre point in a 100-metre straight does not record the wind situation in each of the lanes, nor for the entire length of the 100 metres race. The presence of high grandstands, for example, can cause the wind's strength and direction to vary over the area within which track races take place and, hence, affect individual athletes differently. Such inequalities are inevitable in races held out of doors.

And what about the human environment? Nowhere in the rules of athletics is there any suggestion that spectators are a necessary part of the stadium ensemble. Indeed, it is possible to read the optimal, pure stadium as being spectator-free, particularly if the spectators are partisan and/or can influence the outcome of a race. At the very least, if spectators interact with runners during the course of a race, the competition cannot be treated as the production of the runners alone.[93] Roger Bannister recalls a mile race at the former White City stadium in London when, with 300 metres to go, a foreign opponent came up to his shoulder:

> For the first time I heard the deep-throated White City roar as I made my finishing effort. It seemed to give you new life, like a whiff of oxygen, so that you can leave the field standing, flying away like a wild duck startled from a clump of rushes.[94]

And American runner Steve Prefontaine, running on his home track in Eugene, Oregon, said of the crowd: 'Those people are fantastic. They're my people, man. How can you lose with 12,000 people behind you.'[95] Such support from the crowd could be seen as an external environmental advantage, therefore contravening the norms of fair play. Such norms seem to suggest that the crowd should be silent (or absent), applauding only when the race has finished.[96]

The optimal geography of the running environment, according to this model, appeared in the *Berliner Illustrirten Zeitung* in 1936.[97] It showed a postmodern stadium, predicted for the year 2000. It was to be free of spectators, provided with simulated crowd noise, electronic visualization technology and an automatic starting apparatus (see Figure 2.3). The only human figures would be the athletes. A postmodern arena would be devoid of spectators since, like nature, they provide unwanted noise, creating an unfair advantage when they shout in support of their favourite athlete. The spectator-less stadium would approximate to Weiss's 'normal situation'.

Sigmund Loland sees an alternative to the isotropic plane as a site for running. He argues that sport has become too specialized and that the quest for records has reduced 'the potential for human progress to one narrow capacity such as the ability to run fast'.[98] In order to moderate this obsession, he suggests that the hegemony of the standardized synthetic track should be reduced. If specialization could be softened, and narrow specialisms be replaced by complex skills as an objective of serious sport, what sort of races might take place? Loland argues that track running can learn from the marathon (see below) and from skiing, in which non-standardized sites are used. Grand Prix races, for example, might be run over different surfaces with one race on a track, one on sand, one on snow, another through forests and so on. Races could occur in summer and winter. Sprinters could compete over different

Die XXVII. Olympischen Spiele im Jahre 2000 ...

Figure 2.3 'The 27th Olympic Games in the year 2000 ...' (*Berliner Illustrirten Zeitung*, 1936).

distances – 80, 100, 200 and 300 metres, for example. Loland expands upon his vision:

> When competing in Africa, running can take place on the characteristic red soil. Competitions in Florida could be on the white shores of a beach. In the Oslo wintertime, there could be sprint races on hard packed snow, or even on icy surfaces with spiked shoes. Different surfaces would require different running techniques. Inclusion of one or two turns and a small uphill and downhill area would pose further challenges on technique. Imagine a 30 metres race in an angled curve, or a 300 metres race starting with 150 metres slightly uphill and 150 metres slightly downhill! All these changes would increase the complexity of the performance and represent alternatives to the specialization of the record logic.[99]

Under such circumstances record breaking would become less important, if not meaningless.

The extent to which this, or other futures for running, will emerge remains to be seen, but in considering such projects a conflict between the anaesthetic of sport space and the aesthetics of sport place would have to be played out. And Loland's suggestion of moving out of the stadium, on to the ice and into the forests leads neatly into the next chapter in which I move beyond the stadium and consider the place of nature and the countryside in the culture of achievement running.

Beyond the Arena

Between wilderness and the city is, what Tuan terms, a 'middle landscape' that he labels 'Edenic'.[1] There has been a long-standing sentiment for the rural, the countryside beyond the city. In a machine culture, nature is reasserted in the rural. But wilderness tends to be something different – wild and untamed. Just as the country beyond the city has long been read as an idyll to which urbanites may retreat,[2] many athletes – or their coaches – seek an additional milieu beyond the stadium in which to train, in which to be 'refreshed by contact with the glories of nature'.[3] At the same time, the 'elements' may be thought to harden athletes for the competitions they will undertake on the synthetic track. It is the extra-stadium dimensions of running that form the foci of this chapter.

On the synthetic running track and in the covered arena, runners are estranged from nature and its sensory stimuli. In parkland and the country-side, runners are at least in contact with a more natural milieu and on occasions may even have opportunities to explore it and feel in communion with it. The Finnish distance runner Juha Vaatinen claimed that the stadium is for spectators, adding romantically, 'we have nature'.[4] The sterility of the synthetic track, its anaesthetic qualities, the tedium of interval running, is implied by athletes and coaches who seek to return training to more natural, rural surroundings. Even the most dedicated of scientized runners, keen advocates of interval running, have been drawn to ex-urban places for at least part of their training. Some of the rural locales in which world record breakers have trained have become almost sacred places, providing a sense of place, of topophilia. There is always a dark side to nature, however, and for some, the forest, field or park can be landscapes of fear.

Forests and Meadows

During the 1940s, the centre of gravity of European middle-distance running moved from war-torn Finland to neutral Sweden. A long line of great Swedish runners emerged – Gunder Hägg, Arne Andersson, Lennart Strand

and later Dan Waern and Anders Gärderud. In 1951, eight of the fastest eleven 1,500 metres runners of all time were Swedes.[5] Hägg, the world record holder for the 1,500 metres, mile and 5,000 metres, was the most well known of the Swedish stars. In a number of races in the 1940s, in which he vied with his compatriot Andersson, he brought the world's mile record down from Sydney Wooderson's 4 minutes 6.4 seconds to 4 minutes 1.4 seconds (the record that was to be beaten by Bannister). Although he practiced on the regular confines of the 400-metre track, he relieved the tedium of track training with runs in the meadow and forest landscape of his native Sweden. Gösta Holmér, the Swedish coach, claimed that this form of training 'suited our mind and the nature of our country',[6] associating a 'national mentality' with the physical environment. The Swedish runners incorporated the country-side into their training in a quite explicit way. It is significant that the form of running they practised in the countryside, through its naming, claimed to have a play element in it. The word for his training method is *fartlek* or 'speed-play', a method of training involving the mixing of steady running with much faster bursts in close-to-natural environments such as lakeside beaches, meadows, forests and hills. For Hägg and his companions, trained by Holmér and Gösta Ollander, the area around the training camp (or more accurately, a resort hotel) at Vålådalen, in west-central Sweden, contained routes on which the runners undertook various aerobic activities. A course of about 5 kilometres, which runners completed in pairs, running at different speeds and gaits, involved varied surfaces and topography (Figure 3.1). Unlike interval running, however, the runners were allowed to 'spontaneously call out a distance (say from here to that tree 40 yards up the trail), and they would cover that distance at a different speed'.[7]

The question has been raised about why Andersson and Hägg were able to achieve faster times than the German runners who had used the track-based interval running method. One answer is that the Swedes were permitted to

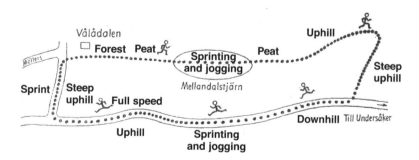

Figure 3.1 Running course (5 km) use by Gunder Hägg at Vålådalen, Sweden (based on Wilt, *How they Train*, p. 27 and Persson and Pettersen, *Svensk Friidrott*, p.349).

choose the distances run, adding an element of freedom or even play to the training.[8] And reflecting the idea of choice as play, Holmér wrote of *fartlek* in a naturalistic and romantic way, arguing that 'nature's rich variety must be used to make its impact on the training', that running must take place on 'smooth paths, on lingonberry and blueberry twigs, up and down hills, along soft, springy paths, over moor and marsh, interwoven with firm, needle-sprinkled paths';[9] or, as the English writer on running, W.R. Loader, put it, 'out in the quiet countryside, over rolling grassland, through conifer forests, along the shores of the tranquil, reed-fringed lakes'.[10] Herb Elliott, the Australian miler, described the joy of running along the 'soft-textured paths that meandered through the fragrant pine forests' in central Sweden as 'breath-taking'.[11] The strain and burden of trivial clock-work was seen as being replaced by the inspiration and power gained from communion with nature.

But it would be deceptive to associate running in nature solely with Scandinavia. Gordon Pirie described lyrically how much of his running, in his early years as a serious athlete, was

> through the woods and over the downs – those rolling hills so typical of the English countryside. The North Downs Escarpment in Surrey, where a great deal of our training was done, is particularly steep and rugged. There are footpaths through the woods and fields, and the going is beautiful, with reasonable green grass in the spring and summer, and lovely mud in the winter. The woods and fields are interlaced with miles of hedge-lined country lanes, barely wide enough for two cars to pass. The surface of these old roads is not particularly hard, and is smooth and firm. The countryside around our home at Coulsdon stretched out for miles like this in every direction.[12]

Pirie's contemporary, Bannister, whose writing also included a romantic and lyrical mode as well as one centred on science, recalls running with his friends down the steep mountainsides of North Wales, following rock climbing in Snowdonia:

> The wind sang in our ears and deafened us. Sometimes we tumbled, falling if we were lucky on a patch of grass, otherwise on hostile stones. We picked out likely landing places, as we jumped on ledge or boulder. Faster and faster we ran, each in turn leading until he slipped and was overtaken. Towards the bottom we could release ourselves from the agony of checking our descent, that tore at the overworked muscles of our thighs.

It was a glorious moment when the level ground brought us under control.

At Penn-y-Pass (sic) we threw ourselves on the grass by the stream, and drank our fill of water. Then we rolled over on our backs and lay there, steamy perspiration rising from clothes that had been inadequate protection against the chill wind on the ridges. We had drunk too deeply of the dangerous mountain air, become too infatuated with the goddess of speed. Waiting to catch up with ourselves we rubbed our aching limbs, tired but happy.[13]

Bannister also recalls, again in lyrical mode, the recuperative effects of a wild landscape, this time in Kintyre in Scotland following a hard racing season in 1951:

I felt I was running back to all the primitive joy that my season had destroyed ... The gulls were crying overhead and a herd of wild goats were silhouetted against the headland. I started to run again with the sun in my eyes nearly blinding me. I could barely distinguish slippery rock from heathery turf or bog; yet my feet did not slip or grow weary now – they had new life and confidence. I ran in a frenzy of speed, drawn by an unseen force. The sun sank, setting the forest ablaze, and turning the sky to dull smoke. Then tiredness came on and my bleeding feet tripped me. I rolled down a heather topped bank and lay there happily exhausted.[14]

The playful gambolling in Snowdonia was followed immediately by a time trial on the quarter-mile cinder circuit where, a year before the four-minute mile, he ran three-quarters of a mile, un-paced in three minutes, one second.[15] And the Scottish adventure was soon followed by a personal best performance over 1,500 metres, even though Bannister modestly claimed to be 'completely out of training'.[16]

The pleasures gained from running in the rural may be matched by running under cover of darkness. Again, it is Bannister who is shown to be a sensitive writer, describing the changing sense of speed that many runners will have experienced when running at night-time. He observes that:

Running in the dark has always had a strange fascination for me. Being unable to see the expanse of ground very far ahead I am not depressed by the distance yet to be covered, and have a sense of going at great speed. The velvety ensheathing blackness makes me feel at one with the world, as if the earth were moving with me.[17]

Such enjoyable sensations contrast with the conventional view of darkness, fear of it being worldwide.[18] For many people, running in darkness is anything other than entering a landscape of fear, one associated with potentially dangerous encounters (see below).

Reading accounts of exuberant running in darkness or in nature, and of 'speed-play', can be rather misleading. Running playfully in the countryside and the spontaneous element in *fartlek* remain secondary to the ultimate performance on the 400 metres track. And in both *fartlek* and in Bannister's Celtic runs, the running element is found to be hard. Aching muscles result from each. Any suggestion of rest – away from the track in North Wales, or the recovery period in *fartlek* – turns out to be an interval before more speed training, more work. The running regimen for Hägg and Bannister was carefully, but not totally, prescribed. Indeed, it has been suggested that in developing *fartlek*, Holmér and Ollander 'simply expanded on the concept of interval running' as adumbrated by Gerschler.[19] Bannister, despite his rural allusions, was a scientist, accepting interval running as 'a rewarding system of training because of its punishing intensity and infinite variety'.[20] And the Norwegian marathon runner Grete Waitz is said to have stopped *fartlek* training because it was too hard.[21]

Beaches and Dunes

One of the enduring images of the film *Chariots of Fire* is the group of runners moving rhythmically (to the swaying tune of the Vangelis sound-track) along the land-sea interface, the beach. A primeval sense of freedom is evoked in this scene. Beyond movie images, the beach and the adjoining sand dunes have been focal points of the runners' environment. The Australian coach Percy Cerutty, who is primarily associated with his star pupil Herb Elliott, placed great emphasis on the beach as a site for running. Like Hägg, Elliott was a world record holder at 1,500 metres and the mile. He was also the 1960 Olympic 1,500 metres champion in Rome. Elliott trained at Cerutty's coastal 'camp' at Portsea in Victoria. Here, he witnessed a coastal idyll where

a gigantic surf pounds along a golden expanse of sand, which extends into towering sand dunes and cliffs … I took one look at glorious, God-kissed Portsea and wanted to run through the sand from sheer joy and exhilaration. Everyone is effected the same way.[22]

Cerutty seems to have had a philosophy of running that was an odd amalgam of the romantic and modern, the idyllic and the fascistic (see Chapter 4). He eschewed the running track except for competitions: 'the artificial track is *not* the place to develop our athletics even if it be the place to demonstrate our ability', he propounded.[23] Combining the words 'stoic' and 'spartan', Cerutty labelled adherents to his ideas as 'stotans'. His runners faced considerable self-discipline; they trained in natural surroundings, on woodland paths and remote beaches at the water's edge, punishing their bodies by hard running up steep sand dunes. A day's training might start at 7 a.m. with a 'five mile run before breakfast in any direction our whim took us, followed by a dip in the ocean'.[24] The water's edge and the beach were signified in Cerutty's atavistic thinking as the site of protohuman beginnings. He claimed (quite falsely) that 'no great athlete grew up in luxury' and he had a romantic view of the working class.[25]

Cerutty's vision has been said to take precedence over 'any merely bio-dynamic count that could ultimately reduce human athletes to some sort of "mortal engines"'.[26] Yet his training regimen included discipline and order. Like *fartlek*, it was based on the interval running principle, though he would have hardly admitted this. The ultimate aim was achievement, with nature being used as part of the search for the record, the Olympic gold medal, the perfect athlete. Nature was being used, though in a different way from the case of the concrete stadium replacing the meadow.

It would be erroneous to assume that all those who have tried to return to nature have enjoyed their running. I earlier alluded to the negative experiences of English private schoolboys with their thankless 'grind'. And Loader refers to his early years of running in the fields of North East England in winter-time. He was greeted with

> showers of sleet and a bitter east wind … the long grass of the meadow was soaking wet … there was no lark on the wing, only a foolish youth sprinting backwards and forwards over a 150 yard stretch of melancholy fields … At the end of the exercise I had no sense of euphoria, no feeling that the blood was coursing redly through my veins, no belief that all was right with the world.[27]

Fictions of Rural Running

The world of fiction graphically illuminates the centrality of nature and the countryside as a relief, not only from the rigours of the track, but also from those of urban life itself. Consider, for example, this description from *The Front Runner*:

We ran softly for about three miles. We wended among the great silver beeches hazed with pink buds. Early violets and wood anemones poked up through the carpet of dead leaves. In the marshy sports, the skunk cabbages' bloom was long past and they were thrusting up their coarse green leaves. We leaped over logs fallen across the trail. We splashed over streams where the witch hazel still bent its frail yellow sprays of bloom. We leapt up hills and floated down on the other side.[28]

Shortly after, the two runners made love. This was running as foreplay. More often, however, running 'free' in such surroundings is seen as a form of therapy, of freedom, away from the constraints of modern, machine living.

In Alan Sillitoe's *The Loneliness of the Long Distance Runner*, Smith, the anti-hero, is incarcerated in a young offenders' institution. He is recognized as a potentially world-class athlete and is allowed privileges that include training outside the institution's walls. In Tony Richardson's movie, based on Sillitoe's book, Colin Smith's languor, depression and misery are converted into carefree happiness as he runs free in his early-morning training sessions through a carefully landscaped garden. Geographer Martyn Bowden sees Smith's running through the lens of William Blake's epic poem, 'Jerusalem'. Smith, outside his cell, is in 'England's green and pleasant land':

His lonely figure plods over dewy pastures closely cropped by sheep and deer. A tall Scots pine or two and the occasional clump of beeches and elms dot the landscape. And then he is across the steam and into the trees … Colin does a hop, step and jump through puddles like a kid, goes through the over-arm bowling action of a cricketer (conjuring up images of that most pastoral scene, cricket on the village green) and does a long backslide down a leafy bank. His flashbacks, as he lies there and as he runs subsequently, are all happy memories.[29]

In the novel, Sillitoe writes of Smith poetically:

By the time I'm half-way through my morning course, when after a frost-bitten dawn I can see a phlegmy bit of sunlight hanging from the bare twigs of beech and sycamore, and when I've measured my half-way mark by the short-cut scrimmage down the steep bush-covered bank and into the sunken lane, where there's still not a soul in sight and not a sound except the neighing of a piebald foal in a cottage stable that I can't see, I get to thinking the deepest and daftest of all.[30]

Bowden additionally draws on the significance of the rural in the running movie *Chariots of Fire*. The Scottish Olympic 400 metres champion of 1924, Eric Liddell, and Harold Abrahams, winner of the 100 metres at the same Games, are the main characters and protagonists. The influence of the rural is, in Bowden's reading, clearly specified in the film. Liddell races in the industrial milieu of Glasgow, in unmistakably working-class settings. He is presented as an untidy runner, untrained and, in Abrahams's character-ization in the movie, 'runs like a wild animal'. As such, he is represented as training in a Highland field and on steep, craggy, uneven mountainsides. At the end of the film he is seen running on a vast and tractless beach with other athletes, noted above.[31] The more disciplined Abrahams is always seen train-ing on a straight and narrow path. The English pastoral is caught, however, in the film's representation of Abrahams running on a carefully laid out, straight, grassy path between two long rows of tall elms. He also runs with the hounds and their master, the essence of the English aristocracy in a rural setting. Even the athletic meetings in which Abrahams runs seem to be bounded by grass and deciduous trees in rural settings. Bowden notes that 'the character and style of each of the major runners are determined by the type of pastoral environment in which each trains'.[32] The message is that when they enter the British countryside, runners flourish.

Landscape Determinism

It has all too easily been explicated that a nation's countryside, its landscape, can be a – indeed, *the* – determining factor in producing runners of high quality. In the 1920s and 1930s, Finland was a nation that produced a disproportionately large number of top-level distance runners. Of the 20 fastest 5,000 metres runners in the world in 1930, 12 were Finns.[33] At the pinnacle was Paavo Nurmi but there were many others, as the record books vividly show. Among them were Kolehmainen, Mäki, Iso-Hollo, and later, Salsola, Salonen, Vuorisalo, Vaatinen, Vasala and Viren. According to the German Jack Schumacher, writing in the 1930s, the over-production of Finnish running talent could be 'explained' by Finland's landscape:

> All kinds of being in these stretches of land were capable by nature of special feats of endeavour ... Running is certainly in the blood of every Finn. When you see the clear, deep green forests, the wide, open luxuriant plains with their typical red peasant homes, the heights covered by massive clusters of trees and the never-ending light blue of the horizon with the lakes merging with the sky, one is overcome with an involuntary feeling of

elation and because you don't have wings, you want to run. Yes, hurry, light-footed through this northern scenery, for kilometres, for hours on end. Nurmi and his friends are like animals in the forest. They began to run because there was a deep need, because a peculiar dreamlike scenery enticed them and pulled them into the spell of its mysteries … It is not merely the pursuit of the naked record, for fame and honour, which spurs every son of the north to near superhuman feats. Their splendid times are also a way of thanking mother earth and the beauty of her many endless trails.[34]

Many Finns employed such sentiments themselves, journalists citing Finland's northern location as a factor that could spontaneously produce elite runners.[35] Lurking within such accounts of the centrality of nature is the widely discredited notion of environmental determinism and the anti-urbanism and anti-intellectualism of Volkish body-cultural ideology.[36] Even so, in the 1950s, when the German coach Waldemar Gerschler visited England he could hardly avoid lapsing into deterministic rhetoric. As a result of witnessing the kind of countryside – the chalk downlands of Surrey – where Gordon Pirie and his brother Peter frequently trained, Gerschler claimed to have understood the results that they had achieved: 'He saw the kind of grass [they] were running on, the conditions under foot, the size of the hills – they were challenging but not impossible. He thought the whole area was visually attractive, and that was important to runners too.'[37]

In *Escapism*, Tuan is at pains to point out that the kinds of escape to nature noted above are more likely 'escapes from nature'. 'What we wish to escape to', he argues, 'is not "nature" but an alluring conception of it.'[38] It is a tamed landscape, the result of human dominance. Vålådalen turns out to be a resort, Portsea a 'camp', Pirie trained on downland, long cleared of its native forest, the fictionalized Abrahams ran in a landscaped landscape. In Finland, long thought of as a land where runners trained in the idyllic forests, one soon finds that running would be impossible in forests that have been left untouched by human contact, a wilderness. The entangled undergrowth, fallen timber, and unsure footing makes running impossible and paths and tracks have to be provided for training to take place. Runners run in a nature that has been tamed.

Tuan notes that the 'countryside nearly always exudes an air of innocence'.[39] He is wise to insert the word 'nearly'. The tamed wilderness and its conversion to countryside or park are not necessarily safer places to run than the inner city. Forests, fields and parklands can, for some runners, be landscapes of fear. So too can places of darkness. Freedom to run where they like may apply only to certain groups, often white, heterosexual males. Drawing on the work of geographer Gillian Rose, sexual attacks on women runners remind them that their bodies are not meant to be in certain places. Racist, homophobic and sexist violence delimits the running spaces of black, gay and women runners. Such spaces constitute Tuan's landscapes of fear.[40]

More Runnings

There are other contexts for serious running where the rural and the quasi-natural form central milieux of the performance. These are road running, cross-country running, fell running and orienteering. Additionally, there are various forms of 'extreme' running. None of these kinds of running require a specialized site. Even so, the tendencies shown towards the rationalization of track running is also found in these other configurations.

Road running has a long history. In the middle of the eighteenth century road running became popular in the era of pedestrianism. Races were focused on gambling and organized by gentlemen's clubs. Later, running for money became popular among the working classes, and races were organized by public houses where wagering was common.[41] Distances run varied with no standardization or bureaucratic record keeping. By the mid nineteenth century the conventional form of running had shifted to the enclosed track and 'running grounds'. Standardization and time-keeping paralleled enclosure and rationalization in the broader society. The marathon, today the most well-known road running event, was re-introduced into the calendar of running at the 1896 Olympics. For many years the marathon was relatively unpopular, and races were composed of a small number of runners by today's standards. Runners were often subjected to ridicule by unknowing spectators. In 1959, five marathon races were held in the USA; ten years later the figure was 44, and by the late 1970s had reached around 200.[42] The big city marathons continue to attract huge numbers. The New York Marathon attracted 29,327 entries in 2000, compared with 55 in 1970.

The marathon has been subjected to cultural analysis, being seen as a symbol of late modernity. Jean Baudrillard, doyen of postmodernists, saw the New York marathon as 'suffering freely entered into as we might speak of a state of servitude freely entered into'.[43] Others have called it a 'flagellantist-delusion'.[44] Reminding us of the first Marathon man, 2,000 years ago, Baudrillard sees the runners seeking death by exhaustion. The sadness of the marathon seems, for him, that the overwhelming majority of the runners do not seek victory; they run 'simply in order to feel alive'.[45] This is in spite of the fact that they become increasingly decrepit by the hour – 'from the competitive athletic types who arrive first to the wrecks who are literally carried to the finishing line by their friends'.[46] 'Do we have to prove to ourselves that we exist?' queries Baudrillard. However, while he seems happy with the 'Promethean ecstasy of competition, effort and success', this may be how the decrepit wrecks (perversely) see themselves performing, 'fetishistic' though it might be.[47]

Road running is a rejection of the synthetic and territorialized nature of the track and a claiming back of the roads and streets or the re-taking of autopolis. Here, running is a kind of oppositional strategy. Christopher Winters has suggested that taking to the streets represented a mild, though sanctioned, kind of rebellion.[48] The marathon can also be read as an uneasy concoction of the pre- and late-modern. The marathon boom made the old look new. Racing was taken out of the stadium and back to the people, back to ordinary environments. The music and carnival atmosphere associated with many marathons and other road running events also hinted at less seriousness. Indeed, elite athletes rubbed shoulders with novices and hobbyist runners. Other incongruous juxtapositions, suggesting a postmodern turn, include whole grain food being taken together with isotonic sports drinks, raw bodies carried on high-tech shoes, and spiritual tendencies coexisting with the results of the latest scientific research.[49] Some marathon races seem to go out of their way to reject seriousness. In the Marathon de Medoc, a run through the Bordeaux vineyards, the organizers have chosen to include wine-tasting during the race.[50] However, the urban marathon has also been read as bearing all the signs of the most modern modernity with its 'staging of individuality as a collective event'.[51] Today the New York and London marathons are business enterprises.

The road-racing boom of the 1970s and 1980s can also be read as a reaction against the 'Fordism' of track running. Fordism is typified by rigid capital equipment, mass production, uniformity, centralization and bureaucratic regulation. Post-Fordism is characterized by small-batch production, flexibility, decentralization and deregulation.[52] Fordism has its analogies in running. Fordist foot-running involves production (of races) being geared to capital equipment (the standardized, synthetic 400-metre track), the optimization of processes (interval running), a growing division of labour and a standardization of outputs (a few Grand Prix spectacles). It is 'tightly' organized with little, if no, space for deviations. Post-Fordist flexibility, however, refers the ability to switch from one system to another with 'non-dedicated' machinery, that is, roads. It is, in Rigauer's words, a 'temporally and spatially looser' kind of running,[53] avoiding the monotony of track running. Road races are not standardized; they are uphill and down dale; they are analogous to 'small batch production' and are able to satisfy the whims of the most recent running fad.

Cross-country running is a widespread winter sport in many nations. The English championship still attracts over 1,000 runners for the men's race. It has grown out of forms of Victorian and pre-Victorian running known as 'hares and hounds' and paper-chasing and other less well-known variants.

The historian J.A. Mangan records that schoolboys at Harrow School in the 1830s engaged in 'toozling' – the chasing and killing of birds in the local hedgerows.[54] Paper-chasing was more well known and widespread. A group of 'hares' set out with sacks of scraps of paper, dropping them as a trail that leads to the finishing point. They also attempt to deceive the 'hounds' by setting fake trails that petered out after a relatively short distance. In *Tom Brown's Schooldays*, published in 1856, the Barby Run was a hares and hounds event that covered nine and a half miles – for schoolboys. Such races took place over open countryside and continued in England until the late nineteenth century when championship events exceeded 11 miles in distance.[55] However, paper-chases did provide the runners with a chance to slow down when necessary. As a result, 'they are better than races' averred Webster.[56] The demise of paper-chasing seems to have been associated with damage to farmland, the prevalence of betting on such events and the growth of by-laws against litter. More rational running would replace it.

Cross-country running requires less guile than paper-chasing and continues today during the winter months. Until the later decades of the twentieth century, cross-country was thought by many to be an important form of conditioning for the summer track season, especially for middle- and long-distance runners. Farmland and parklands were widely used. The climax of the British season was the English championships, run over 9 miles. Mud, streams and stiles had to be negotiated on courses that often included a variety of features such as woods, ploughed fields and meadows.

In recent decades cross-country running has witnessed containment and taming. Rather than open countryside, the needs of spectators and television have been taken into account and existing facilities such as horse race courses, golf courses or urban parkland have been used. The ruggedness of the traditional English course has been replaced by a tamer version. As in track races, runners now tend to run several laps; often, but not always, the mud has given way to carefully tended turf. In one championship, the streets of the city were covered temporarily by soil and turf so that it could become a site for cross-country. Although looser than track racing it displays signs of tightening up.

Founded in Norway in 1895, orienteering is the most geographical of sports. Geographer Jay Appleton comments that orienteering integrates physical activity and environment to the farthest limits so far achieved by any recreational activity: 'It directly exploit[s] the pleasure-giving potential of nature by intimately incorporating the perceptual experience of the natural environment' within the activity itself.[57] The sport is particularly popular in Finland and Sweden but has spread to embrace a large number of nations. In contrast to track running, it is a humane, intelligent, supremely geographical and environment-friendly form of running in which map and compass are essential tools. Way-finding and an attention to detail are crucial. Here speed is subordinated to concentration; the orienteer has to look for things other than the finishing line. She has to run, hurdle boughs and branches, read a map and use a compass. Basically, the orienteer is a runner with a way-finding mission.

Orienteering can be read as a mix of the pre-modern and the modern. It is close to nature, or as close as it can possibly be. It does not destroy the physical environment, nor does it become garden-like. It is a sport of the forest, most popular in Finland and Sweden. At the same time it utilizes modern technology in the form of detailed maps and compasses. Through the use of maps it brings the reality and the simulation together. It uses a model of the world (the map) to find one's way through the real world. As the orienteers traverse hilly, forested terrain, they are doing so by 'reading' the landscape off a flat surface. Courses range from about one to 15 kilometres, variations in terrain determining the level of difficulty.

Yet orienteering also displays similar tendencies to those noted above. For example, in the late 1960s the International Orienteering Federation introduced an internationally *standardized* approach to the design and layout of orienteering maps. A Norwegian computer scientist created the first, modern multi-colour maps based on real photography. The sport of the forest has become technologized.

Athletics, Aesthetics and Sensual Pleasures

As a runner, one experiences many places at a variety of scales. At the local level there are many types of terrain over which running can take place. At the global level it is possible for a migrant athlete to experiences exotic as well as mundane milieux. At the end of a lifetime of running one might look back and vividly recall the sights and sites where one has run and trained. Tuan writes: 'When individuals savor their own lives they recall the good moments, which occur, of course, in a cultural context. Culture strongly influences, though it does not necessarily determine, the character of these moments.'[58] I have already touched on some of the contexts in which good moments take place – the beach, the Stockholm Stadium, the forest paths. It is these kinds of places that can be said to form the cultural models of a good life of running. In an introductory book on running, the former Boston and New York marathon winner Alberto Salazar identifies what he considers the best kinds of places for running, his criteria being based on safety, comfort and aesthetics. He recognizes a hierarchy, ranging from (1) off-road running paths with surfaces of packed dirt, wood chips or asphalt, (2) side streets, (3) running tracks, and (4) big-city sidewalks. He notes that aesthetics is a personal matter, but it often entails getting away from cars – exactly what you want for safety and, often, for the best footing.[59] The safest environments for running, it would seem, are the most rural, the least safe are the most urban. This, as I have already noted, is not necessarily the case, however, and comfort and safety should not be seen as synonymous.

Sharing of experiences, social harmony and teamwork have traditionally been regarded as sources of satisfaction that contribute to a good life (see chapter 7). Teamwork can exist in running situations, as in the cases of relay races, cross-country or road races where aggregated positions are used to calculate team scores. Team races once featured in the Olympics but were discontinued after 1924. Warm feelings are induced by the success of a team and some athletes have been know to achieve faster times when they are members of a relay team than when they are competing as individuals. The efficient performance in a race brings satisfaction and the camaraderie experienced among runners, both before and after a run or race, provides pleasure and satisfaction.

Moral-aesthetic considerations have become increasingly important in sports as athletes promote their bodies as well as their performances, though it would be difficult to envisage an elite athlete sacrificing victory for grace. A degree of asceticism may also typify an athlete's career. A culture of running provides the milieu in which pleasure and gratification may be derived from at least a degree of austerity. Like those who adopt a monastic existence, athletes may appear to lead somewhat austere lives. Tuan feels that 'a trace of austerity is essential for the good life', arguing that this applies to hygiene and mental health and also to moral-aesthetic considerations.[60] Self-denial is an important dimension of a runner's life. Abstention – for varying degrees of time – from alcohol, certain foods and sex is not uncommon among athletes. Perhaps the runner gets sufficient satisfaction from his body-cultural activity for him to be free of worldly concerns. Gordon Pirie chose to ignore fine foods following a victory and ended up being dedicated to herbal remedies. In other cases, however, famous runners have been reduced to alcohol abuse and worldly excess. The great Kenyan runner Henry Rono had been a world multi-record holder before being reduced to a virtually derelict alcoholic.

Christopher Winters has recalled that 'most runners would admit to an esthetic, sensual component to their running ... Long distance running induces intermittent but sometimes extraordinarily intense and pleasurable awareness of the environment.'[61] Recall Bannister's *feelings* of running on the beach and in the mountains of Wales and Scotland. Tuan suggests that 'running at peak form indeed yields bodily pleasure, but it is an embracing happiness, a reaching out to an immersion in the world'.[62] In this form of bodily locomotion, the tactile (or haptic) sense is of considerable sensory importance. Runners notice the difference between running in town and country, on concrete and tarmac, on grass and sand. Some surfaces provide more pleasure than others, the forest floor being preferred by many. Other senses are experienced during running: In T.O. Beechcroft's short story 'The half-miler', he writes that 'the summer was still new enough to greet the senses with surprise'. The runner 'stepped lightly on the elastic turf. The grass breathed out delicious freshness.' For years after, that fragrance was to set the runner's nerves tingling.[63] The smell of bluebells in an English woodland; Smith 'smelling the green grass and honeysuckle' and the sound of 'birds singing from a briar hedge' during his epic (non-) race;[64] the sound of gulls and whiff of salt on the seashore; the gently gurgling streams of the forest; the clear view and enhanced colouration of woodland and meadow in the clean air following a storm: all enhance the experience of running. Additionally, there are the sounds and smells of the city. And, independent of the physical environment, it remains possible to gain a sense of *joie de vivre* through 'the thrill of sheer speed'[65] on track, grass or road, even at my advanced age (though I have to admit, again, that 'speed' is relative).

Tuan has no doubts that sensual pleasure contributes to the good life. He points out that we are 'losing touch, in a literal sense, with nature'.[66] He notes that while children still enjoy 'jumping into a pile of leaves' or 'rolling down a hill of snow', adults enjoy nature by simply looking at it.[67] And, by contrast, if adults 'reach out for the tactile rewards they tend to do so in the context of strenuous sport'.[68] The yearning for a more passionate engagement with nature than that provided by the more conventional forms of running may have led to an interest, among some, for more extreme versions, such as the 'Canadian Death Race'.[69] Claimed to be Canada's toughest race, it is open to individuals or relay teams. The website exhorts: 'Come experience the newest and "baddest" extreme race on the block, and find out why we call it the Death Race.' This macabre event involves three independent races over the same 125 km of extreme mountain trails. The course crosses 3 mountain summits and gains over 17,000 ft in elevation. All events include crossing the Smoky River. Even so, despite a degree of estrangement from nature, a good life of running can still be found in the sensuous pleasure that conventional forms provide. The sense of movement and of speed can still be experienced in the most sterile of environments.

The sensual engagement with running may be at its greatest when all the senses are stimulated. If I assume that 'nature' is more complex than 'culture', then the more artificial the environment the less sensuous the experience. Artificial running environments tend towards the anaesthetic; natural settings tend toward the aesthetic (see Figure 3.2). And here I return to the notion of slowness. Running in the countryside, the beach, the forest or the meadow may refresh the athlete but it does not permit the runner to fully absorb the pleasures and senses of nature in a way that walking can. Tuan observes that it is widely assumed that 'aesthetic appreciation is possible only when one moves slowly, with frequent pauses'.[70] According to Paul Adams it is 'the stroll', not a run, which provides a source of pleasure. One can take in the landscape and its variety more fully; one may pause and contemplate, even communicate. Adams places slowness, not speed, as the main attribute of walking.[71] 'Going

Indoor track	Estrangement
Outdoor track	
Cross-country	Simple contact
Paperchasing	
	Exploration
Orienteering	
Training	
Walking	Communication

Figure 3.2 A typology of sensory relationships in running. The vertical line represents the continuum of human-environment relationships (right) and forms of locomotion (left). (After Paul Rodaway, *Sensuous Geographies: Body, Sense and Place* (London: Routledge, 1994), p.46).

slowly has a good reputation' and 'slowness has traditionally meant the examined life', allowing us 'to take control over our lives'.[72] As Rebecca Solnit notes in her remarkable book on walking, 'a walker does not skip over much'. A runner, however, does. And even an athletic walker is so consumed by endeavour 'as to be unable to participate in his surroundings, particularly when driven by a schedule of competition'.[73] For the serious runner, 'participation' or communication with the landscape is even less. Serious runners seek to eliminate nature from their consciousness, seeing it as an intrusion. Amby Burfoot, in his runners' guide, advocates not looking at the landscape ahead 'or at least, to look at it as infrequently as possible. Stay centred on the moment. Look down the road in front of you. Chug, chug, chug. Concentrate on the basic, essential things that you have to get done.'[74] Serious runners stop at appointed places or times, not when observation of, or concentration on, the milieu beckons.

When it comes to careful observation and attention, running seems impoverished compared with walking. Slowness rather than speed is preferred. The serious athlete *is* engaged in (at least, a kind of) field-work, but when talking about fieldwork, the geographer Carl Sauer stated that 'locomotion should be slow, the slower the better'.[75]

Athletes as Pets

A reading based on Tuan's *Dominance and Affection* might well see some athletic arenas as gardens, displaying as they do a melding of dominance and affection and of horticulture and architecture. How might he read the athletes who populate and participate in these places? His answer might well be as pets. A pet is a zoological version of the garden. Tuan sees pets all around us. Many animals are commonly thought of as pets. Human power is exercised over them to the extent that they may become dependent on their owners. We train them to respond to our commands; we train them to perform tricks; we shout 'Go' and they run. Sporting animals can also be read as pets. Like a pet poodle or cuddly kitten, the greyhound and the racehorse are trained; each suffer domination but also receive affection. But what about human pets? Are athletes pets too? Tuan notes that

> People who exploit nature for pleasure and for aesthetic and symbolic reasons seldom realize that they are doing harm to the plants and animals, distorting them into shapes they are not meant to have and, in the case of animals, forcing them into behavior that is not natural to them. People who exploit other humans for profit or pleasure have, by contrast, an uneasy conscience.[1]

Consider for a moment some of the words used in this quotation. Are athletes 'distorted into shapes they are not meant to have'? Are runners forced into unnatural behaviours? A pet, according to Tuan, is a 'diminished being'.[2] The relationship between the trainer and the trainee is unquestionably one of dominance, but are the trainer's charges diminished in any way? To many people the word 'diminished' would be an inappropriate term to apply to the athlete. After all, far from being diminished, training and racing is frequently thought to have enhanced the human athlete, physically and emotionally. The word 'training' is easily, and unreflectively, applied to animals, children and athletes. But can training display an overwhelming dominance, with affection perverted into abuse? I want to address these kinds of questions in the sections that follow.

Coaching and Encroaching

Running seriously is not forced labour. It clearly has a voluntary dimension, though it is all too easy to aver that the runner always chooses the coach. Even so, athletes have long sought the advice of a coach or trainer, putting faith and trust in an expert. While the coach may then take control, the desire to improve must also carry 'a strong internalized feeling of a "need" of discipline and conformity' for training to be successful.[3] The trainer's external gaze is accompanied by an internalized 'bad conscience' that drives the runner to maintain the training regimen.[4] The coach's record and reflections on the athletes' bodies and souls are incorporated into the subjects' self-knowledge and self-understanding, enabling them to get a grip on themselves. The runner is created: the coach is central to this process.

Gordon Pirie observed that having met, and been impressed by, Waldemar Gerschler, 'I unreservedly put myself in his hands'.[5] From this point onwards, the coach's role becomes one of dominance and though the trainee has the right to leave, the power of the trainer is often durable. The need for a coach may result from runners being implanted with 'a sense of constant lack, of recurring incompletion'.[6] Runners are said to develop a 'need' to train regularly, to obey the coach's demands. Through the coach, athletes are familiarized with a training plan, they will try to meet kilometric goals 'but they do not necessarily intend to develop a conscience (bad or good) relative to the expectations'.[7]

Are athletic coaches altruistic? Do coaches exist for the sake of the athlete or is it the other way around? Tuan reminds us that in ancient Greece, 'in gymnasiums, teachers were exposed to the temptation of naked boys under their charge'.[8] The prolific British writer of inter-war training manuals, Captain F.A.M. Webster, recorded that he trained boys who wore 'no clothing other than a pair of silk shorts while the watery sun and the sharp breezes of October and March bit at their beautifully bronzed bodies'.[9] Undoubtedly, some coaches have succumbed to the homoerotic temptations of youthful flesh.[10] Eroticism is likely to be a factor attracting some to the coaching role. It is a relationship in which young, relatively unclad bodies are willingly and innocently exposed and where the sense of touch is, on occasions, not denied to the coach. In her remarkable autobiography, Leslie Heywood sums up her coach's attitude to a female high-school runner, who trained with the boys' team, as follows: 'You're a girl, so you're garbage, not an athlete, no right to be here with my guys on my field … We use girls for sex, and we don't know why you think you're any different. Come here little girl. Just who do you think you are?'[11] As Tuan comments, '*Play* is such a sunny word that we forget its dark side. It is bad to be "used", but it can be worse to be "played with".'[12] Of course, it is more than plausible that the athlete rather than the coach might initiate such playfulness. In *The Front Runner*, the fictional distance runner Billy Sive searches the eyes of his gay coach at their first meeting and confronts him with the fact that there is nothing in the rule books 'about the sex of the person you sleep with'.[13]

But the erotic – and its possible perversion into abuse – is very far from being the only motivation for those who are attracted to coaching and training young athletes. More commonly, there is likely to be a Pygmalion tendency; that is, to turn the body into something that it ought to be, according to the norms of the trainer. Loader observes that 'some runners get to the point of relying on advice as a cripple relies on a crutch. They finish up by playing Galatea to the coach's Pygmalion'.[14] In doing so, the pride of the trainer will be enhanced. Coaches are often professional and hence the coaching of their charges may carry a strong economic imperative. Additionally, coaches and trainers are motivated by local or national factors – to increase the sporting output of the nation, city or school, to *use* the athlete as a means of achieving national or local prestige. In such cases, the runner is co-opted by the school or nation, assimilated into the larger society, denied freedom to choose what distance and where to run. The runner comes to *represent* a place. Team or national goals subsume the success of the individual and the runner carries the expectations of others who will share or appropriate his or her success. There may be coaches who display genuine affection, the dominance being muted, caring and playful, though inevitably present. Whatever the motivation, however, it is difficult to see how the athlete is anything but a pet. Power is inevitably displayed in training, even if undertaken altruistically. Tuan is emphatic in his view that 'the basis of all successful training is the display of an unchallengeable power'.[15]

When children have been trained in special skills, they are often praised for being good at something. Tuan suggests that they learn to 'place value less on who they are than on what they can do, on the more or less specialized tasks and roles they can perform'.[16] This is certainly true of the young athlete. And during the course of training, dominance is frequently too distant from affection, and control from nurturing care.[17] Apparent dominance may be taken for affection. But the governor of the remand home where Alan Sillitoe's runner, Smith, was incarcerated, talked to him 'almost as he'd talk to his prize race horse',[18] an appropriate simile for situations where child-athletes and teenagers become exploited. In recent years the world of sport has been shocked by the often-abusive relationship between coach and athlete. This is malign domination, though it may be no more (but no less) prevalent in sports than in the wider society.[19]

The coach possesses power (dominance) over his or her charges in several ways. It is one of many examples where human relationships contain a hostile element (Tuan notes that 'hospitality' and 'hostility' have the same root).[20] Celia Brackenridge cites 11 types of power possessed by sports coaches. Some forms of power seem more dangerous than others. Expert power, showing ability in a sport and being able to demonstrate a sporting technique, seems more nurturing than coercive forms of power that might involve bullying an athlete in order to make her compliant. Expert power has the potential to lead the trainer/trainee into a master/apprenticeship situation, to 'learn by doing' by observing the body cultural practices of a gifted practitioner/mentor (not teacher).[21] Similarly, legitimate power, gained by receiving an official appointment from a sport's governing body, is more likely to be benign than charismatic power that results from an attractive personality, which might charm athletes to train harder.[22]

An ethnographic study by Robert Sands of a group of American collegiate sprinters graphically revealed the coach's power over his athletes, though in an ambivalent way.[23] The sprint coach of the track team of which Sands became part was Willie Williams, one-time 100 metres world record holder. Sands writes of him: 'Willie is many things to us, our coach, ex-world record holder, a father figure [...], an authority figure and at times a benevolent dictator.'[24] Despite Williams's benevolence, he is not referred to as a friend, though those in partnerships in many kinds of projects, including the world of business, often see themselves as friends.[25] But the athlete–coach bond is not inevitably felt to be friendless. Gordon Pirie claimed that he felt that his coach, Gerschler, was 'a mentor, inspiration and close friend'.[26] Even so, the German obituary archive *Munzinger* felt that Gerschler, while undoubtedly making contributions to the science of running, 'was authoritarian and self-righteous'.[27]

The United States intercollegiate sport system has supplied much evidence of authoritarian track coaches. In the 1960s, at least, most American student-athletes who wanted to compete for their schools were required to train under the direct supervision of the coach. The application of their own training methods was (and usually still is) denied them and the time of their training is explicitly specified. The coach–athlete relationship tends to be one of 'obeying until it hurts' – and beyond.[28] By contrast, a professor cannot force a student to study in any particular manner.[29] Bruce Kidd, a Canadian distance running prodigy of the 1960s, observed that one of the reasons that he refused an athletic scholarship in the US was the unnecessarily onerous dual meet schedules of most colleges. He remembered telling one coach that he had ambitions to be a six-miler. The coach's response was that with Kidd's strength he might be able to run a leg on the mile relay team in dual meets, after he had run the 880 yards, the mile and the two miles.[30] Such exploitation of the athlete in the name of the university has been far from uncommon in the United States. Power in this form may be even more cynically exploited when the athlete concerned is a foreign recruit from a part of the world unfamiliar with the US college set up.[31]

Percy Cerutty insisted that his athletes ('stotans') follow a training regimen that took them close to nature. His objectives, in terms of training the athletic body, resonate with the fascist philosophy of National Socialist Germany. As noted in the previous chapter, Cerutty's regimen included much running on the land–sea interface, that is, the beach and sand dunes. These idyllic surroundings in no way lessen Cerutty's concern with producing pets, despite his claims to the contrary. His notion of 'inner-time recorders' (rather than the mechanical stop-watch) is precisely the self-administered control that Foucault argued is so powerful.[32] Cerutty has been quoted as saying that as an athlete 'you have got to make yourself hate', and 'all I'm interested in is achievement',[33] an attitude felt by the Australian runner Ron Clarke to be an 'unpleasant philosophy'.[34] The charismatic teacher readily obtains unquestioning acceptance. Cerutty argued that by virtue of their philosophy, his stotans

> will be nature lovers, with a respect and appreciation of all evolved and created things. They will appreciate the sanctity of creative effort both in themselves and others. They will strive to understand the significance implied by reality, will be able to discern the real from the spurious, and see no anomaly in nudity, either in body or mind. But neither will they cast pearls before swine. Stotans, for all the reasons that their philosophy stands for – hardness, toughness, unswerving devotion to an ideal, and many more – will look upon the sea as their pristine element and endeavour to associate themselves with their primeval source of life by going into the sea at least once per month in all seasons of the year. No practice is more disposed to toughen both the body and the morale than this. Stotans believe that neither the body nor mind can be maintained at a high pitch of efficiency unless sufficient regular rest is obtained, and aim for a daily average of eight hours ... Stotans will not be found in social places after midnight. Stotans shall regulate their lives so that at the end of the period, varying with the intensity of the effort, each shall realize what he has attained, without conscious striving, to a state of knowledge and a position of leadership in the community. It is axiomatic that only the pure can understand purity, only the cultivated appreciate beauty, and only the strong measure their strength. Therefore, only the self-disciplined can command genuine respect.[35]

Discipline and fanatical devotion, hardness and elitism, a belief in nudism (Cerutty even rejected the use of the 'jock strap'),[36] strength and nature, and anti-intellectualism, all resonate strongly with ideals advocated by National Socialism in 1930s Germany, where Physical Education was regarded as the most important subject on the school curriculum.[37] Of this period, George Mosse has noted that

> sun, light and unspoiled nature were supposed to steel the body and give it health and strength ... The nude body ... was supposed to be one beautiful object among others, such as meadows, gardens, the sea, or the rising sun.[38]

The difference between Cerutty and the Nazis was that there was no obvious racial message in the former's writing, and, indeed, he displayed an atavistic tendency towards the running qualities of Australian aborigines. However, Cerutty's observations on gender would have rested comfortably with those of a fascistic misogynist. 'I see no good at all in women competitors', he is quoted as saying.[39]

It might be reasonably argued that pet-making in human sports was carried to its extreme in the former German Democratic Republic, which was able to produce high class runners from the sprints to the marathon. In John Hoberman's words, East German athletes were subjected to 'scientific cultivation of high performance' and children became 'experimental subjects for high-performance theorists'.[40] But perhaps the saddest tale does not come from East Germany but from Canada, when Ben Johnson, who was given steroids by his coach Charlie Francis, was disqualified, having won the 100 metres at the 1982 Seoul Olympics. He was treated like a pet who had misbehaved when sent out to perform. The publicity surrounding this event made it all the more poignant – one human being deceived by another.

In addition to the coach, runners at the professional level often have to accept the power of an agent. In recent decades, runners form Kenya and other parts of Africa have migrated to Europe and North America, seeing future wealth in parts of the world where most professional racing is found. The role of the agent is explicated in the following extract from a contract between an agent and athlete:

> I _____ agree to Athletes International Management representing and negotiating on my behalf, on a domestic and international basis for my presence in athletics or related promotions and accept that they will require a fee of 10% of any monies negotiated for the former, including prize money and 20% for promotional/

sponsorship/commercial contracts. I fully accept and understand that I must inform Athletes International Management of any approaches made by race organizers or other such persons.[41]

The extent to which an agent might exploit athletes within the terms of such contracts will vary from individual to individual, but any contractual arrangement necessarily involves power relations that can readily be seen as expressions of dominance.

Performers as Pets

Tuan writes that 'when people are treated like amusing performing animals, the line between condescension and sadistic taunt is thin'.[42] It is often inferred that human athletes are performers. We talk of 'performances' – a time of 9.85 seconds for the 100 metres is a 'great performance'. But 'performing' also carries negative, even sinister connotations. In the 1904 Olympics at St Louis, native peoples from various parts of the world were brought together in 'Anthropology Days' in order to compete (perform) in Olympic sports with which they were totally unfamiliar. The 'savages', as they were termed, took part in a number of running events, displayed to tourists who had come to see the Games and the concurrent St Louis World Exposition. It had been rumoured that such native peoples would be natural athletes and the organizers expected great things from them. Aided by anthropologists, they set out to test their expectations. The results were measured by the stopwatch and then recorded so that they could be compared with those of the Olympic champions. They turned out – hardly surprisingly – to be feeble in comparison with those of the Euro-American standards of the day. Here can be seen dominance without affection. The natives who performed in these sad events were figures of fun, patently shown to be inferior to their western peers by the statistical record of the respective results, used uncritically but powerfully. The Olympic report stated that as a result of their quantified performances it was no longer appropriate to think of savages as natural athletes and that such assertions needed to be backed by evidence rather than hearsay.[43]

In more recent times athletes have also been treated as pets, to entertain and to perform in humiliating contexts. One of the greatest sprinters of all time was Jesse Owens, who set four world records in one afternoon at Ann Arbor, Michigan, in 1935 and won four gold medals at the 1936 Olympics. However, having lost his amateur status late in his career, he was reduced to being little more than a sideshow performer, feeling obliged to compete against a thoroughbred racehorse in Havana. This was an old showmanship gambit introduced by circus magnate P.T. Barnum. Owens beat the horse and returned a time of 9.9 seconds for the 100 yards race.[44] He also exhibited himself in other novelty races, including one against Joe Louis, the champion boxer. Apparently, the race was a farce, Owens tripping and falling at the start of the 60 yards dash; Louis just won.[45] Years later, Owens's reaction to such exhibitions was that he felt humiliated, sick, feeling like a 'spectacle, a freak'; it was 'a new kind of slavery'.[46] William Baker, in his remarkable biography of Owens, is not overly sympathetic. From his 'sideshow'-style performances Owens had made a lot of money, enough to buy two Buicks, and he lived comfortably. Running in these 'freak show' events was seen by Baker as 'extra money in the bank and Owens was glad to take it'; 'to a restless young man barred from amateur competition while not yet freed from the athletic impulse, it was better than nothing'; it was 'good to get out on the cinders again'.[47] Baker seems to be suggesting that human pets are willing agents in their own degradation.

The British runner Gordon Pirie, former world record holder for the 5,000 metres, was ignominiously involved in running around a Spanish bullring in order to supplement his post-amateur earnings. Pirie's biographer, Dick Booth, notes that in 1962, Pirie obtained a 'fairly lucrative contract' to run two races over 10,000 metres in San Sebastian, involving Pirie starting on one side of the track and an opponent on the other. 'It was essentially a gambling occasion', spectators gambled on when one runner would catch the other and the times the runners would take to complete parts of the race. Pirie was not fully fit and reflected later that it was a 'bit of a joke'.[48]

Owens, the black sprinter; Pirie, the white distance runner: 'Difference in physical appearance make it easy for society to justify orders of unequal power and prestige',[49] and for many years such inequality was applied to abilities in sport, including running. The ability to classify macro-groups as less athletic ('no speed' or 'little stamina') often resulted from a belief that differences between groups were greater than differences within them. In recent years local, regional and national differences in running performance have been subjected to considerable scrutiny and analysis.[50] I stress performance rather than ability because it is difficult to convincingly argue that some groups of people have more ability at running than others. Difference is more likely to be 'explained' by historical, economic and cultural factors than by biology and genetics. Indeed, to explain why one place 'produces' more world-class athletes than another will not be understood by looking at a single factor alone. However, this is far from saying that coaches and trainers have not believed that some 'ethnic groups' have more innate speed or stamina than other groups. Teachers and coaches, in coercing young athletes into running, have applied such stereotypes. In the USA and Britain, young black runners have been traditionally viewed as sprinters and have, at high school, been labelled as such.[51] Their expectations of success have been raised but in most cases they are consigned to oblivion.

Cruel jokes have also been levelled at black athletes, often stressing sexual characteristics over athletic performance. Frantz Fanon's famous observation that in white representations of the black man, 'the Negro is eclipsed. He is turned into a penis. He is a penis.' And it is the black athlete that has become most singularly eroticised.[52] Cruel sexual jokes identifying the English sprinter Linford Christie with his genitalia circulated widely in Britain following Christie's victory in the 1992 Olympic 100 metres. Attention was regularly drawn to the outline of his genitals under the skin-tight Lycra shorts that he wore. His genitals became known as 'Linford's lunchbox' and stories about this subject abounded in the British tabloid press. Christie and 'the lunchbox' became interchangeable, an allegation in one of the trashiest papers being that a woman had 'sex with the lunchbox'. As Ben Carrington has pointed out, 'Christie is metonymically reduced to his genitals: he actually becomes, as Fanon foretold, his penis.'[53] Mocking athletic pets is the dark side of praising them.

The pet-like character of athletes is reflected also in the juvenile and animal imagery used to describe them. Condescending language was used in describing women athletes, such as American runners *Little* Mary Decker and *Little* Francie Larrieu, even though the latter was over 21 years of age at the time.[54] Wilma Rudolph, the 1960 Olympic 100 metres champion, was known as the 'black gazelle', while a common allusion to French athletes from Africa was that they were 'feline'.[55] We describe pacemakers as 'rabbits' or 'hares'. Cerutty, the eccentric Australian, argued that athletes should run like animals, himself demonstrating horse-like running styles.[56] But such animal imageries may be much more malign than those noted above. For example, throughout the career of Canadian sprinter Ben Johnson (see Chapter 6), he was defined in relation to animals. For example, he was 'doctored … like a racehorse', a 'caged wild animal', 'a trapped animal'.[57]

The Runner as Machine

'The feelings unleashed by a technological gadget are eminently physical and are described in bodily terms', notes Gunter Gebauer. A machine has a 'purring noise' or it is 'running smoothly'.[58] More usually, however, the body is seen as technological, and the body as machine has been a widely-used image in medicine and sports. In sport, writes Chris Shilling, 'the body is seen as a complex machine whose performance can be enhanced, and which can break down and be repaired, just like any other machine'.[59] Could the machine be the ultimate pet, totally controlled by the flick of a switch? Athletes may become the ultimate pets when they no longer think for themselves. Gordon Pirie commented that his coach Gerschler, who had guided Rudolf Harbig to the 800 metres world record in 1939, 'does my thinking for me'.[60] Roger Bannister, amazed at the sports facilities at Harvard University, observed that there the athlete 'did not have to think, or do anything for himself – he just provided a willing, obedient body, which his university clothed in athletic dress'.[61] Sport had been turned into 'a machine in which the athlete's individuality was submerged'.[62] And Pirie, having been captivated by the performances of Emil Zátopek in the 1948 Olympics in London, returned to his home in Surrey wanting to run like his hero, 'like a machine'.[63] However, even mechanized objects can be shown affection or, at least, cared for or well maintained. Runners may be 'perfect, fuelled and well-oiled machines, taking just enough mouthfuls to keep us primed'.[64] Tuan certainly recognizes that the machine is a powerful metaphor for the body in the realm of work – 'a dark tale that is often told',[65] though the 'dark tale' of the working runner may be less well known than that of the alienated factory worker.

Perhaps having in mind Bannister's carefully targeted approach to the four-minute mile, Tuan explicitly recognizes that the athlete's goal is 'as precisely defined as in factory work' – to reach a certain speed or to defeat an opponent.[66] This view would lie comfortably with neo-Marxist works on sport.[67] However, Tuan tempers his view with more moderate sentiments that tend to reveal his unfamiliarity with critical writing on modern sport. He continues:

> unlike factory workers athletes, to reach their goal, have to be highly conscious of the power and limits of their own bodies. The body is the athlete's instrument of success. It has to be nurtured and trained, mentally as well as physically. The athlete has to rehearse in his mind the necessary motions in relation to the barriers to be overcome. [...] In sport, success may be all-important, but means to it have their own beauty and justification.[68]

There is much in Tuan's comments with which to agree but his focus on the aesthetic, I think, ought to be put in its place. Some runners are obviously aesthetically attractive. Grace, poise and apparent effortlessness are central features of the aesthetically pleasing body in movement. But aesthetics are secondary, almost incidental, to success and the quantified result. Emil Zátopek, regarded by many as the greatest middle- and long-distance runner of all-time, was a highly effective athlete but his apparently ungainly style and tortured facial expressions belied his efficiency (see Chapter 7). The two-time winner of the Olympic 800 metres title Douglas Lowe observed that, 'Whenever it is said of an athlete, "How easy it looks!" one can be sure that he possesses a good style',[69] but in modern track running, there have never been any prizes awarded for style. What counts are measured times. Beneath the apparent beauty of the athlete there lies pain and severe effort, and injuries sometimes induced by damaging substances or excessive training. In running, beauty is often, literally, skin-deep and hides behind the trainer's dominance or the athlete's obsession.

The machine metaphor and its application to the human body was common at the end of the nineteenth century among novelists, physiologists and biologists whose ambitions seem to have been to understand how far the body could be transformed into a machine.[70] The idea of the athletic machine, or the 'human motor', reflected the nineteenth century desire to see the end of exhaustion, fatigue and neurasthenia that were associated with industrial work.[71] Hoberman quotes Horkheimer and Adorno who noted that the fascistic extolling of the body above all else sees 'the body as a moving mechanism, with joints as its components and flesh to cushion the skeleton. They use the body and its parts as though they were already separated from it.'[72] And only on the premise of the body as a machine, surely, could coach Franz Stampfl, an avid advocate of interval training, boast on his arrival in Melbourne, Australia, 'that he could turn any man in the street into a world champion'.[73] Likewise, the colonial project frequently engaged literally and metaphorically in 'processing' natives as part of a rhetorical 'conversionist fantasy'.[74] The body could be quickly transformed, as if by some mechanical process, from a savage into an athlete.

The notion that the athlete's body could be broken down into parts was assisted by the photographic work of Etienne-Jules Marey and Eadweard Muybridge, who were able to visually break down the body into its essential components, a task subsequently undertaken by the science of bio-mechanics.[75] Brohm is quite unequivocal and observes that sport 'is basically a mechanization of the body, treated as an automaton, governed by the principle of maximizing output'[76] – in this case the maximization of results and records. In a rare allusion to sport, Walter Benjamin noted that there was nothing more typical of 'the test' in its modern form 'as measuring the human being against an apparatus'.[77] The motor analogy was vividly drawn by Douglas Lowe, who observed that 'general training is analogous to overhauling and conditioning the engine of a motor-car. Special training is equivalent to tuning-up.'[78] Here, French and German neo-Marxists appear to be speaking the same language as a 1920s English liberal. The philosopher Howard Slusher wondered if such mechanization of the body 'increases our "efficiency" at the cost of de-humanizing mankind'. He sensed that he was witnessing a situation where control 'over self and environment becomes a higher priority than freedom', illustrating the great importance of discipline in the sport experience.[79]

At the end of the nineteenth century, some observers labelled Finland as 'non-athletic'.[80] By the 1920s this image was totally overturned and replaced by one of a small, Nordic nation being a source of many brilliant runners.

Figure 4.1 Paavo Nurmi as machine (Itkonen and Knuuttila, 'Aika voi sun ainoastaan', p.202 and 210).

The first of these was Hannes Kolehmainen, winner of the 10,000 metres at the Stockholm Olympics in 1912. The British coach F.A.M. Webster believed that 'short, slightly built, flaxen haired Hannes, [was] the best piece of running mechanism ever seen on any track at that time'.[81] The machine metaphor was encouraged by the use of mathematics and the stopwatch. Paavo Nurmi, Kolehmainen's successor as the best Finnish athlete, combined the two, the stopwatch (a machine) becoming an extension of his body – and something that could control his body movements. He became 'an imperturbable and apparently unconquerable automaton'.[82] Martti Jukola observed that having left the army

> Nurmi entered the Industrial School at Helsinki, passing the three-year course with very high marks. He was especially strong in mathematics, a branch of study of which he made good use in his later record runs. During the year 1921 he made a special study of training methods, reading everything on the subject he could lay his hands on. He now began to carry a watch on his training runs. With the aid of the watch he could judge after two or three laps his current form for different distances. His mathematical instincts took him further. Soon he *needed* a

watch in competitions, for having drawn up a schedule that was to yield a result beforehand, it was necessary for him to *control* his speed. This was an entirely new feature of distance-running and one that was to provoke a good deal of comment. Nurmi's dependence on the watch was responsible for all the talk about a 'running machine'.[83]

The rationalized body and the machine metaphor were not lost on artists and cartoonists who saw Nurmi in a variety of ways.[84] Far from being simply a creature of the wild, romantic Finnish physical environment, Nurmi was also likened to a human stopwatch and a machine (see Figure 4.1). He was described as being 'like a machine which, chugging away in businesslike fashion, ground down opponents'.[85] The man–machine nexus was seen, of course, as part of an 'entire system in which [all] men are turned into machines'.[86] John Heartfield, the anti-Nazi exponent of photo-collage, saw the 'running machine' as a reflection of the time-obsessed industrial age and of 'mechanical serfdom' (see Figure 4.2). It could have also reflected the rise of a Nazi masculinity – firm, prepared and programmed to respond to the demands of a powerful leader. Heartfield captioned his image as a spectre haunting Europe, meaning not only Nazism but also the march of rationalization. Additionally, he may not have missed the mechanically–minded products of the National Socialist physical education system. Here, the objective of any running, welfare and sportized, was ultimately to fuel the war machine.[87]

The stopwatch aided the popularity of a form of training that has been widely seen as an analogue of time and motion studies from the world of work. This is known as interval running. Rigauer described it as exemplifying the

> repetitive division of the tasks of training and the law of psycho-physical loading, both of which are copied from the methods of industrial labor. Continuous repetition of temporally, spatially and quantitatively set training tasks, interrupted by controlled pauses for recovery is exemplified in interval training.[88]

For example, the former Russian world record holder for 5,000 metres, Vladimir Kuts, would run 400 metres 20 times in 70 seconds with a 200 metre jog recovery between each one; it is reported that Zátopek, the great Czech record holder, could run 60 'fast' 400 metre laps (that is, between 56 and 75 seconds) with 200 metres recovery.[89] Here, as noted previously, the running track becomes a machine for training (*pace* Le Corbusier)[90] – indeed, a machine for producing machines. The continuous repetitions found in both daily training and interval running make up what can be termed 'time-space

Figure 4.2 'A spectre is haunting Europe: Rationalisation on the march' by John Heartfield (Akademie der Künste, Berlin).

routines'. As David Seamon notes, such routinized body-practices are difficult to break or modify because of the strength of the attachment people have to them. Runners, for whom running is their life, often forget that life could be otherwise. A time-space routine such as training is, therefore, a conservative force.[91]

The clock is a powerful simile for athletes' lives, let alone their training. Marty Liquori was told by his coach to 'live like a clock'. This meant rising every day at the same time and eating and training at the same time each day. In Liquori's words, 'I must live regularly if I'm going to progress ... I fit my life into a groove ... It's like being a zombie ... I'm like a communist athlete (sic) who's confined at a training camp.'[92] Leslie Heywood found that she could readily run at four in the morning because she was woken by the discipline of her 'internal clock'; she added, 'I don't need any machines, I'm one myself'.[93]

These days, techno-science has moved on sufficiently to make the mechanized human more than a metaphor. Indeed, postmodernist observers of the world of sports see in the athlete the perfect model for the cyborg, which destabilizes dualisms such as human/machine, healthy/unhealthy, pure/impure and natural/prosthetic.[94] When the body is damaged through running, no efforts are made to change the running. Instead, repair to the body must be made as soon as possible.[95] The athletic body is subordinated by the power of technology, the natural body becoming superfluous. It is fitted with spiked shoes, covered with aerodynamically designed clothing, shaved for speed, invaded by diuretics, hormones, high-calorie food and vitamins, pure blood and numerous drugs.[96] This may be not such a recent development as is sometimes assumed. Jack Lovelock, the 1936 Olympic 1,500 metres champion, is said by his biographer James McNeish, that in the period leading up to the Olympic final he (Lovelock)

> [c]hecked the phials of vaccine, hypodermic syringe and needles I had brought, also my sleeping draught. It was my usual mud-coloured sleeping draught, chloral, bromide and tincture of opium mixed in equal quantities. For emergency I had brought trional, a longer-lasting hypnotic. I hadn't taken trional before, but then I hadn't been in a situation like this before. I knew it was addictive.[97]

The natural body disappears and its ownership becomes ambiguous. The power of the coach, buttressed by medical scientists and by the ideology of achievement sport, converts the athlete into a pet.

The horrors to which the pet metaphor can be taken are demonstrated in the novel *The Olympic Hope*, a sporting science fiction about running by Danish writer Knud Lundberg. Published (in English) in 1958, it features the athletes competing for the 1996 Olympic 800 metres title. In the brave new sports-world of the 1990s (as seen by Lundberg), all of the 800 metres finalists (except, it appears, the Dane) are, in different ways, pets who been offered little affection. The Russians, Konev ('the human locomotive from Georgia') and Vlasov

> had a peculiar appearance. It seemed as if they consisted only of a lower part of the body and chest. Their arms could not be seen – though they *had* arms. The Russian tests for athletes with amputation of the arms just above the elbow had been a failure. It spoiled the rhythm and the balance. It was now known to be a blunder, and Solknikov, who became a hero of the Soviet Union after his victories of '84 and '88, would possibly have been still more superior if he had kept his arms.[98]

The two Russians had been in a training camp without any connection with the outside world from the age of four. They had been discovered at the 'Pan-Russian baby Championships', subsequently living at 'sports schools', their parents receiving compensation in the form of a 'bronze cross' and a luxury car.[99] Hasenjäger, the German

> had been brought up, together with 399 half-brothers, in the castle in the Black Forest, only by men, and only for athletics. They had been taken away from their mothers after exactly eight months. They stayed with their mothers only while they were at the breast, for health's sake. Afterwards they had been forced to literally stand on their own feet. And to *run* on them.
>
> They were 400 half-brothers. They had trained and trained in keen competition through the years. Every day and every hour of the day they had fought to see who could run the fastest 800 metres.
>
> It was an experiment. Friedrich Hasenjäger was the first 800-metre runner who had been brought up on completely modern principles. He was the best of the 400 sons of the old Hasenjäger – the double Olympic victor – and the best 1,000 women 400-metre and 800-metre runners in Germany.[100]

Jim Stoker, the American, had been cared for by 'The Black University' once his 'exceptional respiratory system, the slow pulse and the rare elasticity of the skeletal muscles had been fully appreciated'. The university 'saw to it that he lived a healthy, simple, sexual life, and he was congenitally indolent, contented with a carefree existence in which the only real problems were the big races'.[101] The other American, Ted Jackson, 2.30 metres in height, was the product of parents who, for $100,000, had allowed him to be experimented upon with hormone replacement treatment from the age of three. He was 'a little backward' (with an IQ of 85) but was given growth-promoting substances and 'exhibited at universities all round the country'. Sexually impotent, he remained a 'giant boy' all his life.[102] The last of the finalists, the Dane, Erling, was, of course, a residual amateur from a bygone age.

Lundberg's prognostications are exaggerated but they are not entirely unrecognizable in the late modern world of achievement running. In 1936 the German journal *Sport und Rasse* had included an article by Dr Bruno Schultz in which he declared that it was the duty of top athletes to 'bequeath their aptitudes' to as many offspring as possible.[103] And in recent years it has been stressed that training and its associated human and non-human agents do serve to physically change, and in some cases distort, the body of the athlete. The pharmaceutical substances given to many runners of elite and even school and club level are well documented.[104] Additionally, diet can equally affect body shape. Because it is widely thought that peak performance by distance runners is, in part, related to weight and body composition, athletes often seek to reduce weight or to lower the percentage of body fat. The effects of disorders such as amenorrhoea (absence of menstruation) and anorexia and bulimia (related to diet) are thought to be more prevalent in sportswomen than in the general population.[105] A 1986 survey revealed that 47 per cent of female college long-distance runners in the United States 'used techniques such as self-induced vomiting, laxatives, diet pills, and diuretics to keep their weight down'. And this also becomes competitive. Heywood recalls that in the training room her high school colleagues compete there too:

> All of us get quiet and shifty, dropping eye contact, looking at each other's stomachs for the faintest shift gathering in front of the shorts, a bulge to indicate an ounce more weight. We hold our stomachs in, keep our steps smaller, heads and shoulders below the ground.[106]

Coaches are often complicit in such practices – practices that can be read as rational or even necessary for their athletes to succeed.[107]

But even with rigorous training alone, the body can be changed quite dramatically in a relatively short period of time. As a young runner, Paavo Nurmi's face appeared quite chubby (see Figure 4.3 left). He seemed to have round shoulders, lacking 'good posture'. After a few years of hard training he had a much leaner look, upright, 'a winner' (Figure 4.3 right). So body-transformation should not be associated only with the shift towards the use of anabolic steroids and other exogenous technologies. Yet it is certainly the body changes in athletes, witnessed form the 1960s onwards, that draws us most forcefully to accept the idea of the disempowerment of the individual over his or her body and the dominance of 'the system', if not an agent of it.

But what is 'the system'? In the 1960s it was possible for the Finnish sports sociologist Kalevi Heinilä to talk about a 'totalization process' in sport in which an individual was no longer responsible for his own training because it had been taken over by agencies of the state.[108] The athlete was now a pet of the state, her success and effectiveness depending more on the effectiveness of the total system of national sport and less on individual effort. However, the world of sport had already moved on at the time Heinilä was writing and globalisation was well under way, including the international migration of athletes. Today, their futures may lie in the hands of American university athletic departments, multinational sports shoe

Figure 4.3 Paavo Nurmi (Sport Museum of Finland).

companies, pharmaceutical organizations or the global athletic federation itself (see Chapter 6).

Were the bodies of steroid-boosted and anorexic athletes any less distorted than that of topiary art or the breeding of freakish dogs?[109] Hoberman noted that 'it is well known that steroids modify female physiology, anatomy, and sexual drive, and that they can cause irreversible masculinising of the female organism, including clitoral enlargement, a deepened voice and baldness.[110] But although human runners are not (yet) bred like dogs and horses, Brohm averred that in the former German Democratic Republic it was 'thought acceptable to hold a sports file on every child', a 'Stalinist, cybernetic and technocentric conception'.[111] If this is correct, Europe has already experienced a pale shadow (but a shadow nevertheless) of the horrors of Lundberg's Olympians. Machines do not feel pain. And if the capacity to catch athletes taking dope becomes increasingly successful, the outcome may well be that even more severe training will be necessary. Should that be the case, Hoberman notes that:

> Harder training will mean more pain, and the athlete will require a trainer of some kind to help him or her inflict and endure this suffering. One extreme development ... would be 'torture contracts' between athletes and their handlers that would attempt to establish the trainer/torturer's legal immunity from prosecution. In this scenario, the athletes of the future ... would literally require protection from their 'trainers'.[112]

It would be the retention of pain that would define their humanity.

The running milieu as motorway and the athlete as pet combine to provide a dystopian image. As painted by Hoberman it is depressing indeed: 'a dehumanized, robot-like athlete operating in a state of hypnosis, a creature immune to pain or unable to stop it.'[113] I could add that this creature would also be genetically engineered and competing in a sanitized, sterile, anaesthetic hall, devoid of spectators, the object of a televisual gaze.

The role of the teacher, trainer, coach, agent or handler is clearly pervasive in the modern world of running. Can a runner exist without a mentor? Some runners still feel the need for their coach, even following abuse and exploitation. Without him, progress in performance may be retarded.[114] Marty Liquori, a US record holder at 2,000 and 5,000 metres, stated that 'in distance running, the coach is everything – you can overcome everything if you have a good coach'.[115] However, recalling his schooldays, Roger Bannister recognized

how delicately one's individual freedom is poised. Though
most of us were perhaps unaware of it, the school was in fact
governed more by fear in one way or another, than by respect or
tolerance ... Under these conditions, freedom to explore and
expand was always in danger.[116]

Bannister, who claimed that Stampfl was more an adviser than a coach,
displays awareness of the tension in Tuan's notion of dominance and affection. As a serious runner, Bannister argued that an athlete should coach him
or herself as much as possible. Only the athlete 'could assess his reactions
to different training programmes; it was part of the fun of the sport to exper-
iment, and if he did not win he only had himself to blame'.[117] Bannister felt
that he 'learned more from other athletes than from professional coaches
who have never been runners themselves. Though qualified in the techniques
of events, coaches sometimes have difficulty in applying their textbook
information.'[118] If he really was learning from his athletic peers, he seems to
have regarded himself as undertaking an apprenticeship, subscribing to the
view that 'without the models who exemplify cultural movement patterns, it
is doubtful that performance standards could be raised repeatedly'.[119]

To attend to people in the spirit of altruism, for their own good and with no
expectation of reciprocity, is rare. As a result, Tuan feels that 'exploitation
to some degree is unavoidable in any hierarchical society'.[120] However, let us
remember that the coach can also be diminished through the over-exercise
of dominance. As geographer David Lowenthal has added, the 'exercise of
power transforms the potent no less than the weaker partner ... [W]e should
not ignore the self-inflicted injuries of the mighty, the effects on human
nature of habitual exercise of power'.[121]

Running as Pain and Elation

Tuan recognizes that the problem with the pet metaphor is that of distin-
guishing affection from 'teasing playfulness, patronage from condescension,
or cruelty from love'.[122] Does the patronage of a coach or trainer inevitably
lead to negative feelings? No, since it is clear that pleasure can be obtained
from running, even if aspects of the overall running experience may be
painful. But let me first explore the pain.

Through pain and agony the specifically human in the machine is
expressed.[123] And pain is greatly encouraged in running. 'No pain, no gain'
goes the well-known locker-room saying, an exhortation to train and race
hard. Pain, according to anthropologist Robert Sands in his study of top-class
sprinters, is the deposit, the investment, through which speed is extracted.[124]
In training for the 1,500 metres, the former French record-holder Michel

Jazy noted that pain 'starts to hurt deep in your throat. The blood rushes up. You feel sick, your stomach muscles knot up and your legs feel like lead.'[125] Even in her first year at university, Leslie Heywood sometimes felt that she had

> already given too much, all my blood and my driving, pounding heart and guts, I cannot possibly keep doing it, giving it more and again ...Since I don't know what else to do, I just keep giving more but I am so tired.[126]

At the age of 19 her joints thought they were 50.[127]

In some cases, the pain induced by long-distance running leads to considerable distress, collapse and hospitalization. Recall the collapse of Pietri Dorando in the 1908 Olympic marathon, and of Jim Peters, staggering into the stadium and collapsing, dehydrated, before the finish line in the 1954 Empire Games in Vancouver. In the latter case, perhaps the athlete had gone beyond pain: he came close to death. In similar, more modern performances, athletes appear to torture themselves to make a living and to provide entertainment. In the cases noted above, however, their grotesque perseverance and distress was felt to be worth rewarding. In the case of Dorando (the 'moral winner' according to Coubertin),[128] the King of England awarded him a special medal; the Duke of Edinburgh similarly rewarded Peters.

Pain can undoubtedly become emotional distress but it can also become emotional satisfaction. Running as training need not necessarily be a lonely experience. Interval running, when undertaken as a member of a group where each member may share taking the lead, while painful, can be an object of group satisfaction (see Figure 4.4). During training, for example, painful fatigue may be satisfying because it signifies improving strength. In a race, however, there is more at stake for the athlete: 'In a close race, runners experiencing painful fatigue will probably react with distress because the pain means they are running out of steam.'[129] But pain may also be ameliorated by the body's natural opiates (endorphins) that make running a pleasure rather than a pain. Such natural opiates allow runners to continue running with minor or even major injuries. This suggests that natural opiates, by encouraging the body to run while injured, contribute to the body colluding in its own oppression. Opiates may also contribute to running addiction, which may be read as a condition to improve fitness but, at the same time, a means of self-destruction – a machine out of control.[130]

Is there a point at which self-torture becomes heroic? What are we to make of the courage of the long-distance runners who overcome the pain of fatigue and injury, perhaps endangering their health and even life in so doing?[131] One way of reading such a condition is that some runners refuse to

Figure 4.4 Interval training as a group activity. A rare example of the
author in the lead, Cardiff, 1963 (Photograph by Jan-Erik Karlberg).

not only grow old, but also up,[132] addictive running being infantilizing and
alienating. Addiction may constitute escape (see Chapter 6). In such cases,
Jeffrey Segrave suggests that perhaps 'the greatest challenge for those of us
who live in a culture besotted by sport is to learn how to escape from the
world of sport as escape'.[133]

   Can the pain endured by athletes be a perverse source of pleasure? Pain
is often presented as an inevitable part of running. It is not the result of injury
(with which most references to pain in sports science seems to be associated)
but simply the effect of effort. Herb Elliott likened pain caused through training to a religious experience, perhaps that of an ascetic. He observed that
the 'purifying quality of the pain that has to be suffered is like that of a
confession'.[134] Alternatively, Lovelock, in James McNeish's novel of that

name, recalled: 'I suddenly realized what running had given me, an enjoyment of heightened tension. I actually enjoyed the agony.'[135] Perhaps he had learned this from the German world-record holder Otto Peltzer, who was said to possess 'a fanatical quality'. He was seemingly able to 'submit himself to the worst kind of body-abuse' and 'to run at varying speeds to the point of exhaustion, and then to answer a summons and run three hundred yards more'.[136] Cerutty urged his charges to 'love suffering'.[137] Gordon Pirie went somewhat further, stating that 'an athlete who isn't enjoying himself even in moments of the most agonizing effort at the point of exhaustion, might as well give up'.[138] To enjoy oneself at the point of exhaustion may be related to the fact that the runner has achieved a target, for example, achieving a record number of repetitions during a session of interval running or setting a world record. Exhaustion may be the result of having run a personal best time. In such a case, it may be the personal best, not the exhaustion felt in obtaining it, which provides the enjoyment. Agony showed on the face of Roger Bannister as he crossed the line in his 3 minutes 59.4 seconds mile. He writes that he

> collapsed almost unconscious [but] it was *only then* that real pain overtook me. I felt like an exploded flashlight with no will to live; I just went on existing in the most passive physical state without being quite unconscious. Blood surged from my muscles and seemed to fell me. It was as if my limbs were caught in an ever-tightening vice.[139]

Yet within a few minutes Bannister was on his feet scampering 'around the track in a burst of spontaneous joy'. For Bannister pain is separated from the pleasure. The pain is the result of exhausting running; the pleasure comes from breaking the record. The pain that seems to be experienced is not described as pleasurable. However, the pain Bannister recalls having felt as a schoolboy rower seems different. He remembers 'the intense pleasure of utter exhaustion from rowing'.[140] Here it *was* the exhaustion that seems to have provided the pleasure.

The notion of pain being pleasurable takes us into the realms of masochism, which Tuan has touched on in more than one of his works.[141] It is a subject that seems to be linked to running but about which we have little information. The former British 400 metres runner, Adrian Metcalfe, described the experience of racing over that distance as 'the virtual masochism of pleasure through prolonged pain'.[142] Cerutty argued that 'the more it hurts, the harder we try to run' and, more explicitly masochistic, observed that 'it is not normal to dislike pain, since all true men realize that nothing worthwhile was ever accomplished without it'.[143] Describing the running of a marathon as masochistic is common enough in popular writing but such language tends to be used frivolously and the actual pleasure (sexual or not) that might be derived from painful running is hardly ever mentioned. Allen Guttmann claims that there exists, at the start of a race, 'that strangely masochistic sexualized sensation of mingled pain and pleasure known to every serious athlete'.[144] We seem to know little about pain being enjoyed in sport and it borders on the perverse. Yet it is hard to deny the possibility that pleasure during pain is experienced by at least some runners, while running.[145]

In addition to physical pain, running may be associated with emotional pain and distress. Such distress may be related to pride. During the women's 3,000 metres final at the 1984 Los Angeles Olympics, the American favourite Mary Slaney was accidentally knocked over by the South African-British runner Zola Budd. The collision affected the performance of each of the athletes but Slaney left the track, distressed and in tears. For someone who undoubtedly attached great importance to winning the race, it was more than physical pain that she endured as she fell and withdrew to the infield. Her pride was more than simply dented. Athletes who fail to win races are often reduced to tears, perhaps from pain, perhaps from chagrin. From a Christian point of view, it can be argued that 'perfection is not a human state, and to aspire too highly, to fail to forgive even ourselves the occasional transgression, is mere vanity. And vanity is yet another sin'.[146]

How does it feel when a runner no longer feels like participating? Consider the example of Jim Denison, an American college miler who had ambitions to compete in the Olympics:

> That whole season I had been running right around four minutes – 4:04 in Philadelphia, 4:05 in Durham, 4:02 in Indianapolis. And in practice the week before I'd run 4:03 all by myself. But for some reason I had started feeling like I was just going through the motions. As if I really didn't care anymore how fast I ran or whether I won or lost, which just made no sense at all. I mean, considering the years of training I'd put in, you'd figure I would've been raring to get out there and get it done. It didn't add up that I was willing to chuck all of that hard work away. As if suddenly running had become something I did for somebody else – a job, a requirement, a responsibility – when it always used to be so fun: heading out to the track each day, spending time with my friends, pushing myself, feeling so strong.[147]

The loss of any fun, its replacement by work and co-option and 'going through the motions', seemed to be crucial.

Some 18-year-old runners look into the mirror and see that they are starting to look old.[148] Here is the start of the emotional pain for athletes whose promising careers are terminated by illness or injury. Emotional pain may be greater and may stay with them for many years. Jim Denison recalls how his route to athletic ruin began:

> I should have listened when the pain started. But it was hardly anything at first. Just an occasional ache, nothing I couldn't tolerate. I kept training on it every day, most days twice. [I]t was my senior year and I had big plans. When it started to get bad I swore to myself every night before going to sleep that if it still hurt in the morning I'd take the day off. Rest it. Give it a chance to heal. But I never did.[149]

For Denison, watching from the sidelines would not do. He was a runner, not a spectator. He continued running, each morning breaking his promise to stop. He was addicted, despite the pain. In August 1984, instead of meeting his friends for a twenty-first birthday celebration in an Irish pub, he was at home with his parents. Neither knew much about running; they had no idea what a 'good runner' was; the only runner with whose name they were familiar was Roger Bannister. They watched the 1984 Olympics on television. He wrote:

> While I was at home with my parents watching the Olympic Games on television a queer feeling in my gut told me it was too late, that I was in serious trouble. And somehow I knew it to be true. So like a man who senses his lover drifting away, who realises that he's about to get dumped, I began to prepare for the worst.[150]

In the case of Leslie Heywood, her doctor told her that she had a female athlete triad: eating disorders, exercise compulsion, leading to amenorrhoea. Unless she stopped running her immune system would eventually start attacking her vital organs, her heart and her liver. She would have to do something other than running.[151]

Ethnographic studies of former runners reveal the emotional pain they experience following retirement. Michael Messner has recorded how runners act differently to a 'mid-life crisis' when their speed diminishes and younger athletes surpass their achievements.[152] One of his respondents noted that he had managed to transform himself from a 'racer' to a 'runner', shifting his focus from achievement to welfare. He learned how to take pressure off himself, he dared to be a 'normal person'.

My wife had a T-shirt [made] for me. It says 'Dare to be average', and it gets funny reactions from people. I think it gets at that place where somehow we all think that we're going to end up on the cover of *Time*, or something, you know? Do you have that? That some day you're gonna be *great*, and everyone will know, everyone will recognize it. And I think I used that to somehow disengage from that, because that's part of the competitor, the racer, the vicious person. And it's a *disease*! It's *hard*! I'd rather be great now because I'm *good*.[153]

The emptiness in a life that has had to leave running behind can also be a relief.[154]

However, there is no guarantee that all racers will turn into runners upon retirement from serious competition. The marathon runner and apparent running addict Ron Hill continued to maintain a meticulous record of his training and racing performances and cannot be said to ever have retired from serious running. In the second volume of his autobiography, he writes:

although I am fully aware that advancing years inevitably produce a slowing down of my times, my own demise has been too rapid and the purpose of my further training will be to decrease the downward slope of my performances, perhaps even reverse the slope in the next few years.[155]

While for many runners, pain of various kinds exists, it is the pleasure gained from running that is most vividly recalled. Indeed, 'most of the photographs in our albums depict significant moments in our lives, and usually happy ones'.[156] In *The Erotic in Sports*, Guttmann quotes *Village Voice* journalist, Laurie Stone's view that sports are typified by their 'innate eroticism',[157] but allusions to erotic pleasure derived from involvement in running seem more likely to be found in the world of literature than in the biographies of runners. Guttmann cites the French author Henry de Montherlat, who, in his *La Paradis à l'ombre des épées*, visits the stadium where the narrator, Riry, witnesses 'athletically trained young girls ... what a revelation! Like that of new sex. I realized that a woman's body could be beautiful – if it is trained.'[158] Here it is implied that it is the *trained* athletic body that contributes to a heightened eroticism: 'adding to musculature is always beautiful, a woman's as well as a man's, if it is not excessive.'[159] Sara Maitland likewise stressed that the leanness of her lover's body was a gift from her marathon training. She had the 'most beautiful legs, hard, stripped down, with no wastage, and her Achilles tendons are like flexible rock.

Running does that for her.'[160] And Harlan Brown, the gay track coach in Patricia Warren's *The Front Runner*, observes that a 'man's body is good to look at only when it is conditioned, because of the muscling'.[161]

Homoerotic pleasure is also available at the athletic arena. It is likely that the proportion of runners who are gay is greater than that in team sports and possibly than in society as a whole. Former runner Jim Pullen argues that this is because running can be done independently:

> I think if you are uncomfortable being part of the mainstream heterosexual thing, if you are a little different, if you are a little effete, shall we say, and you're interested in sports, then it's easier to do something on your own, where you don't have eighty people in the locker room together, which is intimidating anyway, I would think.[162]

At the same time, however, the locker room could be a great site for the voyeuristic gaze, despite the inhibitions faced by some gay men and women, noted above. The fictional Harlan Brown was able to confirm that 'every day' the coach is 'in the locker room with those beautiful naked bodies, close enough to touch'.[163]

The arena provides a broader venue for gratification if muscular, half-naked bodies are around. While competitive running suggests dominance, winner and loser often display physical intimacy. These may reflect forms of equality, brotherhood or fondness, like Jack Lovelock 'being affectionately embraced' by Luigi Beccali shortly after the latter had defeated him and equalled the world 1,500 metres record at the World Student Games in Turin in 1933 (see Figure 4.5).[164] Here are men enjoying close bodily contact with each other. Of course, this form of physical intimacy is almost always read as being part of 'sport', not as part of 'sex'.[165] The direct bodily contact with another man is legitimated through such a post-race embrace, something that would be out of place, even disgusting, and considered perverse in non-sporting settings.

Sensual and sensory pleasure from running (see Chapter 3) – even racing – is more often associated with 'runner's high' and 'flow' than with the erotic. Each refers to what Tuan termed a feeling of 'visceral pleasure in the ease and naturalness' of deep engagement in physical activity.[166] Struggling for words to describe the feeling, Gordon Pirie observed that this 'liberated condition is one which you have to experience to appreciate'.[167] Perhaps Pirie would have found the words easier if he was a poet. The poet and runner Stephanie Plotin felt running liberated her from the simple, daily routines of conventional women's clothing. Her high heels 'gnawed at her toes', her 'skirt was a hobble'.[168] Running rids her of these hindrances. In Devon Sykes's 'Women who run':

Figure 4.5 'After defeat at Turin, an affectionate embrace from jubilant Luigi'

Heels tense, ready to let feet fly.
These free spirits
have found a common foothold
in womankind
because they run;
yes they do, they run.
Freely and forever.[169]

Running is here seen as a revolt against the conventions and constrictions of women's body management.

I earlier alluded to Roger Bannister's reminiscences of his life as a child and his running on the beach. How different is it from James McNeish's (fictional) description of Jack Lovelock's feelings about a training session at Oxford? Following a period of self-doubt about his ability as a runner, Lovelock

half expected my knees to buckle underneath me. Instead, as my feet touched the cinder crust and I began to run, I experienced a physical shock, half physical, half sexual, like a blade cutting through the flesh. I probably exaggerate, but in that moment I felt a faith, a wavering faith in myself, had been reborn.[170]

Some might argue that Bannister and Lovelock were experiencing what has become known as 'runner's high' – a widely reported euphoric sensation, of heightened well-being, an enhanced appreciation of nature and transcendence of time and space. Runner's high – 'an unreflective, lived, culturally specific, bodily reaction' – cannot be explained by accurate representation. For one runner

Every once in a while, when I'm running, I feel a sense of tremendous well-being come over me. Everything about me feels in harmony. I feel smooth, and my breathing is so relaxed that I get the feeling I can run forever. I'm not aware of time or space – only a remarkable sense of calm.[171]

But runner's high is not likely to be a frequent occurrence. Marathon runner Amby Burfoot claimed to experience it about twice a year.[172]

In *Geographies of Resistance*, Nigel Thrift suggests that dance is a form of play, an exaggeration of everyday life that 'eludes power, rather than confronts it'.[173] Like dance, runner's high takes the runner into an unstoppable, imaginary world as runners find themselves neither dominated nor suppressed. The state of runner's high slides around systems of power in runners' virtual worlds.[174] In this state, which cannot be predicted, the runner escapes the teacher, the coach, the trainer. Such a state is not restricted to training. During his 100 metres victory at the Seoul Olympics, Ben Johnson, the Canadian sprinter, has said that he felt his 'whole body was in space, in the middle of the ocean, silence, calm, calm as can be'.[175] And while the writer Joyce Carol Oates puts it differently, her message is similar:

> Running! If there's any happier activity, more exhilarating, more nourishing to the imagination, I can't think what it might be. In running the mind flees with the body, the mysterious efflorescence of language seems to pulse in the brain, in rhythm with our feet and the swinging of our arms.[176]

But what kind of running is she describing here? We are not told.

Whereas 'runners high' cannot be predicted or specifically trained for (though it is unlikely to be achieved by the totally unfit) the state of 'flow' can. Something approaching 'flow' was defined by Gordon Pirie, who advised that 'the first essential is to teach the athlete to enjoy the basic exercise of running by being uninhibited in movement and thought. He will then revel in the mere rhythm of running and never tire of it'.[177] A manual on flow explains how it involves gaining a balance between a runner's challenges and skills.[178] Feeling in control is central to flow but it involves training in the transcendence of normal awareness and a balancing of control and release. It results in time seeming to stop moving, as one becomes so absorbed in the running. One runner noted that:

> It is being totally in control of what's going through your head, and totally in control of your own body and how hard you're pushing, and to be able to go faster when you say, OK, let's put on a bit of a sprint or let's drop this person'. And being able to do it and being in total control of what's going through your head. Like if pain comes to you, to be able to say 'OK, fine, I expected this. That's all right, I'm not going to dwell on it'. And to be able to do that … get away from it … total mental and physical control.[179]

The objective of experiencing a flow situation is to improve athletic performance. So flow turns out to be a technique. Indeed, the previous quotation seems to bring the human close to the machine with its emphasis on control. And, as Webster noted, 'for myself, the joy of athletics has ever been a mastery of technique'. The 'indescribable feeling of personal well-being which is the result of the production of perfect effort, by the just combination of mind and muscle, speed and effort'.[180] Running need not be all pain.

Running with friends, and the camaraderie generated by a long-distance road race, can be companionable and enjoyable. Competition suggests the need to dominate but racing is not violent in the same way as body contact sports. Occasionally, athletes do make contact, mainly accidentally and only sometimes purposefully. In racing, dominance is mainly benign. But particularly in races of more than about 10 miles, the emphasis may turn from camaraderie to loneliness. Kevin Lewis, a theologian and 'recreational marathoner' (if this is not an oxymoron), observes that the banter and bonhomie that occupy such events are essentially collective. When he ran the New York Marathon, however, he never once recognized a single person in the race or among the spectators:

> Not a single face I saw for three and a half hours knew mine. The shouts of the spectators were meant for all of us collectively or for others, never me in particular ... My 'scanning' of the crowd for anyone who would 'recognize' me proved fruitless. At one of the great moments of my life, for which I had worked patiently and hard, I realized I was awfully alone. Something was missing.[181]

Solitude is different from loneliness. And Loader, perhaps one of the most sensitive of runner-writers, felt that 'all runners are lonely'.[182] So what lesson did Lewis take home with him?

> The sheer sensual joy of running may come to be tempered by a sense of loss if the irresistible needs of one's central humanity are shunted to the side and not met. The very rewards (self-discovery, self-esteem, or more) a runner may reap contain the seed which, if allowed to take root and grow, may infuse recreation with deceptive selfishness. Taken past a certain point, what ought to enhance life will begin to diminish it. The heralded 'positive addiction' of running, like every other good thing in life, can and will be abused.[183]

These words not only recall the drift from recreational running into achievement sport but also the Tuanian tension between dominance and affection. How and why do people get dominated by running, where some suffer and others gain?

> Why some of us cross over a line that kicks us free of the earth and into a space where there is nothing, literally nothing, but reps and sweat and improving your times, and why for others sports is a shining thing that gives them blood and a backbone that holds them up, makes them part of this world, wide awake and ready for more?[184]

Some runners will have visited both places but either way, to be dominated by running could mean that much is missed along the way.

5

Running as Transgression and Resistance

In *Dominance and Affection*, Tuan pays scant attention to the possibility that dominance might be resisted, or that its results might be transgressed. Likewise, in *Escapism* he seems to avoid explicitly linking escapism with resistance and instead identifies it more with literal or metaphorical forms of migration, a topic I will explore in the following chapter. This avoidance of a focus on agency seems contradictory in view of humanism's traditional concern with the human agent. However, it is widely accepted that power is not simply top-down and one-way but is 'a process in which dominated groups may partially redefine, negotiate or even reject, the ruling group's rules, values and meanings'.[1] It becomes necessary, therefore, to think of both dominating power and resisting power. And, as I implied in Chapter 4, it seems possible (through Tuan's *Dominance and Affection*) to disentangle power from dominating power.[2] For example, in certain situations the athletic coach may display a form of power but one that is distanced somewhat from dominance and which may even be benign.

The focus of this chapter is on the athlete's power to transgress or resist. Resistance is distinguished from transgression. Tim Cresswell, one of Tuan's former students, takes resistance to mean the *intentional* 'action against some disliked entity with the intention of changing or lessening its effect'.[3] Transgression, on the other hand, 'does not, by definition, rest on the intentions of actors but on the results – on the "being noticed" of a particular action' or 'to have been judged to have crossed some line that was not meant to have been crossed'.[4] This is not to say that unintentional acts cannot contribute to change. Indeed, transgression is often unintentional. The notion of 'crossing lines' resonates strongly with C.L.R. James's notion of 'beyond a boundary' (and with the territorialized nature of sport per se) – a central motif in what follows.[5]

What kinds of 'disliked entity' might a serious runner wish to transgress or resist? There are many possible stimuli for resistance – opposition to a political regime in which the athlete is competing, opposing the very idea of competition when religious conventions condemn it, contesting the role of one's national sports federation, displaying resistance for 'racial' reasons, against drug abuse, against a former 'colonial master', or against a sense of not competing solely for oneself.

Michael Messner claims that people may use sport 'as a means to resist (at least symbolically) the domination placed on them'.[6] How is it possible to reconcile this view with that of that critics who read sportized running as a conservative activity? Walter Benjamin, reflecting on the 1936 Berlin Olympics, observed that the Games were reactionary.[7] Forty years later, Jean-Marie Brohm viewed sport as 'justifying the established order ... playing an integrating and never an oppositional role'.[8] Indeed, there seem to be inherent qualities of sportized running that make it an unsatisfactory – even impossible – site for resistance. Sportized running is, I suggest, more rule-bound in terms of how the performer (athlete) participates than is the case of the actions of the novelist, actor, dancer or playwright. Books, plays and dances – each possess the potential for individual expression and improvisation; their rules are not so rigidly enforced. In the 100 metres the script for each race is the same. Non-sportized body-cultural forms have the potential for displays of political resistance. They provide more space (literally) for resistant acts than the constrained sites of foot racing.

Here it seems appropriate to distinguish two dimensions of the micro-geography of the athlete's action-space. There is, first, the track or route on which he or she competes. As noted earlier, this is clearly demarcated from the second dimension, the area of spectators and beyond. I want to draw the distinction between the possibility of resistance within and beyond the boundary of the track.[9] I would suggest that while participating on the track, Messner's message would more appropriately read: People may use sports as a means to resist the domination placed on them (but usually *only* symbolically). I suggest that oppositional strategies *while actually running* are rather specific in nature and that resistance is best achieved beyond the track's boundary. This can be illustrated by a well-known example. At the 1968 Olympics in Mexico City, several black American track athletes displayed acts of resistance in opposition to the discrimination against black people in the USA. Orchestrated by the radical sports sociologist Harry Edwards, runners such as John Carlos and Tommy Smith *symbolically* represented the Black Power movement by wearing black socks during their races. This was a minor transgression. After the race they engaged in the more publicized act of performing Black Power salutes at the medal ceremony and, through their body language, displayed what appeared to be indifference to the national anthem and flag. My point here is that the most effective form of demonstration (resistance) took place after the athletes had completed their races and won their Olympic medals. Their post-race protest may have been in the context of a sports event but was not on the track during the race; it was 'beyond the boundary'. Once on the track the runner is confined to strict rules of conduct. Athletes follow a well-defined script. A track race cannot be an anti-race race, an anti-colonialism race, an anti-class race or an anti-drugs race in the way a book, dance, play or poem might be.

It could be argued that the act of, say, a Kenyan runner defeating a European champion can be read as an act of resistance – the beating of a 'white' man at his own game, so to speak. However, it could equally be pointed out that such events take place within a framework conceived by, and still largely controlled by, former colonial powers. Hence, 'the African' who defeats 'the European' does so on the latter's terms. And even if they are defeated, European runners who subscribe to the notion of 'fair play' will be magnanimous in defeat. In this conception of sport, losing is simply part of the game, well played. Likewise, the notion that success in running is a means of national expression can be read as untenable. When African runners are domiciled in Italy or Monaco, it is difficult to think of them as anything but workers in a globally organized business.[10]

Even so, it is likely that some runners use the running track to resist the actions of those in power over them. Little is known, however, about the motives of those athletes who might deliberately choose to lose a race, or to fail to expend sufficient effort, to feign an injury while running, or under-achieve in order to resist the exhortations of a coach, trainer or parent. Such acts seem likely to have occurred within the boundary of the track but they are difficult to authenticate. Even so, I believe that the idea of the boundary has some value in exploring transgression and resistance in sports.

In this chapter, I will first explore some examples of transgression by runners, exemplifying rebels but hardly rebellion. I will proceed to show how 'border crossings' – the intentional stepping off the track (beyond the boundary) and the stepping on to it (inside the boundary) – can each be read as forms of resistance. The boundary may exist but resistance can work across it.

Rebel Runners

Runners may be rebels beyond the boundary of the track but conformists on it. Their rebelliousness may, or may not, have anything to do with running. Consider, for example, the case of Otto Peltzer. Born in Schleswig-Holstein in 1900, for part of his youth Peltzer was confined to a wheelchair with polio. It is said that he overcame this disability through running, modelling himself on the ascetic Nurmi.[11] As a student, Peltzer studied an interesting combination of subjects: engineering, physical hygiene and social politics. In his early twenties he was achieving a high standard in middle-distance running. In July 1926 he took part in the British half-mile championship, run on a grass track at Stamford Bridge, London. He defeated his British adversary Douglas Lowe in a world record time of 1 minute 51.6 seconds.[12] Many track *cognoscenti* regard his greatest feat to have been his world-record breaking 1,500-metres-run of 3 minutes 51 seconds at Berlin in September 1926, defeating Nurmi and bettering his record. Apparently, 30,000 German spectators tearfully, but joyously and spontaneously, sang the *Deutschland Lied*.[13] Peltzer was a national hero but was injured during the 1928 Olympics at Amsterdam and under-performed in his event. During the 1930s he practiced medicine and developed a lasting interest in athletic training and coaching.

Peltzer was widely known in Germany as *Otto der Seltsame*, translated into English as 'Odd Otto'. This labelling of Peltzer as odd is generally represented as the result of his willingness to contest status quo opinions, particularly in relation to officialdom in the world of sports: 'He seems to have been a man always in opposition.'[14] However, his 'oddness' could also have referred to his habit of lying 'naked like a cat in a pool of sunlight in a forest. At one point he went to India and walked about in a loincloth.'[15] He was also gay.

Peltzer's anti-Nazi outspokenness is often presented as the reason for his suppression by Nazi officialdom but his admission of homosexuality in the 1930s could be read as being of equal, if not more, significance. In several accounts of his life his gayness is simply not mentioned.[16] Such an admission would have been unusual in the 1930s, especially in the world of sports. In Nazi Germany it was a confirmation of a degenerate society – a perversion of the kind of masculinity promoted by the Aryan ideal type.[17] Given his high profile as a world-record holder and hero of German sport, his admission of gayness conflicted strongly with a Nazi ideology that insisted that athletes of the Reich should be essentially soldiers; that is, athletic training had military motives as its conclusion. Gayness was anathema to Hitler and homosexuals were, like blacks and Jews, stigmatized as degenerate and effeminate. Homosexuality and other degenerative tendencies could, according to Nazi dogma, be seen in the body;[18] Peltzer confounded the stereotype. In 1935 he was imprisoned for 18 months for criticizing the Nazi appointed *Reichssportkommisar* and in 1941 he was interned in Maultausen concentration camp for four years. Following the Second World War Karl Ritter van Halt, who had been named as a war criminal by the Nuremburg court, was elected as Honorary President of the German Track and Field Federation. Peltzer's anti-fascist politics argued in favour of a 'new start', opposing a prominent Nazi in high office. His arguments were countered by the continued use of the derogatory '*Otto der Seltsame*', 'this assuming that the argument of a gay is valueless in the straight world of sport'.[19]

Peltzer seems to have intentionally set out to resist Nazism and the continued presence of far-right-wing politicians in the German track and field movement after the war. All this, however, took place off the running track and, to a great degree, after his serious running career was over.

Another athlete who was labelled a rebel was Gordon Pirie. Compared with Peltzer, his rebelliousness off the track was related more to his participation on it. Pirie was world-record holder for the 5,000 metres, three-time Olympian and silver medallist in the 5,000 metres at the 1956 Games. He was an immensely popular British sportsman during the 1950s. Pirie, variously dubbed a 'bank clerk' or 'paint salesman', was represented as a rebel, partly because of his grammar school background at a time when Oxbridge runners were still a prominent force, but mainly because he was read as the man who dragged British athletics into the 'professional' era, the man who titled his autobiography *Running Wild*, and the runner who aped Zátopek's huge mileage. If he lost a race, he would train harder, not less. Pirie would train hard up to the day of a major race.

Pirie ran a world record at 5,000 metres, when beating the Ukrainian Kuts, in an epic race in Bergen, Norway, in 1956. His performance was (I think) intrinsically superior to that of Bannister's four-minute mile. Pirie also ran in three Olympic Games, finishing fourth in the 5,000 metres at Helsinki and second in Melbourne in 1956, behind Kuts. He was a huge disappointment in Rome in 1960 where he was apparently over-trained and dehydrated. Pirie was a brilliant cross-country runner and also became a British orienteering champion in his forties. But it was Bannister who went on to be knighted and to run an Oxford college. Pirie simply went on running until he died.

Pirie was a running fanatic.[20] This may initially be read as demonstrating resistance to the 'amateur' ethos that typified much British sport at the time. His fanaticism inspired many protégés to fanaticism, leading to untold physical and emotional damage. Pirie brought the methods of mechanised production to his own body by adopting interval training. Pirie saw this method as a way of improving his stamina and, of more significance, his speed. Running through the countryside, while providing the stamina required of the long distance runner, did not provide the predictable surface needed for speed training. Yet the *distances* that Pirie ran in training were generally thought to exceed anything previously seen in British athletics. Asked how many days a week he trained, Pirie replied, 'seven, there are no more'.[21] This was Pirie the rebel – confronting the outmoded amateurism of the British sporting establishment.

The logical trajectory of a mind set that sees the body as a machine (see Chapter 3), constantly increasing its output of results and records, is to supplement it with additives of various kinds and, especially towards the end of his life, Pirie became addicted to various health foods. During his athletic career, he had adopted a somewhat ascetic stance to the various junketings that followed international events or the breaking of a record. More, not less, training would follow a poor performance. Somewhat paradoxically, however, one of Pirie's many excuses for a bad performance was that his opponents had taken 'drugs', which at the time were not subject to any kind of systematic surveillance. This excuse was used to help 'explain' his defeat by Kuts in the Olympic 5,000 metres in 1956.

The problem with Pirie's dedication to running was that it was incompatible with any (other) kind of full-time job. Running was his life and when running finished how could a full-time athlete sustain himself? As an 'amateur' Pirie was denied the possibility of gaining earnings from advertising Brylcreem, a product endorsed instead by cricketer Denis Compton. Fellow cricketer Len Hutton could benefit financially from advertising jock straps, or euphemistically, 'Litesome supporters'. Pirie had to make money in more surreptitious ways – such as earning 'expenses' from running in Scandinavia.

Pirie, knowing little else but running, was forced to turn to setting up businesses of various kinds. He offered 'fitness' courses for aspiring athletes and the average man. He was years too early for the fitness boom and his ventures invariably failed. As noted earlier, he was reduced to running in a bullring in Spain. He wrote guides on the sport of orienteering, took up coaching young girls in New Zealand and developed a relationship with a woman much younger than himself. The relationship, like that with his wife – the British sprint international Shirley Hampson, did not last. In his final years Pirie became a sad figure. He seems to have scrounged accommodation and work off his acolytes and admirers. With no means of self-gratification except driving his body to the limit, he became something of a misery.[22]

Publicized as a rebel, Pirie turns out to be, in many ways, an ultra-conformist. He followed a trajectory of rational, scientized running initiated at the end of the nineteenth century with its great emphasis on programmed training, dominated by the measured times of interval running. He transgressed the norms of the English 'gentleman amateur' but can, at the same time, be read as a specialist in an age of growing specialization. Pirie's life revolved around running. Indeed, he was such a specialist and a conformist that he could do very little else with his life.

Roger Bannister who was to become the well-heeled Master of Pembroke College, Oxford, was a contemporary of Pirie. Bannister, acknowledged as the first man to run faster than four minutes for the mile, is still widely read as the *amateur* – the Exeter College toff representing the establishment, for whom there was more to life than running (but see below). In 1954 Bannister took the world mile record beyond the 'barrier' that had proved impenetrable to the Swede Hägg. Bannister won gold medals at the Empire Games and European championships. He retired at his peak to follow medical studies and to make, later, somewhat outrageous pronouncements on the natural sprinting ability of black athletes.

As a 17-year-old fresher, Roger Gilbert Bannister entered Exeter College, Oxford University, in 1946. Soon after arriving there, he ran his first-ever mile race in a time of 4 minutes 53 seconds, at the time a moderate performance even for a 17-year-old. At Oxford he steadily improved so that by graduation he had reduced his time to 4 minutes 11.1 seconds.[23] Bannister continued running during his postgraduate years as a medical student in London and by 1952 his methodical progress produced performances that were good enough to make the British team for the Helsinki Olympics. Indeed, he was, for many, favourite to win the 1,500 metres. However, he finished fourth. He was disappointed with this result but was determined to continue running – in search of the elusive four-minute mile. His training was systematic and based on scientific principles. He was, after all, a medical student and researcher. He planned some years ahead that he would make the record attempt at the Iffley Road track in May, making sure that he was at his peak early in the season so that he could outdo his main rivals, the Kansan Wesley Santee, and the Australian John Landy, in breaking the elusive four minute barrier. His timing was meticulous, off and on the track. Bannister achieved his ambition on 6 May 1954, when he ran 3 minutes 59.4 seconds at Iffley Road. Less than two months later this record was broken in Finland by Landy, though later in the same year Bannister was to defeat Landy in the so-called 'mile of the century' at the Empire Games at Vancouver. Bannister also won the European 1,500 metres championship in the same year. He then retired from competitive running. Unlike Pirie, the Oxbridge set – Bannister, Chataway and Brasher – with the necessary educational and cultural capital, could slip into 'proper jobs' (medicine, management and media) when their running days ended.

This bland account of Bannister's career hides the ways in which Bannister was read by the British public and represented by the UK press. Despite Bannister's considerable improvement during his Oxford years, he was widely reported as something of a 'natural athlete', rarely running more than 25 miles per week. Bannister claimed he trained three times a week, taking 45 minutes for each session, and was unable to specify the nature of his training because, he said, that depended on how he felt.[24] Bannister had the reputation of light training, taking six days off before his epic run to retreat with his friends, Chataway and Brasher, in mountain climbing in Snowdonia. This lack of rigour with regard to training was antithetical to the self-imposed training regimen of Pirie.

Bannister was presented to the mass media as an image of the English sporting gentleman – the very ethos that Pirie contested. Bannister was written and read as an amateur, living and running in a pre-modern world, transgressing the norms of serious running and going against the grain. However, such an image was, to a large extent, a legacy of the Oxford lifestyle of the time. Bannister wrote that at Oxford

> Undergraduates are, without exception, haunted by the fear of being thought to take anything too seriously. I know that I

developed a pose of apparent indifference, to hide the tremendous enthusiasm which I felt for running, from the day I set foot
in Oxford. You had to be almost as careful in Oxford not to
appear to take games too seriously as you had at school to avoid
the stigma of being called a 'swot'.[25]

It should not be surprising to learn, therefore, that Bannister was almost
certainly doing more than he admitted. His Oxford colleague Chris Chataway
claimed that, in total contrast to Pirie, 'Roger went to great lengths to conceal
the amount of training that he did'.[26] And, as noted earlier, the influence of
Stampfl may well have been far greater than Bannister claimed.

In many ways then, Bannister and Pirie were both truly modern athletes.
Pirie was coached by medical scientists but Bannister *was* a medical scientist:
Who better than he to monitor his training and engage in experimental
methods – learning by doing? As early as 1951 he was undertaking 'exper-
iments in Oxford on the control of breathing'. He stated that he prepared his
training programme and his physical reactions with the same precision that
he had learned in the laboratory; he 'used the motor-driven treadmill in the
laboratory on which the speed and gradient could be altered so as to exhaust
the toughest athlete in a few minutes'.[27] Here was a man driven by a machine.
The shoes he wore for his successful assault on the mile record were specially
made for him and, with their designer, Bannister 'worked out modifications
which would reduce the weight of each running shoe from six to four ounces.
This saving of weight might well have 'made the difference between success
and failure.'[28] Such scientific detail was matched by the fact that on the
morning of his world mile record he meticulously sharpened the spikes of his
bespoke running shoes on a laboratory grindstone.[29] He was utterly achievement oriented, setting himself the carefully planned target of being the first
man to break the four-minute 'barrier'. Far from transgressing modern
methods by harking back to bygone ways, Bannister can be read as the
epitome of the modern athlete – the scientist and record breaker.

Transgression

It has long been believed in Europe that Africa is a storehouse of fantastic
athletes. Disappointed by their nation's perceived mediocrity in the 1936
Olympics, French journalists suggested that their coaches should venture into
the colonial bush and bring home African athletes to compete for the mother
country.[30] The British colonial system was different and sport tended to be
taken to the African rather than vice versa. A large number of change agents
were involved in setting up sport in Africa. These included missionaries,

schoolteachers, local administrators, plantation owners and military and police physical education instructors. They did not find it necessary to disguise their motive – that of social control.[31]

In the early 1950s the prevailing western view was that African track athletes, like African Americans, possessed 'great speed but little stamina'.[32] Middle-distance running (that is, track racing beyond 800 metres) was read as being the preserve of the 'white' athlete, epitomized mainly by Nordic runners such as Paavo Nurmi in the 1920s, Taisto Mäki in the 1930s, and Gunder Hägg in the 1940s. During the 1950s it was the Czech Emil Zátopek who was the nonpareil of distance running. To be sure, in the 1948 Olympics Alain Mimoun from Algeria, who ran in the colours of France, gained second place in the 10,000 metres. He went on to win two silver medals, in the 5,000 and 10,000 metres at the 1952 Games, and capped his career by winning the 1956 Olympic marathon. In 1952 he was the only African in the top 60 5,000-metre runners in the world.[33] But by representing France Mimoun could immediately be read as an ambiguous African hero. Indeed, he could be argued to have represented France in more ways than one. He assumed 'French-ness' by dropping the Algerian element in his surname (O'katcha) and supported France in the war against Algeria. He was the colonized athlete and did not represent 'blackness' in the way that athletes from central and southern Africa might. It was the 'Arab north' rather than 'Black Africa' that Mimoun represented – if he represented Africa at all. Not until the Rome Olympics in 1960 was the black athlete with stamina made visible to a global audience, when the Ethiopian athlete Abebe Bikila claimed victory in the marathon.

In contrast to Mimoun, consider the example of Nyandika Maiyoro, born in 1930 in the Kisii district of Nyanza province in the Rift Valley of western Kenya. As a young man he took part in district and provincial track meetings before becoming a national champion and record holder. Maiyoro seems to have made his first international appearance, at least outside of British East Africa, in a meet in Madagascar in 1953. He was entered for the 3,000 metres race and emerged a local hero. Apparently, he failed to arrive at the start in time and only started when the rest of the field was 100 metres down the track. He closed the gap after 4 laps and proceeded to win the race by 50 metres. The following year a team of Kenyan athletes took part in the Empire Games in Vancouver. En route they broke their journey in London and took part in the AAA championships held in the (appropriately named, from an ethnic perspective) White City Stadium, London. Maiyoro competed in the 3-mile event and surprised many of the 30,000 British spectators by leading for much of the distance. During the course of the race he periodically opened up a considerable lead on the pack of English runners behind him, only to let them catch him and then sprint off again. Eventually, they over-took him, and the British runners Fred Green and Chris Chataway each broke the world record. Maiyoro finished in fourth place, breaking his Kenyan record in the process.

The British press far from predicted Maiyoro's performance but it was a defining moment in the history of athletics. Following the race a British track expert noted that 'never again shall we nurse the idea that the coloured races (sic) are no good at anything beyond a mile'.[34] The world of British track and field, if not the world beyond, had been alerted to the fact that Maiyoro was an exception to the notion that black athletes lacked stamina. Maiyoro also achieved fourth place in the 3 miles at Vancouver and again improved on his Kenyan record. The next major international event in which he competed was the 1956 Olympic Games at Melbourne. This was the first time a Kenyan team had competed at the Olympics and Maiyoro was entered for the 1,500 metres and the 5,000 metres. He met with little success in the former but finished seventh in the latter, in a race that included global luminaries such as world record holders Kuts and Pirie. Maiyoro did not run particularly well in the 1958 Empire Games in Cardiff but in 1960 he brought his career to a climax by achieving sixth place in the Olympic 5,000 metres in Rome. He did not achieve the global visibility of Bikila but his time of 13 minutes 52.8 seconds was an 'African record'.

Maiyoro was the first black athlete from Africa south of the Sahara to achieve world-class status as a middle-distance runner. His achievement in the 1960 Rome Olympics made him the only black athlete among the 70 fastest runners over the distance in the world.[35] He ventured where black athletes had been traditionally absent, transgressing the 'purified' space of the 5,000 metres track race. He broke with tradition and drew attention to what had previously been considered 'natural' and 'taken for granted'. Cresswell would argue that in doing so he revealed the 'historical and mutable nature of that which is usually considered "the way things are"'.[36] Maiyoro can be read as a transgressive athlete who crossed the boundary between the perceived preserve of the 'white' and that of the 'black'. He confounded the prevailing stereotype of the black athlete by this 'out-of-placeness' and his 'being noticed'.

Another form of transgression is exemplified by an image of Carl Lewis, a sprinter who is regarded by many as one of the greatest athletes of all time.[37] On the face of it Lewis was, during his prime, a classic conformist to sport's ideology. He had, according to the sub title of his autobiography, a 'professional life in amateur track and field'.[38] He was Olympic champion in the both the 100 and 200 metres in 1984 and won the 100 metres and gained second place in the 200 metres in 1988. His performances and his style revealed masculinity writ large – tall, powerful, well muscled. And this was, of course, black masculinity.

As a world star, Lewis has been photographed many times, usually in full flow or crossing the finishing line ahead of his rivals. In the mid 1990s, however, a photograph was published of Lewis on the starting line in the

Figure 5.1 Carl Lewis, photographed for a Pirelli advertisement (Pirelli).

'set' position, though in this case he was posing as an individual with his gaze, not focused on the horizon of the finishing line but on the camera (see Figure 5.1). What are we to make of this image? First of all it must be noted that the photograph appeared as part of a calendar published by the tyre firm Pirelli, associated with calendars featuring scantily clad women, thought by the producers and some consumers as sexy. Although the image would be recognizable to many people as Carl Lewis, the stereotypical representation of Lewis as a super-masculine athlete is disturbed by the fact that he is wearing red, women's high-heeled shoes, invoking his femininity. As the sociologist Stuart Hall notes, when reading this image, 'the super-male black athlete may not be all he seems'.[39] The image is ambiguous when compared with the stereotypical images of black athletes.

It is possible to read the high heels as central to one meaning of the image, explicated in the caption running across the top of the photograph: 'Power is nothing without control.' Lewis has the power but in those shoes he will lack the required control. But is there more to it than that? What is Lewis, the black athlete, the super-male, doing here? Compared with photographs of many black athletes, this photograph goes against the grain. It could be simply a joke on his part or that of the photographer or producer. He could have been exploited into posing in this way. He may have deliberately set out to challenge and contest the traditional image of black – or even straight – masculinity. It is certainly a transgressive image; whether it is a demonstration of resistance is more doubtful and this could only be established if we knew Lewis's intentions. He may have intended some kind of resistant act, but against what is unclear.

Taming Transgression

As noted earlier, Steve Prefontaine was a teenage phenomenon, a world-class athlete while in his teens. While successful competitively, he never held a world record nor achieved an Olympic medal. His successes were mainly in the USA. At high school and at the University of Oregon, he was a youthful prodigy.

Theresa Walton, in an insightful study of Prefontaine, sets out to explore the ambiguous nature of the runner's media image in the light of his initial rebelliousness and his posthumous co-option and commodification.[40] Prefontaine's career can be seen as fitting into three stages. The first sees him as a rebel of sorts, not quite fitting the all-American athlete. He was brought up in a working class home in Coos Bay, Oregon, and was to be labelled a rebel for much of his life. He projected a non-conformist image in a conformist sport: 'He had a tough, front running style and … outspoken candor.'[41] He was said to be controversial and the most outspoken of America's amateur athletes, criticizing the track and field establishment. He especially criticized the US sports bureaucracy for not providing enough assistance to athletes. He argued against the US sports system:

> People say I should be running for a gold medal for the old red, white and blue and all that bull, but it's not gonna be that way. I'm the one who had made the sacrifices. Those are my American records, not the country's. I compete for myself. To hell with love of country … If you asked me if I'd give up my American citizenship, I would say never. But if you asked me if I'd trade our sports program for a Finnish sports program or a Russian program, I'd say darn right.[42]

Prefontaine had the reputation of being something of a womaniser but it was alcohol that may have led to his death. Four hours after his last race on 30 May 1975, he met his death in the accident that I referred to in Chapter 1. He died from a form of suffocation called traumatic asphyxiation. His blood alcohol level was found to be 0.16 per cent. Drunkenness is presumed under Oregon law if the blood alcohol level is 0.10 per cent.

Although his name lived on among fans, it was 20 years after his death that Steve Prefontaine returned to the consciousness of the broader US public. In the 1990s three movies were made of him and, unusual among biographies of runners, his biography, first published in 1977, was revised and reprinted in 1997.[43] His image and name were used in Nike advertisements and in running magazines. There remain numerous web pages dedicated to him. The connection between Nike and Prefontaine is very strong and goes back to Prefontaine's running days in Oregon. The Nike company was set up by his coach, Bill Bowerman. One of the Prefontaine movies, *Fire on the Track*, is said to be as much about Nike as it is about Prefontaine. First, the shoe company funded the film; second, Nike features prominently, occupying 15 per cent of the 58 minute film. During the 1990s, therefore, Prefontaine can be read as no longer representing Coos Bay but, instead, representing Nike.[44]

Fire on the Track tended to sanitize Prefontaine. It showed him as having one steady girlfriend, it showed him bowing to the consummate father figure of coach Bill Bowerman – who nurtured Prefontaine in a paternalistic mode, it showed him employing the Puritan work ethic of the United States. According to Walton, he was constructed by Nike as an ideal person, 'uncolored, ungen-dered and able to "rise above his class"'. An 'ideal' person does not alienate the kind of consumers that Nike desired.[45]

Though a rebel off the track, Prefontaine was always a conformist on it. He criticized American track but also took part in it. Once on the track, the script prevented him from any oppositional strategy, leaving any resistance beyond the boundary. He was posthumously transformed into a conformist off the track by the forces of consumerism as exemplified by the globalised, exploitative and seductive world of the sports goods industry.

Towards Resistance

Recall that resistance involves intention. The British record holder for the 5,000 metres, 10,000 metres and marathon, Paula Radcliffe is (as I write) widely admired in Britain for both her racing style and her stance against doping. She invariably sets the pace in her races and attempts to run the other athletes off their feet. All too often, however, she had been unable to match her adversaries, who tended to have a faster finishing sprint than her. In 2002 she won both the London and Chicago marathons, the latter in a world-best time. In the same year she ran the second-fastest ever 10,000 metres race and won the European 5,000 metres championship.

However, it is upon the events of the previous year, at the World track and field championships at Edmonton, Canada, that I want to concentrate. Radcliffe had run a good, but losing, race in the 10,000 metres. It was then her turn to be a spectator of the 5,000 metres event in which the Russian athlete Olga Yegorova was a major contender. This race had assumed more than normal significance because of the problems Yegorova had encountered in a drug testing session in Paris. She was apparently tested for the natural hormone erythropoietin (EPO), a substance banned by the IAAF. This product is used to increase red blood cells among leukaemia patients, but is also an important medical product used by many athletes in cross country skiing, cycling and distance running. However, she only took a urine test, failing to follow it with a blood test that someone had forgotten to administer. Her first sample tested positive for EPO. Under normal circumstances she would have been banned by the sport's governing bureaucracy but due to the lack of correct procedures in Paris, Yegorova's test was dismissed. She was retested for EPO but she did not test positive on that occasion and was allowed to compete.

There was considerable controversy before the 5,000 metres race and many athletes and spectators labelled Yegorova a 'cheat'. If other competitors took part in the race against Yegorova they could be read as being complicit in providing her with an unfair advantage. The other athletes could have demonstrated against drug abuse by going on strike and refusing to compete. After all, if she had no one to race against, any 'victory' would have been meaningless. But none did. The only mildly transgressive act was for Radcliffe to publicly display a poster stating 'Drug Cheats Out', which was quickly removed by an official. Although Radcliffe claimed she was aiming her critique at all 'illegal' substance abusers, it was rather obvious that her target was Yegorova.

Radcliffe was mildly reprimanded for her action and it was more or less suggested that she should concentrate on her running and distance herself from the 'politics' of sport. In the weeks following the Edmonton championships she took part in several races against Yegorova (in all of which the latter emerged as the winner). Can Radcliffe, a severe critic of proven substance abusers, be interpreted as colluding in Yegorova's success by racing against her? Should she have refused to race against her? Radcliffe's tacit response was that she should not opt out of running (that is, making a living) when it was Yegorova who was the 'cheat': She stressed how much she loved running and did not want to be denied participation.

Radcliffe's continued engagement with an athlete she had labelled a cheat and her inability to engage with a more resistant act (for example, going on strike, making a protest while on the running track, failing to complete the race) illustrates the power of modern sporting ideology and hegemony. It also reveals the inappropriateness of the running track as a site for resistance.

Fictions of Resistance: Alf Tupper and Wilson

Resistance and transgression often contain dimensions of social class. Two examples of transgression can be found in the post-war British boys' comics *The Rover* and *The Wizard*. These, and other similar publications, were common reading material for boys in the post-war years of austerity, before the years of mass television consumption and a youth leisure market. During the harsh years of the 1940s and 1950s – and for some time prior to then – the elite, Olympian runners of England were disproportionately represented by members of the Achilles Club, the sole preserve of graduates of the two 'ancient' universities, Oxford and Cambridge. Olympic gold medallists Arnold Strode Jackson (1912), Bevill Rudd (1920), Harold Abrahams (1924), Douglas Lowe (1924), David (Lord) Burghley (1928), Tom Hampson (1932) and Jack Lovelock (1936) exemplified this long-standing line of superior runners who reflected the Achilles tendency. Later, Roger Bannister, Chris Chataway and Chris Brasher, the architects of the first mile recorded in less than four minutes, were members of Achilles. Bannister's achievements have already been noted; Chataway broke the world 3 miles and 5,000 metres records and Brasher won the 1956 Olympic steeplechase. Most of these athletes, like most of the students attending Oxbridge at the time, were privately educated. These were not runners who were, literally, hungry for success but were affluent and sophisticated. In the pre-war period they dined in college halls and took tea and scones in their studies, served by their 'scouts', as the Oxford dialect would have it.

Where were the working class heroes who could contest the hegemony of the Achilles club in post-war Britain? Arguably the most inspirational was to found in the pages of the British comics *The Rover* and, later, the *Victor*. His name was Alf Tupper, dubbed 'the tough of the track'. In an age of austerity, he symbolized the sporting success of working-class runners, their social values overcoming those of the ancient universities, occupied invariably by snobs and toffs. Ron Hill, the British marathon runner and winner of European and Commonwealth titles, implies that Tupper was his childhood idol and inspiration. Hill lived in Accrington (Lancashire) in a 'stone terraced house, two up and two down, with a cellar and a drop lavatory at the bottom of the garden'; his mother worked as a French-polisher at a factory making billiard tables and his father was a locomotive fireman.[46] In his autobiography, Hill observes that one morning, sometime in the mid 1950s, he

> sat down, put aside the *Daily Herald* without even a glance at the headlines, and started to turn the pages of the *Rover*. Quickly I came to the story I was looking for – 'The Tough of the Track'. I felt a tingle of excitement as I began to read and was transported into another world ... I had been so absorbed that I didn't notice that our kid had come down and practically finished his breakfast. I glanced up at the clock again. 8.30. Late for school.[47]

What was the 'other world' into which Hill, and countless other boys, including myself, were transported? Well, it was the world of Alf Tupper. This working-class hero appeared in various guises over the half-century in which he featured in British comic books and boys' annuals. He was first and foremost a proletarian runner who lived in the appropriately named Greystone, a large manufacturing town in the industrial north of England. He was variously employed as a millwright at Greystone Aviation Factory, a plumber's mate to Charlie Chipping and by the early 1990s a self-employed welder with a factory built under the unmistakable workingman's milieu of railway viaduct arches. It was in the working-class streets of terraced houses, amid factories with their chimneys belching smoke, and along canal towpaths that Tupper trained in the rain, driven by the prevailing westerly winds, fuelling the dreams of working-class grammar school boys of the 1950s (see Figure 5.2).

Tupper was an anti-hero: working class but also amateur. He rejected the scientific approach pioneered by German scientists of the Gerschler era and trained on fish and chips and a few hours sleep each night. One image of Tupper shows him surrounded by scientists, instantly recognizable in their long, white coats. They are shown measuring the optimal angle of the body at the start of a race. Tupper rejects their geometries and formulae, sticking to his own homespun approaches. On another occasion, Tupper failed to qualify for the England team for the marathon in the 1970 Commonwealth Games because of sickness. He immediately gained a place in the team representing the south-Atlantic island of Tristan da Cunha. He won the race,

Figure 5.2 Alf Tupper (D. C. Thomson & Co. Ltd).

consuming a bag of chips at the halfway point, and beating African adversaries (Kippo of Kenya and Gezi of Nigeria) in the final 400 metres.

Rivalling Tupper as a hero in the boys' comics of 1950s England was another running idol, Wilson of the *Wizard*. Whereas Tupper drew on working-class sentiments, Wilson's attraction seemed to lie in an atavistic yearning for a glorious, natural, mystical yet rugged, rural past. Born on 1 November 1795, Wilson was still running in the 1950s and 1960s. At 160 years of age he was breaking world records. Wilson lived in a cave on Ambleside Moor in Cumbria and was advised by an aged hermit, Matthew, who advocated a natural diet of herbs and various elixirs, one of which was the elixir of life. Wilson ran in an antique black running costume. He was able to take on all comers and break world records. He ran the half-mile in 1 minute 40 seconds, defeating a German who was known to be using drugs. He ran the mile, at London's Stamford Bridge grounds, in 3 minutes 48 seconds – outrageous at the time but well within the reach of several present-day milers. He ran backwards up Mount Everest and ran the marathon in 2 hours 22 minutes – his most modest performance.[48] Having done so he would return to his rural retreat. In contrast to Tupper, Wilson was a sporting polymath. He represented a triumph of the rural and the traditional over the urban and the modern. He also represented the traditional non-specialist over the modernity of the narrowly-skilled 'expert'. Wilson was a high achiever in many sports. He could jump and throw and played a good game of cricket. He reflected an age when W.G. Grace, regarded by many as the greatest English cricketer of all time, could also win the 440 yards hurdles (involving the clearance of 20 hurdles) at the 1866 London Olympics, a precursor of the more well-known Coubertinian games 30 years later.[49]

In their different ways, Tupper and Wilson can both be read as transgressing the norms of mid twentieth-century running. Their attraction was that they ran against the grain in a period when running was becoming increasingly serious, technical and modern. One was an urban, working-class hero; the other celebrated a disappearing world of the rural. Each was clearly out of place.

Resistance: Stepping off the Track

A further literary creation which, I think, is worthy of more serious consideration is (Colin) Smith, the key figure in Alan Sillitoe's novella *The Loneliness of the Long Distance Runner*, alluded to earlier, and who geographer Martyn Bowden has termed a neo-Marxist athlete.[50] Smith's exploits best illustrate, perhaps, resistance through running. Sillitoe achieves this by 'inverting and falsifying' the truisms of the conventional world of sports writing. The story smacks of subversion and can be read as a 'critical stance' against 'athletic careerism'.[51] An inmate of a youth detention institution, Smith is encouraged by the governor to develop his running skills. This will not only serve the function of social control but also rehabilitate the incarcerated athlete. Furthermore, it will promote the image of the institution. Smith (the commonest English surname) will be turned from a criminal into a supporter of the status quo. He finds himself in a situation where he is expected to train on his own (his self-created identity) in the service of the penal institution (team identity). The story tells how Smith uses the mismatch between the two identities for his own purpose, to resist the ambitions for him espoused by the governor of the institution.[52]

The climax of the story is the race between the offenders' institution and another, Gunthorpe. In the movie, Gunthorpe is changed into a posh private school in order to heighten the social difference between the two competing teams. That Smith, a convicted criminal from one of the working-class areas of the city of Nottingham, is able to compete in a race against social elites shows the bonding function of modern sport. It also reveals the social class tensions of post-war England. However, Smith uses the race as a dramatic and intentional form of resistance. Well in the lead, with a short distance to go, he tells his story thus:

> I'm slowing down now for Gunthorpe to catch me up, and I'm doing it in a place just where the drive turns into the sportsfield – where they can see what I'm doing, especially the governor and his gang from the grandstand, and I'm going so slow I'm almost marking time… I'd got them beat at last.[53]

Smith had beaten the system by deliberately losing the race. He had shown resistance, planned and implemented. 'I lost the governor's race alright, and won mine twice over' says Colin, meaning that if he hadn't raced his race he wouldn't have developed an illness that kept him out of military service and permitted him 'the sort of work' his 'itchy fingers want to do'.[54]

In his analysis of the movie version of the story, Martyn Bowden reads Smith's pact with the governor as a compact with the Devil. In a series of flashbacks during the race, Colin is forced to think about who's side he is on. There are the temptations of a middle-class life and the tension between athletics and his 'embryonic Marxist-Socialist thought'.[55]

A furlong ahead of the rest of the field and only a few yards from the finishing line, with both sides urging him to win, he stops dead. With his face wreathed in a devilish smile, he bows in mock servility to Ranleigh School's official winner, Gunthorpe, and to the other runners who eventually pass him to cross the line. The camera pans first to the three symbols of the Establishment – the churchman/padre, the army general and H.M. Governor of the Borstal – for whom incomprehension turns to disbelief and, in the governor's case, to angry frustration and the certain knowledge that he will not make the Queens New Year's Honours List.[56]

The Loneliness of the Long-Distance Runner is one of the few pieces of writing that is able to demonstrate the hegemonic nature of achievement running and the way in which it is resisted by the anti-hero opting out of one of sport's basic norms – achievement. Smith prefers personal honesty to hypocrisy and the 'slow dying of being or becoming bourgoisie'.[57] It is possible to read running, therefore, as a vehicle for moral triumph.[58] The paradox here is that the moral triumph comes not from sport but, at the last minute, from opting out of it – spoiling sport. In other words, it is difficult, if not impossible, to be subversive by 'playing the game'. Invariably, one has to take oneself 'beyond the boundary' in order to demonstrate resistance. Smith 'deliberately loses the race that he could easily win; in doing so, he unmistakably asserts a fundamental *human* freedom not to suborn himself, not to conform, and not to comply'.[59]

Robert Zeller suggests that the fictional Smith, who feels compelled to commit what many would regard as an anti-social, resistant and self-destructive act, can be related to a real world example. He suggests that the relationship lies more in the nature of competitive, representational running and the way in which it forms runners as subjects, than in their psychological make-up.[60] He cites the case of Kathy Ormsby, a student-athlete at North Carolina State University in the mid 1980s. Her coach, parents and peers regarded her as a perfectionist who fought to overcome events beyond her control. She put pressure on herself to achieve. According to Zeller, she had internalized the lesson that motivation for athletic achievement should not be for individual glory but for the service of others – her school or her team. Additionally, as told by Frank Murphy, she held the view that her running could serve God – a 'desire to glorify the ungendered Him by her accomplishments'.[61] In May 1986 she set a National Collegiate Athletic Federation (NCAA) 10,000 metres record of 32 minutes 36.2 seconds while competing in the Penn Relays in Philadelphia. Her success increased the expectations others had of her. Like Smith, once she achieved success her name was no longer hers.

Her success in Philadelphia made Kathy Ormsby favourite for the 10,000 metres at the NCAA Championships, held in Indianapolis a month later. She felt nervous before the race, partly because of the high expectations that had been heaped upon her and partly because in a race a few weeks before the championships she had 'blacked out'.[62] It was also a hot day. Once the race started Ormsby ran with the pack of runners but by half-way she recognized that she was struggling to keep up with the leaders. At the 6,500 metres point she ran off the track. But she did not stop running. She said that 'it was like something snapped' and 'a burst of energy' carried her across an adjoining baseball field. She climbed a chain-link fence and ran on for two-and-a-half blocks until she reached a bridge, about 45 feet above the White River. She jumped. She missed the water by about 20 feet. As a result, her running career ended: she suffered paralysis from the waist down.[63]

It has been suggested that what happened to Kathy Ormsby at the White River Bridge 'was the most important single event in the developing sport of women's track and field in the United States'.[64] It revealed, in terrible form, the way in which driven-ness could lead to disaster. What had 'snapped' as she ran off the track? Had her previous success increased expectations that may have exceeded or even contradicted her own view of her ability?[65] Could it have been her affiliation to the university and her regimen of control that had snapped, leading to a sense of release from the responsibility and stress of representing the university to the wider world? Had she failed in the glorification of her God? Psychiatrists claimed it was a panic attack, related to anxiety and depression.[66] Zeller suggests that the relationship lies more in the nature of competitive, representational running and the way in which it forms runners as subjects, than in their psychological make-up.[67] Was it a jump or a fall? Who knows? And no single factor could 'explain' such an event. Ormsby claimed that it was not a deliberate act and that she was not think-ing rationally.[68] If that is the case, it was not a suicide attempt. In Ormsby's diary she had made meticulous plans about how she would spend her time in Indianapolis. She had planned to run in the heats of the 5,000 metres championship the day after the 10,000. Leaving the track during the first of her two planned championship attempts was not part of her agenda.[69] A clinical sports psychologist described it as 'an act of impulse. If it had been calculated, it would have succeeded.'[70] Because of this, and because she was struggling and unlikely to win the race, it seems to me that it was a funda-mentally different act from that of Smith, for whom stepping off the track was a rational and well-planned strategy of resistance rather than one of despair. Smith's motivation is clear – 'he wants to defy authority, including its construction of the value of athletics, and undermine the legitimacy of the system'.[71] Stepping off the track can act as a metaphor for the kind of other resistant acts noted earlier – for example, dropping out of a race by feigning injury, deliberately losing a race, or not giving one's best.

Resistance: Stepping on to the Track

I have suggested that stepping off the track is a powerful, visible form of resis-tance, most graphically exemplified by the fictional Smith. But stepping on to the track can also be read as an equally, if not more dramatic, resistant act. Running on the grass, rather than keeping off it, has for a long-time been a form of resistance to municipal authority by children everywhere. Similarly, the road running and jogging boom of the 1970s has been seen as a mild, though sanctioned, form of rebellion, claiming the streets back from the motor vehicle.[72]

Running on to the track is a metaphor for the increasing presence of women in sports; Coubertin and Cerutty would have found no space for them and it is only in recent decades that several long-distance races have been available to women. Claiming the purified space of the track, road or cross-country course is also a potential strategy for radical non-athletes, though as a tool for political activism it has been relatively infrequent.

A particular area where running on to the track has been a cause of resistance lies in the recent history of women's participation in long-distance running. Stepping on to the running track or the road race course can, of itself, be read as an act of resistance for women per se. Running has always been strongly gendered. For many years women were excluded from racing more than 400 metres on the assumption that they were intrinsically unable to run such distances without incurring injury or distress. To see women in a distressed state of exhaustion was considered more displeasing than seeing men in a similar state. Here lies an example of paternalism which treats women as pets before they even start taking part in serious athletics. A number of initiatives have shown women resisting the hegemony of male bureaucracy and entering, sometimes undercover, races from which they were notionally barred. This exemplifies power from below and reveals that athletes are not necessarily dupes. The intentional disruption of running protocols was demonstrated by several women marathon runners in the 1960s at a time when, in some races, women were officially banned. The failure to acknowledge the feats of early women marathon runners is not unusual. However, as Annemarie Jutel has skilfully demonstrated, while resistance provided a framework for the emergence of women's long-distance running, expectations of femininity were preserved, many runners conforming to gender expectations and many races being sponsored by cosmetics and make-up companies.[73]

To all intents and purposes, it is a necessity for the body be exposed if a runner is to perform at the highest level. Yet to expose the body to the male gaze, to dress as a western athlete does, is alien to certain strains of Islam. The strict Muslim code of *purdah* decrees that women should be covered from head to toe when in public places. In much of the Islamic world women are forbidden to take part in sports and to display their semi-naked bodies to the spectatorial gaze of the sports arena. Yet this is what the Algerian middle-distance runner Hassiba Boulmerka has done.

Boulmerka attracted the attention of track fans in 1991 when she won the world 1,500 metres championship. This was also the year in which the Islamic Salvation Front (FIS), more popularly known as Islamic fundamentalists, established a struggle with moderate Muslims. A year later, she consolidated her fame by gaining a gold medal at the Olympics. She dedicated her medal to Mohamed Boudief, the former president of Algeria who was allegedly assassinated by fundamentalists in June of the Olympic year. Following the Olympics, she was at first widely applauded by her fellow Algerians. Later, however, she was the subject of much criticism by the FIS, who objected strongly to her contravention of the traditional dress code of Muslim women. Boulmerka had become a symbol of anti-fundamentalism. She claimed that her international experience as a runner provided a powerful chance to express herself. In addition to her self-expression through running she also claimed to have developed a deeper love of Algeria. Bill Morgan's reading of what she expressed through her running was a blend of European individual initiative and Islamic community-inspired discipline.[74] Her 'pluralist cultural expression' was

> an occasion to speak out, to convey, especially to young Algerians not yet enamored with or daunted by fascist fundamentalists, and to Westerners not yet enamored with the stereotypical views of Muslims that greet them at every turn, that Islamic culture is not the hotbed of fanaticism it is often made out to be and that it is not necessarily hostile either to individual effort or to the plight of women.[75]

To take one's place on a running track in relatively scanty garb does, therefore, makes the 400-metre circuit a site for resistance, a site for a demonstration to the world of cultural pluralism.

Although the context of modern sport may be seen as a site for resistance, the precise sites at which running takes place rarely witness resistant acts. Foot racing is not generally a site for radical interventions of a political nature. Compared with the novel, the play and the dance, achievement running and achievement sport per se, remain limited in their potential for resistant acts, unless, of course, actually taking part in running can, of itself, be read as resistant.

The stories told in this chapter reveal that runners such as Pirie, Bannister, Prefontaine, Lewis and Radcliffe were conventional athletes, accepting the rules of running and its achievement ideology. They were able to accept labels as rebels of various kinds but in no real way transgressed or resisted the norms of modern sport. Maiyoro was certainly out of place in his running; he transgressed the racial boundaries of conventional running, as did Tupper and Wilson. So too did Ormsby who, through transgression, may have had more impact than any of the other athletes mentioned in this chapter. At the same time, however, they did not intentionally deviate from the right and proper track (literally). The cases of the fictional Smith and the actual Boulmerka are different. They appear to have exemplified resistance, a conscious effort to resist the status quo. In the former's case he did this by stepping out of the ideological track of achievement sport; in the case of the latter it was by stepping on to it.

Escape: Runners as Cosmopolites

To 'run away' and to go 'running wild' suggest escape of some sort, a resistance to containment – to break free, to escape from the confines of control. In a track race the athlete seeks to escape from the confinement of the starting line. But serious athletes must not run wild as they require a controlled regimen, they are tamed and civilized by their trainers and are confined by the spatial parameters of their course. But running as escape can be read more literally, and this forms the subject of this chapter.

As Tuan points out in *Escapism*, he is a geographer, part of whose business it is 'to study why and how people move'.[1] Running itself can, of course, be seen as not only a *vehicle* for escape but also a *form* of escapism. On the one hand, running assists escape from a threat or as a means of time-space compression. On the other hand, running per se may be a means of replacing the ordinary with élan and freedom. And as I pointed out in Chapter 3, the runner may escape from the track to the country and from the scientific to (what may be perceived as) the natural, be it Portsea, Vålådalen or the Surrey Downs. Even during a sprint race the experience can be one of escape, as, also in Chapter 3, Ben Johnson's comments show.

Ordinary athletes (of which I was one) escape from their mediocrity by dreaming of becoming champions, Olympians or record holders. In such (day) dreaming we become absorbed in another body and/or event, escaping the unsatisfactory body that we occupy. We take temporary flight from our own 'corporeal wrapping'.[2] Reading about running is another form of escape. Reading about Hägg, Nurmi, Pirie and Bannister were ways in which I could escape from my own ordinary athletic performances in the late 1950s athletic backwater of South Wales. Transported to the Nordic forests and lakes, on the one hand, and to the metropolis of London and its mystical White City Stadium on the other, I could at least dream about greatness.[3] On awakening, of course, I and others like me, are well and truly put in our place. There is no place for dreamers in serious sport and those who might try to project their dreams into reality are forcefully dealt with. Just before Frank Shorter had entered the Munich Olympic Stadium as winner of the 1972 Olympic marathon, a German student, Norbert Sudhaus, escaped from the spectators' area and ran on to the track towards the finishing line. Officials quickly removed him. There appeared to be no political motive attached to his entry into the last seconds of the race. It was his moment of glory, his dreams translated into reality before he was summarily removed. He had contravened the protocols of Olympism; the phantom runner had transgressed the sacred space of the Olympic track – no place for a joke. The kinds of escape noted above reveal sport as providing a 'brief and often intoxicating respite from the complexities and confusion of everyday life', that is, escape.[4]

It is escape as mobility or migration that forms the subject of most of this chapter. Migration is clearly a form of escape and has been studied in considerable detail by students of both geography and sports. Traditionally, such studies have attracted positivistic approaches. As part of such an approach, human migrants can be aggregated into 'flows', networks, or 'talent pipelines',[5] or be objects of the 'gravity model'.[6] The positivist approach emphasizes patterns above experiences. The humanistic geographer David Ley critiqued such studies by stressing that they exemplify a style where 'description takes place over interpretation'.[7] More recently, Tim Cresswell has noted that the spatial science approach encourages the view that migration is, in some way, 'dysfunctional'. This is because spatial structures should be arranged in such a way as to minimize the need for movement. This, he suggests, 'points towards a wider suspicion of all things mobile',[8] a reaffirmation that there is a place for everything with everything in its place.

As noted above, the migratory movements that runners may experience range from local to global. Such a range of geographical scales is central to the hierarchical nature of sports organization. A runner starts a career by representing a school or club against other schools or clubs. This usually involves relatively local movement. As a runner's career progresses, he or she may become good enough to represent the county, state or nation. Such representation was traditionally regarded as the highpoint of a runner's career. The runner grows into a larger world, moving from what Tuan terms 'hearth' to 'cosmos'.[9] For the serious runner, as for people generally, the nurturing hearth can be too confining; but the 'cosmos, though liberating, can be bewildering and threatening'.[10] Serious runners leave the hearth of necessity. The cosmos liberates them but some runners could also see the promise of global competition as a threat. Yet the world of running is made less threatening by its standardized rules, its sameness, its placelessness.

Sports migrations also range in time from short-term moves to compete, through medium-term stays overseas for varying times in a career, to permanent settlement and even naturalization in another nation state. While short distance migrations may be periodic, in the modern age of time-space compression, long-distance migrations may not necessarily be anything near permanent. For many athletes, a long-distance, short-term, inter-continental visit to the Olympics (an emotionally distant event even if in his own country) may be a once in a lifetime experience. In this chapter I concentrate on the human experiences of migration and how such movement may impinge on a person's identity.

Migrating to Compete

I now want to consider those migratory runners for whom running is relevant or central to their migration. First, however, note that migration and movement are not the same thing. Nor is mobility the same as migration. During the course of a 100 metres sprint, or of a marathon, the runner cannot be said to migrate. Like other workers, athletes experience (often short-distance and short-term) periodic mobilities. These have traditionally included the regular seasonal movements to compete in national and international meets. In the course of their running careers, athletes who desire to progress inevitably have to make migrations to places far from home.

It would be wrong to assume that long-distance movement to compete is a twentieth-century phenomenon. The American Lon Myers, the first man to improve on 50 seconds for the quarter-mile and US record holder at various times from 100 yards to a mile, competed in Britain during the mid 1880s. The Jamaican-Scottish sprinter Alf Downer competed in the United States in the 1890s. During the 1896 professional season he claims to have travelled 5,000 miles, covering over 2,500 miles in the months of May and June alone and competing at such varied venues as London and Lancaster, Glasgow and Crewe. Not surprisingly, he observed that 'changes in water, air, beds and food, are bound to affect any man, still more someone who is expected to be in the "pink of condition" at every meeting at which he runs'.[11]

If athletes accept the world of serious sport, such movements can hardly be called voluntary. They have to be undertaken if the athlete is to succeed. As a result, their eyes may be opened to new situations, and new experiences may stimulate the senses. Through international contact, pre-existing images of place may be changed (into other images); national stereotypes may be formed or countered; lasting friendships may be made. However, during very brief overseas visits, made solely to compete, athletes may see virtually nothing of a foreign place, beyond an airport, hotel and running track. American Marty Liquori's experiences of such travel were described as follows:

> I'll usually get into a city and either work out immediately or eat immediately, so the food will digest in time for me to work out. The night and all the next day I rest, then I race, and afterward I invariably party in some local bar. This is a tradition when you're making the circuit. The following morning I collect myself

and my luggage, check out and head for the train depot or the
airport; there will be another country and another race in just a
couple of days.[12]

Liquori's experience presents the mobile athlete as a nomad. In Bauman's
terms nomads, unlike settlers, 'are on the move. But they circle around
a well-structured territory with long invested and stable meaning assigned
to each fragment.'[13] The nomadic athlete's territory is well known – a pre-
arranged list of cities on a global circuit. Such movements to compete in
foreign places, as part of a Grand Prix circuit, for example, is almost a habit,
with the circuits being their habitat.[14] Roger Bannister felt that his visits
to compete overseas filled in the gaps in his 'rudimentary knowledge of
geography' with 'images and pictures from [his] own experiences'.[15] However,
his images were, nevertheless, images and Liquori describes graphically his
images of the placelessness of the runner's world:

> It is an eternal series of airports, bad weather, delayed flights,
> plane rides, plastic trays, reheated foods, lost luggage, surly cab-
> drivers, expensive cab rides, unknown cities, surly hotel clerks,
> small hotel rooms, bustling hotel lobbies, crowded coffee shops,
> overpriced coffee-shop food, surly coffee-shop waitresses, and
> cold coffee-shop food. Cities look alike, each is a lump of concrete
> buildings, and the rooms all smell alike, each is musty, and the
> days of races follow a simple pattern.[16]

Central to each visit is the 400-metre track, standardized because of the
centrality of the record and of the comparable global currency of the result.
It is a world of well-known sights/sites even if they have never been visited
before. On the running track and in the hotel one could almost believe oneself to be at home. As in many things, 'the arrow of change – modernization
in its many guises – points the way, the way led by the west'.[17] The star athlete
appears at ease in such situations. Like the peddler he is a cosmopolite 'not
only because he is at ease in the midst of strangers', but also because he or
she 'operate[s] on an extraregional and even global scale'.[18]

Impressions of cities, within which races take place, may be bland and
superficial. Gordon Pirie's travels to international track meets in the 1950s
included a visit to Moscow to compete against athletes from the former
Soviet Union. He generalized his visit by observing that 'Russians are simply
luckless people who are unaware of the wonderful world outside their dismal
homeland'.[19] On the other hand, the Czech Emil Zátopek (or his biographer)
felt that visiting Moscow in the 1950s to compete against the Soviet Union at

the Dynamo Stadium, was a world where the 'shop-windows and department stores, which are open late into the night, were full of goods. The runners were accommodated in 'spacious, comfortable rooms in the "National" hotel'.[20] A summary of Pirie's running visit to South Africa, also in the 1950s, included the observation that 'on the whole we found white people were kind to the natives'.[21]

Liquori produced instant stereotypes of runners from the countries that he had encountered. Scandinavians 'appear the most relaxed, and they are light on their feet ... They appear almost effeminate [or] homosexual'; Japanese 'get along any way they can ... flapping furiously'; English and Irish 'tend to wear black or red socks'; Kenyans 'pay little attention to form'.[22] Such ludicrous, if not essentialized or racist, comments such as these are in large part the result of the fleeting impressions such world-class runners may have of the untypical representatives of the nations they encounter on their brief international visits. When visits abroad to take part in sports are combined with a modest view of the broader picture than that obtained by Liquori, awareness may be enhanced, but the resulting image may still be simple in comparison with that of a native. And as Tuan puts it, the 'visitor's viewpoint, being simple, is easily stated';[23] visitors tend to have viewpoints rather than complex attitudes. Coubertin was aware of such fleeting sporting visits. In the late 1920s he observed that such travel ('the incessant travel associated with championships and sub-championships') must be stopped, adding that it was 'the worst way to see a country'.[24] This is not to ignore the likelihood that athletes making brief visits overseas will be able to sample the joys of running in unfamiliar environments, away from the city and the stadium. Many runners visiting Scandinavia, for example, have 'got drunk on the air and silence of the northern forests'.[25]

It is possible for athletes to be seduced into visiting places that may have been temporarily transformed in order for such visits to take place. Such was the case with the German capital, Berlin, at the time of the 1936 Olympics. Berlin was normalized by the Nazi regime in order to give the impression that the repression of Jews, blacks and homosexuals simply did not exist under National Socialism. Hitler was subsequently normalized by Leni Riefenstahl's filmmaking. James McNeish describes how Jack Lovelock, seduced by both the ideology of achievement sport and Nazi propaganda, rejected any suggestion that he should boycott an Olympics hosted by a nation from whose team Jews were excluded.[26] By resisting the political pressure to boycott the Games, Lovelock, and other runners who chose to compete, can be seen as resisting one ideology in order to collude in the practices of another. McNeish presents Lovelock as a naive colonial whose Oxford education and enthusiasm for running served to not only inculcate a scientific approach to sport and athletic achievement but also as a cloak that obscured the cancer of fascism in Germany from his gaze.

Migration as Escape: Runners as Cosmopolites

Yi-Fu Tuan observes that the relation between a sense of place and mobility is complicated. The star runner can be likened to Tuan's description of the high-salaried executive. As the comments of Liquori suggested, 'he moves abroad so much that places for him tend to lose their special character. What are his significant places? The home is in the suburb. He lives there, but home is not wholly divorced from work.'[27] For a professional runner, home is often a base from which he trains: it is where he can plan and record his mileage and methods. The runner takes her work home with her. She takes periodic trips abroad combining business (running) with pleasure (resting). 'The circuits of movement are complex; even then they may represent a stage' on the runner's upwardly mobile career: 'His goal still lies ahead. His pattern of movement may yet expand and his constellation of places increase before they shrink inevitably with retirement and the onset of age.'[28]

In *Cosmos and Hearth,* Tuan draws the distinction, and tension, between words that respectively mean 'world' and 'home'. When migrant runners become cosmopolitans, do they retain affection for, and identification with, their hearths and homes? In 2002 the Commonwealth Games were held in Manchester. The English sprinter Darren Campbell returned to his home-town to represent England in the 200 metres. He often alluded to the fact that by returning home to compete, the meaning of his athletic performances was enhanced. It would never happen again; he could never again participate in a top-level event in his own city. But, as noted above, it is almost impossible for the modern, world-class runner to be anything but a cosmopolitan. A world view (of sorts) is inevitable through the nature of their sport. But not to have obtained it, suggests Tuan, 'is to lead a stunted life'.[29] It is difficult to think of a modern runner as anything other than stunted if (s)he has not competed in another country, even if what they encounter is often limited and where they compete is necessarily familiar. Elite athletes can have both world and home; they can be cosmopolitan but return to their homes when they feel the need to do so. Runners of modest ability or lack of ambition or achievement are restricted to a life of sport mainly in their home locales. On balance, Tuan favours the life of the cosmopolitan because it is liberating while home is confining. But how does international sporting competition liberate the athlete? And from what is (s)he liberated?

Commonly, runners migrate for longer periods of time and reside in a foreign land, temporarily or permanently severing connections with their homes. Tuan writes that '[m]igration is clearly a type of escape'.[30] More than this, however, it could be read as being transgressive – the crossing of bound-aries, 'an antidote to the monumentally seriousness of fixity and stability'.[31] At the national and global levels, running can be a means of escape, made voluntarily, in search of better racing (earning) opportunities or for better training conditions. Young runners are restless and seek release through geographical mobility. Most track racing at the elite level takes place in cities and in Europe. Here we see 'cosmos' dominating 'hearth'. Elite athletes are compulsory cosmopolitans, facilitated at the global scale by time-space compression and the variety of human agents who are concerned with the production of an athlete from a runner. This involves a number of networks and many hands, devices and places before the runner becomes a performer. He or she has to be recruited (almost hunted down), transported to a new environment, accommodated in a runners' dorm or a cramped city house, trained by a possibly aggressive coach, and then made to perform in more meets than (s)he might freely choose. Looked at this way, the 'tracing of networks and bodies is implicitly concerned with the moral terrain of athletic recruiting'.[32] But what does the escape from the traditions of say, Kenya, to the milieu of northwest Europe or the United States mean for a Kenyan athlete? Is his or her identity changed? What does such escape say about sportized running itself?

In answering such questions it can be suggested that crucial moments in recruiting are not those where athletes act as agents but rather those where they 'are defined, measured, observed, listened to, or otherwise enacted'.[33] Consider the following account that poignantly reveals an early stage in the 'production' of a migrant athlete. Recorded by Jon Entine, without the slightest sense of irony, Fred Hardy, a veteran recruiter of athletes from Kenya to the University of North Carolina, arrives at the home of Josiah Kurgat, the runner he is bent on recruiting.[34] To impress the Kurgat family he brings with him Kipchoge Keino, a national hero and the first Kenyan runner to possess a global reputation. Hardy had already recruited Josiah's brother and says to his father, 'You've given me one son. I want to be sure that I have permission to *take* the second son.' The details of the scholarship deal are outlined and Hardy is elated at having obtained permission to take the young athlete to the USA. 'Thank you', he says to Josiah's father; 'Thank you for the *gift* of your son.'[35]

How many people have used achievement running as a means of escape from poverty and hardship? In doing so, do they become pets? A large number of African athletes have accepted track scholarships from the athletic departments of numerous American universities.[36] Escape from what is perceived as the limited sporting, economic and educational opportunities of Kenya, Ethiopia, Nigeria, Ghana and other African nations is welcome indeed when confronted with the lavish training facilities (sporting and educational) of the American college campus. The same has traditionally applied to the escape of Caribbean athletes to US colleges. Since the decline of the Soviet empire, several eastern European runners have likewise made the escape from their relatively impoverished facilities to take advantage of those in the United States. Evidence of such migration is readily quantified.

For example, in 2002 about 450 foreign recruits were on the rosters of US college cross-country rosters.[37]

Recipients of athletic scholarships see escape from their homelands as a welcome means of furthering their sporting and academic careers. Foreign track athletes have a long history of migration to the colleges and universities of the USA. There they have sought athletic training and in many cases an education and a university degree. They have been able to do this as a result of the long-standing American institution of the 'athletic scholarship'. Many Olympic gold medallists have had their running skills honed in the groves (or on the running tracks) of American academe. The 1956 Olympic 1,500 metres winner was Ron Delaney of the Republic of Ireland who had been trained by 'Jumbo' Elliott at Villanova University; in 1976 the 100 metres title was won by Hasley Crawford of Trinidad and North Carolina State University; in 1968 the 400 metres hurdles was won by David Hemery of Britain, who was educated at Boston University; the Moroccan Nawal El Moutawakel, a student of Iowa State University, won the 400 metres hurdles at Los Angeles in 1994; and Peter Rono, a Kenyan who was a student at Mount St Mary's College, won the Olympic 1,500 metres in 1988. Stories of such escapes are legion and raise certain questions about their period of sojourn, their identity and representation.

Running away from somewhere always means running somewhere else. The experience of being a foreign student-athlete at a US university (a form of co-option mentioned earlier) is ambivalent. The basic role of the recruit is to represent the university, to be co-opted by it as noted in the previous chapter. More accurately, student-athletes represent the athletic department, the quasi-autonomous organizations that run intercollegiate sports. The role of such bureaucracies, in treating runners as pets, has already been noted in Chapter 4, as has their associated exploitation. One migrant runner, recruited by the University of Texas at El Paso (UTEP), said that many foreign recruits at UTEP were admitted 'on the basis of a full scholarship that for no reason was cut immediately after their arrival'. A South African runner arrived at the same institution expecting a full scholarship. When the track coach offered him a partial scholarship the runner confronted him but received the answer: 'Do you want to go home or what?'[38]

A romantic view of the foreign student-athlete in small town America is one of the global in the local – a mixing of peoples and the establishment of lasting friendships through the common language of sport. However, foreign athletes tend to mix mainly with other student-athletes.[39] Kenyan runners in Britain mainly mix with other Kenyan runners, often living five or six to a house, running, sleeping and watching TV. They rarely experience people who have significant interests outside of sports. Very few Kenyan runners – even world-record holders – are known to the general public and rarely appear as interviewees on telecasts. On occasion, foreign sports-workers have regrets about domicile abroad but the achievement sport ideology and the present or future financial benefits usually hide any sense of regret that they might have had about accepting a scholarship or spending some time overseas. Bad experiences tend to be outweighed by good – or, at least, this is what attitude surveys reveal.[40]

Foreign athletes are read by members of host nations in different ways. Migrants may provide role models for local runners to follow. On the other hand, especially when they are receiving scarce college scholarships, they are accused of taking the places of homegrown Americans. To what extent does this latter attitude boil down to racism, or at least, jealousy of the 'other'? It certainly reveals a suspicion of the migrant, reading the migrant runner as exploiting his nation of sojourn.

Tuan notes that

> before people make a risky move, they must have information about their destination point. What kinds of information is available? To what extent does the need to believe in a better world at the horizon overrule or destroy the 'hard facts' that people know? Is reality so constraining and unbearable at home that it becomes the seedbed for wild longings and images?[41]

Each of these questions is important for the migrant runner. It seems that information about the place of residence is partial, the 'need' to live abroad is more important for some than for others. After all, European runners can treat the running experience of a US college as a 'year out', a treat, a once-in-lifetime experience. For a runner from the Sudan or Kenya it can be a route to a better, richer world. For runners with high ambition, home really is constraining.

Escapist Runners and Identity

Traditionally, the international runner's allegiance was to the nation state that he or she represented in international competition. If he or she lived in a country there was little doubt which country they would represent in international competition. On hearing that he had been selected for the British team in the 1948 Olympics, Jim Peters, former holder of the world's fastest time for the marathon, exclaimed: 'The Union Jack had materialized at long last – and so had my first track suit. I was an international, my ambition had been realized.'[42] Wearing one's national uniform, representing the nation (especially in the Olympics), was the pinnacle.

Once the individual runner, more or less, took responsibility for him- or herself with regard to training. By mid-century, however, it was the 'national system' that had 'produced' the athlete – the 'totalisation process' that Heinilä applied to the world of modern sport.[43] At the same time, national victory was, to a large extent, seen as the ultimate incentive and reward in the system that conferred prestige on the winners. In the late-modern (some would say postmodern) world, however, things have moved on from the nation towards the scale of the globe. Globalisation has resulted in a 'reshaping of the minds and imagination of individuals and of community in general'.[44] Western countries have witnessed an influx of unfamiliar groups of peoples, included among them runners of a high standard; there has emerged the presence of 'a nontrivial number of those footloose persons called transmi-grants'.[45] As a result of these changes there seems to have been a growing interest, and concern, about what is called 'identity' – a word to be reified (or 'thingified'). Who do we belong to? (Who owns us?). Who should we exclude? Have national territories become increasingly permeable? Whereas once the boundaries of nation states seemed secure, are nation states today better seen as 'leaking containers'?[46] Or does globalisation also mean 'deter-ritorialisation'?[47] The relevance of these themes to the migratory athlete should be obvious. There seems to be a global crisis of identity as we seek out ways of constructing our identity. Or has place attachment and identity in sport disappeared?

Today the nation state no longer attracts the allegiance of all its members. However, it still serves as the *nominal* label for the majority of the global population, 'but with ever diminishing emotional salience'.[48] Sources of identity have increasingly included the region, the local, multiculuralism and fundamentalism. Sport is another cultural form that has been claimed to build group identity, as discussed in connection with patriotism and topophilia. However, geographer Wilbur Zelinsky, for one, is disturbed by this 'ersatz type of belongingness', one that excludes those thousands of bystanders lacking interest in sports.[49] For many, watching track races on television is simply boring, especially if it goes on lap after lap. But 'belonging' is not an emotion reserved for fans or bystanders. It has traditionally also been applied to athletes – runners who re-present their countries in international sports competitions, be they dual-meets or Olympic Games. Although the vast majority of those who represent their countries in such events continue to be citizens of that state from birth, there is today an increasing and not insignificant minority who seem to have little, if any, commitment or relation to the nation they superficially *appear* to represent. Running is now a globally integrated sport. Trans-national athletes reveal the state as a 'leaking container' and a challenge to conventional notions of national identity. Hence, athletic migration may be upsetting to norms of stability and the status quo. Modern elite athletes seem to have a sort of 'dual citizenship' that devalues service to the nation in favour of service to sponsors or themselves.

The migration of elite runners may also reflect what Cresswell terms 'cunning and sabotage', and these terms may not connote solely 'weapons of the weak'.[50] It seems that it is those with power at their disposal for whom cunning is common. Consider, for example, the case of Zola Budd. She is recalled, by many track fans, as the British runner who effectively dashed the gold medal chances of US heroine Mary Slaney in the 1984 Olympics in Los Angeles. The demolition of Slaney's chances of victory resulted from Budd seemingly (accidentally) tripping her up during the later stages of the race. Unlike Lasse Virén, Slaney was unable to pick herself up in time to claim victory. The other side of Budd's career is the story of her obtaining British citizenship in order to take part in that race.

In the mid 1980s Budd was a child athletic prodigy, resident and competing in South Africa. In 1984 she had run a remarkable 5,000 metres time of 15 minutes 1.83 seconds in South Africa at the age of 17. Had South Africa been accepted as a member of the International Association of Athletics Federations (IAAF) it would have been an official world record. She was clearly a potential medallist at the Los Angeles Olympics but at the time, however, South Africa's apartheid policies had resulted in the country being banned from the 1984 Olympics. Budd's grandfather was British. By becoming British herself she could take part in the Games. Her British citizenship was awarded in record time (13 days), the cunning ruse having been orchestrated and funded by the English right-wing newspaper the *Daily Mail*. Budd's willingness to represent Britain was no gesture of resistance against the apartheid regime. Indeed, Budd was repeatedly questioned by the British media about her attitude to apartheid, about which she failed to indicate any disapproval. She pleaded, paradoxically, that politics should not enter into sport.

It seems unlikely that Budd ever 'felt English', despite the comments about going back to her roots in a hastily produced 'official biography' composed by the *Daily Mail*.[51] The flag of convenience under which she now ran had provided the vehicle for her to put her sporting ideology into practice. She was not entirely popular with fans or runners in her adopted home and even attracted the attentions of the rock group Chumbawumba (see Figure 6.1). Following the disaster (for her) at the Olympics, Budd broke the world 5,000 metres record with a time of 14 minutes 48.07 seconds and also won the World Cross-country championship. By 1986 her running was declining in quality and her popularity in Britain waned, partly because of her unwillingness to live in Britain as a permanent resident. She could never shake off the Slaney controversy and faced protests that her change of nationality had more to do with sporting ambitions than with a condemnation of apartheid. She was banned from taking part in the Commonwealth Games and returned to South

She's a slip of a girl to be out of school

She's a product of apartheid

She won her spurs under minority rule

She's a product of apartheid

Afrikaners run the best

In bare feet and British vest

"She's a slip of a girl but at least she's white"

"She's a slip of a girl but at least she's white"

Figure 6.1 Zola Budd by Chumbawumba.

Africa in 1988 to disappear from the serious running scene for many years. Later, in 1992, she re-emerged as a South African but never regained the success of her teenage years.

Budd's compatriot Sidney Maree is today a South African. Previously he was an African American. Before that he was a South African. Born in South Africa, Maree became a good runner in his teens. However, like Budd he was frustrated by the apartheid system and his country's resultant isolation from international sport. Like Budd he sought international competition by migration, in his case to the United States. The US, after all, had a collegiate system that provided proven sports, as well as educational, facilities. He was recruited by Villanova University. He waited the required time to assume American citizenship and became American record holder for the 5,000 metres and world record holder for the 1,500 metres. He represented his adopted country at the 1984 Los Angeles Olympics and the 1988 Games in Seoul, where he finished fifth in the 5,000 metres. He spent 18 years in the United States where, compared to residence in South Africa, most people would say he had a good life. When the apartheid system was dismantled, Maree returned to South Africa, where today he lives as a successful businessman. Was his return an admirable response to the promise of the new South Africa or a deep yearning for his 'hearth'?

Like Budd, the flexibility of his *nominal* nationhood reflects a kind of identity that seems to last 'no longer than the satisfaction of one of the partners: commitment is from the start until "further notice"'.[52] National affiliation is dependent on contingency. The cases of Budd and Maree[53] cannot be fully understood by looking at their actions alone. In the former case there were the intermediaries – the *Daily Mail* and its various representatives. In the

Maree case, Villanova University and its recruiters were agents involved in the fluidity of citizenship, if not identity.

As noted in the previous chapter, Nyandika Maiyoro was among the first Kenyan runners to compete in Europe as a visiting member of the Kenyan athletics team in 1954, aged 24. Thirty years later, his young compatriot Wilson Kipketer was brought to Europe at the age of about 17 in order to live and train in Denmark. Whereas Maiyoro typified the emerging modernism of African running, Kipketer is arguably an example of the 'postmodern athlete'. He was born in Kenya and attended St Patrick's High School, the Alma Mater of a large number of world-class Kenyan athletes, where he was nurtured by Father Colm O'Connell. He showed great promise as a runner and in 1988, despite a lack of clarity about how old he was, competed for Kenya in the world junior track and field championships in Canada. He was disqualified in his 800 metres heat. He arrived in Copenhagen on a cold December day in 1990. With him was another Kenyan, 18-year-old Robert Kiplagat Kiptanui. To arrange to have two Kenyan boys together made sense in an alien milieu. But Kipketer did not become an instant Dane and had to follow the correct protocol before he could become a Danish citizen.

What is transgressive about Kipketer is not simply that he is out of place literally – a black Dane in Scandinavia – but also in his attitude towards representation. It appears that he is a model of the cosmopolitan or, perhaps, the cultural hybrid. He appears to represent different agencies as it suits him – a sort of chameleon man. Who does he represent in his racing? He initially represented his school in district championships in Kenya. He progressed to representing Kenya in the world junior championships. Then he moved to Denmark. For a short time his status was ambivalent: he could represent Kenya in the world championships, where he won the 800 metres in 1995, but not in the Olympics a year later. He eventually received Danish citizenship via the official route, married a Dane, and competed in the Olympics and World Championships.

The Danish people don't quite know what to make of him. He is not seen as a 'real Dane', mainly because of his skin colour and his inability to speak adequate Danish. Yet they accept him somewhat more, but not totally, when he carries the Danish flag on a lap of honour. In 1997 he broke the 800 metres world record with a time of 1 minute 41.11 seconds – the first world class Danish 800 metres runner since the days of Gunnar Nielsen in the 1950s. To be sure, in the Olympics he wears the Danish uniform and following a track victory he stands beneath the Danish flag and its national anthem. On this occasion he represents Denmark, his adopted nation. In a Grand Prix track race he is seen wearing a uniform with the word 'Puma' written on it. This is the name of his sponsor, the German sportswear company. (Previously, he had been sponsored by the US company Nike.) Now he is representing his employer. Or is he? For after all, he lives much of his life in Italy where a

Polish expert coaches him. He seems to be a postmodern athlete – and a post-colonial one too. So whom does he really represent? Perhaps he is reclaiming a sort of individualism. An interview with Kipketer in 1995, published in the Danish sports magazine *Sport på Stregen*, contained the sub-heading: 'Kenyan or Danish? The king of runners is quite certain: "I am Wilson Kipketer".'[54]

Ambivalent Representations

For most of the migrations undertaken by serious runners, running is either relevant or central to the migration decision. For some runners, however, the decision to move to another place was taken for them; running was of no significance. These are the athletes who were born in a nation other than the one in which they lived most of their lives and, through their running, may represent. They are the children of immigrants who may have arrived on foreign shores as infants or young children. Consider the case of Linford Christie, born in Jamaica but a long-term British international sprinter and European record holder. After several years as a good sprinter, Christie emerged in the 1980s as a world-class athlete, climaxing his career with a gold medal at the Barcelona Olympics of 1992. Although a household name in the UK, Christie was often the butt of racist jokes (see Chapter 4) and was constructed by the press as 'ungrateful, rebellious and paranoid about his persecution'. He has been quoted as saying that he wanted to be treated as a man, not as a black man.[55] He was said by another black British sprinter, Derek Redmond, to be a perfectly balanced runner – he had a chip on both shoulders.[56] He was critical of British and international athletic organizations, displaying frequent 'fits of pique'.[57] However, following his Olympic win he paraded the Union Jack flag around the arena, seemingly displaying patriotic fervour and show-ing pride in his adopted nation. Indeed, he was captain of the British team and as such was expected to show a patriotic example to his team colleagues.

But as a black Briton, Christie's identity can be read as being fluid – moving between his Britishness, Jamaicaness and blackness. Sociologist Stuart Hall has brilliantly deconstructed Christie's reaction to victory in Barcelona. He suggests that Christie, draped in a Union Jack, may be read in four possible ways. First, it can be seen as a triumph for Linford Christie; secondly as a triumph for Christie and a celebration for all black people; thirdly, a triumph for the British Olympic team and for black people; and fourthly, a triumph for black people and the British team – you can be black and British.[58] There is no 'right' reading of Christie's behaviour; each of the above meanings is plausible. Ben Carrington suggests that Christie with his apparent acceptance but at the same time criticism of Britishness, displays the fact that there is at least some black in the Union Jack.[59]

Runners from aboriginal nations can illustrate having allegiance to a nation in a different way from that of runners such as Christie. Kathy Freeman is an Australian citizen; she is also an aboriginal Australian. Just as Christie has part of his self-identity still in Jamaica, Freeman still takes pride in her aboriginality. She can be said to have migrated – escaped, perhaps – from her aboriginal nation to that of modern Australia. Following her victory in the 400 metres at the Sydney Olympic of 2000, Freeman, like Christie, was bedecked with the Australian flag – again a statement of Australian-ness. As Billy Ehn has pointed out, such icons are 'over-specific' forms of national identity.[60] However, unlike Christie, Freeman also carried an unmistakable yellow, red and black flag denoting the aboriginal nations of Australia, a statement of her aboriginal as well as her Australian identity. This represented a degree of transgression – going against the grain, questioning the hegemony of the 'Australian flag'. The aboriginal flag had not been traditionally seen as a sign of victory but one of resistance – or worse, squalor and degradation.[61] Freeman's conjoining of the two flags at least set the tone (an appropriate term) for a hybrid Australian identity – one where two forms of identity kept their distinctiveness but together produce something new.[62]

A third runner who migrated before he became a runner is Ben Johnson, who moved from Jamaica to Toronto, Canada, as a boy. He became an excellent sprinter, attained international class and, by the 1990s, was a world star. He also became a Canadian sports hero, to a degree replacing the formerly iconic figure of ice-hockey star Wayne Gretzky who had left Canada, having been 'appropriated' to play in the USA.[63] Johnson's career climaxed in 1992 at the Olympic 100 metres final in Seoul, Korea. This race was a head-to-head confrontation between Johnson and Carl Lewis. It was a race that Johnson won easily, well ahead of Lewis (and Christie), breaking the world record. This, and the immediate aftermath, will be a well-known story for sports fans. Johnson was discovered to have taken anabolic steroids, a substance banned by the IAAF. As a result, he was stripped of his gold medal and was publicly paraded as a disgrace.

In a media analysis of the post-Olympic reaction to Johnson in the Canadian press, Steven Jackson reveals how it is not simply personal identity that is revealed through representational running but also the ways in which the runner is *identified* by the broader constituency of the nation that he represents. Identification as well as identity is constructed through running and its representation. Jackson explored the Canadian media's representation of Johnson, before and after the stunning exposure of his doping abuse. His analysis reveals what he terms a 'twist of race' – 'shifting, mediated representations of Johnson's identities within specific contexts'.[64] Before Johnson's rise to fame, it seems that he was represented as a 'Jamaican' or a 'Jamaican immigrant', even though he had been officially granted Canadian citizenship as early as 1980. As his athletic achievements grew, he was re-labelled as a

'Jamaican-Canadian'. Following his 1987 World Championship victory over Carl Lewis he was more regularly termed a 'Canadian'. Finally, following the disqualification in Seoul, he was being represented again in terms of his 'Jamaican' identity. Throughout this period, Ben Johnson was the same person but his 'national' and 'racial' identities 'were socially constructed, deconstructed, reconstructed and reproduced through the media'. In other words, his 'Canadian' identity was contingent upon the mass media translating his personal achievements into a symbol of national pride.[65] Identification (though not necessarily personal identity) can therefore be twisted according to context.

Christie, Freeman and Johnson are athletes for whom 'escape' from Jamaica and the aboriginal world of Australia were not primarily induced by running. Nor was one of the two migrations undertaken by the Jewish-Finnish runner Elias Katz, who had won a gold medal in the 3,000 metres team race and a silver in the steeplechase in the 1928 Olympics. Following his Olympic success, he was invited, in the late 1920s, to join the Bar Kochba track club in Berlin, one of the oldest Jewish sports clubs in Europe. In Germany, he would be an encouragement to other Jewish athletes and could live as part of a much larger Jewish population than existed in Finland. He accepted the invitation and for a few years the migrant Finn competed for the Berlin club in competitions in Germany. Such inter-national movement was not an escape, a term that implies the presence of some form of 'push' from his point of origin. However, a few years after his arrival the virulent anti-Semitism of the Nazi regime forced Katz to really escape from Germany, making a second migration and settling in Palestine.[66] Likewise, the great German 800-metre world-record breaker in 1926, Otto Peltzer, fled Germany for England because of Nazi dogma and homophobia. More recently, Ethiopian runners have settled in Europe, USA, Australia and Israel as political or religious refugees. For many others, escape was never a possibility, or it was thwarted.

While 'some mobilities are acts of freedom, transgression and resistance in the face of state power which seeks to limit movement, … it would be a mistake to think of mobilities as in any way essentially transgressive'.[67] Mobility is required to keep the global sport system running smoothly. In serious sports migration has become a necessary convention. Transgression would be reflected in the decision not to join in the global circuit of modern running and to take a step beyond its boundary. Here exists a paradox – the runner is imprisoned by mobility.

Running and Racing: Moral Dilemmas and a Good Life?

Surely all runners, like all humans, aspire to a good life. But how is it conceived? In his books, *The Good Life* and *Morality and Imagination*, Tuan grapples with this question. In this chapter I want to consider whether the running track or the marathon route are sites through which a good life may be bred? Is running a bodily activity that contributes to goodness? Are athletes good people? Certainly Tuan accepts that body cultural practices and experiences can be contributions to a good life, including among them 'peak experiences'. These fall into the three broad categories of the world, the body and personal relations. These correspond, roughly, to the aesthetic, the sensual and the moral.[1] The first two have been alluded to earlier. I will refer to them again briefly below, but in this chapter more emphasis is placed on the moral.

Aesthetic and sensual pleasures undoubtedly contribute to a good life. However, as Tuan points out, 'the moral reading overshadows the aesthetic'[2] – and, one might add, the athletic/sensual. Robert Sack adds that while the moral and the aesthetic are closely linked, a difference arises when the two are compared in terms of effort.[3] Sack states that 'seeing someone undergo moral effort – even a gargantuan moral struggle by an individual to do the right thing – does not detract from that moral act'. Indeed, it may enhance it.[4] But a runner, sweating, straining and agonizing in the later stages of a 10,000 metres or marathon race, detracts from any possible aesthetic performance. Eric Liddell was said to be a runner 'almost entirely without style'.[5] Zátopek's grimacing would win no style prizes (see Figure 7.1). If 'style' or artistry prizes were awarded to runners, the performance should appear effortless.[6] From the perspective of Asian aesthetics, 'the image of a tortured runner in the west, with face distorted in agony, is grotesque ... More important is the Chinese belief that strain in itself is a sign of inefficiency.'[7] However, even aesthetic acts 'may not stand up to moral principals'.[8] Witness the ideals that led to the construction and decoration of the 1936 Berlin Olympic stadium; witness the grace of some of the Nazis who participated there.

Figure 7.1 Emil Zàtopek (author's collection).

A lack of 'style' is not always denigrated. Indeed, on occasions it has been praised. The French writer, Pierre Magnan, said of Emil Zátopek that, above all, he should be respected because he ran like a man – a human being – and 'not like a formless product of modern technique'. He was a runner who 'paid dearly for his victory ... a man whose face is in anguish while running and who struggles for breath'.[9] Half a century later similar comments were made about the British long-distance runner Paula Radcliffe, whose inelegant style, far from detracting from her popularity, made fans love her more because of the visibility of her efforts. Today, notes Gunter Gebauer, 'the audiences want to see passion in all shapes and forms'.[10]

Few deny that running (in the welfare mould) enhances physical values such as health and fitness. Similarly, running, even in its most achievement-oriented forms, encourages some values of the spirit – those of self-confidence, self-discipline, teamwork, competitive spirit, and fair play.[11] Success in running, it has been argued, 'is very much like attaining success in the great Game of Life', implying that the values of sport are related to, or contribute to, a good life.[12] The runner Herb Elliott asked his mentor Cerutty how running round in circles could make him a better person. Cerutty retorted: 'you only ever grow as a human being if you're outside the comfort zone'.[13] Elliott was taught to believe that 'pushing yourself ... beyond what you thought were the borders of endurance is of great moral benefit' and admired his mentor for so encouraging him. He would walk away from such training sessions 'with a clear conscience'.[14]

But not all spiritual values would necessarily be qualities of the good life. The competitive spirit and that of teamwork are arguably incompatible and team races (apart from relays) in the Olympics were discontinued after the 1924 Games, giving individual competition a free rein. The competitive spirit, engendered by hard training, and the encouraging of runners to push themselves to the limit – and beyond – might be seen as an act of overbearing dominance, even irresponsible or immoral. Gebauer suggests that all athletes seek to use their wits to influence a race in their favour. The rules of a track race do not define the spirit in which it is run and this means that there is great scope for the imagination to range widely over the many ways of gaining an advantage.[15] There is latitude within the rules for the intelligent athlete to gain tactical advantages, a quality that many coaches feel defines the great athlete.[16] Others might feel such stratagems are dubious and even unfair, leading to the popular comment that 'nice guys finish last'.

Running and Spirituality

A 'spiritual experience' is often likened to a 'religious experience' and it is that interpretation – one that more or less identifies spirituality with morality or the good life – which I will concentrate on first. To identify running with spirituality is to invoke the notions of 'muscular Christianity' or 'muscular Judaism'. The former, mimicked by the latter, was (and, maybe, still is) 'an association between physical strength, religious certainty, and the ability to shape and control the world around us'.[17] The ideology of muscular Christianity was arguably most manifested in Thomas Hughes's *Tom Brown's Schooldays* though the term itself may have originated in the United States and initially was applied to writers such as Hughes and Charles Kingsley rather than to athletes.[18] Harold Abrahams, the winner of the 1924 Olympic 100 metres, echoed these views in connection with the Christianity of his adversary, Eric

Liddell (see below). He said that Liddell's 'intense spiritual convictions contributed largely to his athletic triumphs ... but for his profound intensity of spirit, he surely could not have achieved so much'.[19] The rhetoric that sport induced morality was taken up by proponents of competitive sport, for example, the English coach and runner Guy Butler, a competitor in the 1924 Paris Olympics where he was an opponent of Liddell in the 400 metres final. Addressing the moral effect of athletics in 1929, Butler admitted the danger of a successful runner being conceited, but felt that two things militated against such immodesty. The first was an enthusiasm to do well for a team – that is, a school 'house', a club, county or nation. The second was a real interest in running (as an art and a science) for its own sake. Training would 'test and strengthen the moral fibre'.[20] But this 'fibre' appears to have little to do with morality. Instead it seems to be the string that attaches and co-opts the runner to a group, something that made running similar in function to other 'team games'. 'Moral fibre' for Butler, turns out to be the qualities of 'keenness and persistence in the face of disappointment' and doing one's bit, 'great or small, for house and school'.[21] This almost amounts to morals as mores,[22] something that Tuan is anxious to deny and a theme I will take up later. Here, I will concentrate rather more on runners for whom the practice of their religion was fully consistent with their athleticism.

It is widely felt that a good life is a spiritual life and several writers on running have implied a causal link between participation in athletics and spirituality. The pinnacle of 'muscular Christianity' or 'Christian manliness' was reached in the mid nineteenth century. Its essential message was that of manly ideology – 'that the healthy body will foster a healthy mind and a healthy morality'.[23] Norman Vance has suggested that the inaugurator of moral manliness was St Paul: 'Athletic and military imagery enliven his account of Christian life, the word *agon*, "race" or "contest" being used as is a description of running the race for the prize of the high calling of God.'[24] The so-called muscular Christian hero should discipline his body in the service of Christ and mankind.[25] However, this mentality could lead to the scholarly philistinism of Old Brooke in *Tom Brown's Schooldays*, whose view was: 'I'd rather win the School-house matches running than get the Balliol scholarship any day.'[26] Legacies of Christian manliness linger on. The 1968 Olympic 400 metres hurdles champion, David Hemery, has suggested that 'to do one's best, to get the most out of oneself athletically – that can be a spiritual experience'.[27] Running guru Mike Spino observes that running becomes boring when access to its spiritual aspects is denied.[28] Nor is muscular Christianity a male preserve. Kathy Ormsby is read as a 'muscular Christian': 'She would permit God to use her through her running ... to serve God by doing her best.'[29]

According to some observers, running has become a religion. Indeed, Coubertin said that the 'first essential characteristic of ancient and modern Olympism alike is that of being a religion'.[30] It follows, therefore, that running (in the Olympian mould) is also (at least like) a religion. But what does this mean? Ove Korsgaard suggests that the stadium is 'an important holy area'. In it 'you do not run to catch the bus but rather to represent the ideals of your culture and in this way, to create a reality for the world outside the holy district of the stadium'.[31] So it is not so much a shift from ritual to record (as Guttmann would have us believe) as one of the record as ritual (according to Korsgaard), the latter pointing out that the physical activity in serious running (for example) is itself a ritual.[32] This is a philosophical debate that has attracted considerable attention and, rather than discuss this subject in greater depth here, I would prefer to move on to the questions of running and spirituality, or the relationship between running and the good life.[33] After all, it would surely be an illusion to assume that a good life and the practice of religion per se are in any way synonymous.

An area where spirituality and running have met is in the work of missionaries, seeking to convert peoples from Africa, Asia and the Americas to Christianity. Sport was central to the work of missionaries. Football fields and running tracks were inscribed on the landscape of colonial territories, their straight lines and geometric dimensions contrasting with the winding ways of the African landscape. They were as symbolic of western power as the railway line from Mombassa to Nairobi.[34] Christianity and running continue to coexist, both in Africa and in the USA. In Kenya, for example, members of the Chepkero Athletics Club, which has supplied runners to the Kenyan national team, seek to improve themselves in spirit, mind and body. For a time, members of the club '*insisted* that daily Bible study and worship be as integral a part of the training program as the running'.[35] In the United States, Jim Ryun, the former high school running prodigy, world mile record holder, Olympic silver medallist in Mexico City, and now US congressman, runs a Christian summer camp as part of his evangelical organization. In a letter to prospective campers he writes:

> My camp is unique in that the instruction is geared toward developing the total runner – physically, mentally and spiritually. Campers will learn how to apply racing, training strategies, and diet as well as hear from top Christian athletes who will share how their faith has helped them reach their fullest potential.[36]

Muscular Christianity is also to be found in a mid 1990s British government publication, inspired by the former sport-loving prime minister John Major. In *Sport: Raising the Game* – a plea for future Olympians to be initiated into sport and its ethos in the primary school – it was noted that in achieving a healthy society, the nation must ensure that 'young people must be introduced to it [that is, sport] early in life'.[37] But it was not simply health that was targeted: 'Competitive sport teaches valuable lessons which last for life', wrote Major.[38] So the Victorian tradition of muscular Christianity continues to flourish. The 'total runner' and the 'Christian athlete', however, seem to lie uneasily together and Norman Vance feels that by as early as the 1910s the idea that a healthy body fostered healthy morals was well wide of the mark.[39] And as noted earlier, the sportized body has little to do with health. Sports may, or may not, inculcate desirable values. However, we 'should not be naïve about how much of their value is transferable to the rest of life'.[40] Additionally, much of the running practiced in missionary sports can be likened to that of the private schools of nineteenth-century England, which were, writes J.A. Mangan, 'essentially an instrument of social control, rather than moral improvement'.[41]

Yet the presence of religion – or, at least, religious postures – continues to feature in sports events. Watching track and field meets on television, I am often struck by the number of runners who make the sign of the cross, or kiss a crucifix before a race or at the end of it. They are respectively asking God to help them win or thanking Him for so doing. On bended knee, some runners thank God for their success. It appears that religion – or a religious faith – forms part of the ritual of many runners' races. Jim Ryun, went further than this. Following a period of inconsistent performances, he claimed that his 'new found peace in being a Christian did indeed carry over on to the track'. His dream was to win an Olympic gold medal and be able to say, 'God helped me get here'.[42]

Tuan would recognize a contradiction here – 'the contradiction of seeking spiritual values selfishly'.[43] The runner is asking God for victory for him or herself; it is inconceivable that s/he could pray for an opponent's victory for such an entreaty would contravene the norms of sport. Even so, it is possible to observe occasional selfless acts during a track race. As a young runner, the Australian Ron Clarke was competing in a mile race that included John Landy, the miler who took the world record away from Roger Bannister. During the race Clarke had his heel clipped by another runner and, losing his balance, fell sprawling on to the track. Aware that Clarke had fallen, Landy turned back to see if the younger runner was fit to continue. Having seen that he was, he set off again to catch the leaders and win the race. Many runners would regard staying on one's feet as part of the race; there is nothing in the rules that says that a runner should help a fellow competitor who falls over. Landy was unable to explain his action. Journalist Harry Gordon described it as a 'senseless piece of chivalry'.[44] Landy wilfully refrained from exploiting the very latitude allowed by the rules, an attitude approximating to Coubertin's meaning of *chevalerie* but quite at odds to our present day convictions of how races should take place.[45]

Tuan regards a moral person as someone who is 'irresistibly drawn by the good'.[46] The term 'good' is left undefined so that it may 'continue to serve as a luminous horizon for aspiring society and individuals'.[47] It is not necessarily good to go along with the status quo – which most runners do. A moral person, Tuan suggests, is a 'thinking and reflective individual, alive to the paradoxes and dilemmas of life, critical of the crude generality of behavioral codes'.[48] However, he avers that a good person is in possession of both morality and imagination. One is not enough and one should not outweigh the other. For Tuan, morality has connotations of set rules of behaviour and a certain rigidity of outlook. Imagination, on the other hand, is appealing because it challenges such rules. As a result, however, imagination can lead to fantasy and irresponsibility.[49] It is where a person lies, on the spectrum between morality and imagination, which determines the 'good person'. Where do serious runners lie in this spectrum? Some runners seem to display extreme forms of morality while others reveal what amounts to criminal irresponsibility. In fiction, the bias seems to be towards athletes, including runners, being morally flawed characters; it is rare in sports fiction, suggests Guttmann, that 'sports are a vehicle for the protagonist's moral triumph'.[50] A consideration of a small sample may serve to reveal that runners, famous and not so well known, can be located at various points on the morality and imagination spectrum.

Pride and Participation – Dilemmas and Time

Tuan notes that 'culture makes it possible for people to be pleased with them-selves'.[51] But where does self-pleasure give way to overbearing pride and arrogance? A moral question facing athletes, their performances and their success, is that of pride. Most of us would find it understandable for athletes to be proud of their achievements, as would their coaches, parents and relations. And observe the pleasure of the proud parent, often basking in the reflected glory of their offspring's result. However, pride is one of the seven deadly sins. Indeed, Tuan regards it as the deadliest – 'the distinctive sin of Satan'[52] – and easiest to mask under the claim of glorifying both God and athletic performance. As Magnan wrote:

> Woe to the athlete who lets himself be deceived by the dazzling speeches of his admirers. The moment the victors feel that they are considered among the giants of the stadium, they only possess the value of their purely physical ability. At best they will only be admired by visitors to the circus.[53]

Collective pride results from athletic performances achieved while the athlete is representing a collectivity – a school, city or nation. Local pride (not disassociated from topophilia) is often reflected in the welcoming signs along America's highways where the victories of the local high school track or cross-country (or other sports) team are projected to the outside world.[54] And, in this context, one might add envy to pride – the envy of other clubs, high schools or universities with superior facilities and runners.

The problem of resolving the tension between athletic achievement and the sinfulness of pride must have figured centrally in the mind of Eric Liddell, the 1924 Olympic 400 metres champion. According to one of his biographers, he was 'probably the most illustrious type of muscular Christian ever known'.[55] It is claimed that for Liddell, reverence for the Sabbath was as natural as breathing 'and infinitely more precious than a gold medal'.[56] However, a serious runner who is also a serious Christian faces many moral dilemmas. Liddell faced such a dilemma in 1924 when, having been selected for the 100 metres sprint for Great Britain in the Paris Olympics, he discovered that the heats of his event were to be held on a Sunday. According to one of his biographers, attempting to rationalize a decision to race on the Sabbath was not part of Liddell's mind set. He could have argued that he would be honouring his God by winning a race for Him rather than having Sunday away from the track. But he did not, despite being called a traitor and having to face jibes about 'national honour'. Instead, Liddell went on and won the 400 metres on the 500-metre Paris track in 47.6 seconds, a world record. He subsequently settled in China to undertake missionary work.

But where does imagination lie in Liddell's life? Was he too far towards the morality end of the morality–imagination spectrum? Was there life beyond proselytizing? His missionary work suggests that there was not; he had demonstrated that God came before sport. But even in China he continued to run and race – and encouraged his charges to do so.[57] It was thought that he was fit enough to compete in the 1928 Olympics but he appears not to have been invited. This seems to have been an oversight as it was reported that he had run 400 metres in 47.8 seconds that year.[58] In 1929 he defeated the peripatetic German Otto Peltzer over 400 metres in Tientsin.[59] He also won the North China Championship in 1930.

Liddell's continued athletic career while in China suggests that at least part of the good life lay in his sense of vitality and speed. He was not entirely an unthinking moralist: there was space for both a sense of godliness and a sense of the athletic in his life. And perhaps he did enjoy the adulation of the crowds and the affection of the fans. At least, he never stopped exchanging letters with one of his greatest fans, Elsa McKechnie, who formed an 'Eric Liddell Club' and hero-worshipped him. Liddell is revealed as a man who was able to display both physical and moral manliness. His continued running during his time as a missionary implies that his imagination was far from absent. He died in a Japanese internment camp in 1945.[60]

Dilemmas and Place

If Liddell faced moral questions concerned with time (that is, *when* to compete), several athletes in the United States in 1936 faced similar dilemmas concerning place. Perhaps the most well-documented example is when athletes had to decide whether to try out for, or compete in, the Berlin Olympics. At the time, anti-Semitism was rampant in Germany and moves had been afoot to ban Jews from the German team. Moral dilemmas faced foreign Jews, and non-Jews, who might be selected for their national squads. Of course, many non-Jews went, burying their heads in the sands of National Socialism. But consider Jewish athletes. How should they react? The cases of four Jewish sprinters, Milton Green and Herman Neugass, on the one hand, and Martin Glickman and Sam Stoller on the other, are exemplary. Each of these athletes had a chance to make the US team in the sprints, hurdles and/or relay. Green, from Brookline, Massachusetts, was a Harvard student in 1936, having excelled at the high and low hurdles and had qualified to take part in the Olympic trials at Randall's Island, New York, a few weeks before the Games. He claimed that he did not have a clear understanding of the situation in Nazi Germany where Jews had been excluded from the national team, despite the Germans' success in convincing members of the International Olympic Committee (IOC) to the contrary. He was shocked when his rabbi informed him of the situation in Germany and despite pressure from his track coach he insisted that he would not participate in the trials.[61] Herman Neugass came from New Orleans and was a student at Tulane University. He became one of the nation's top sprinters. However, on learning of the September 1935 'Nuremburg Laws' he declined to try out for the Games. The Olympic track coach wrote to Neugass telling him that 'we take seven sprinters, that is three for the 100 metres and four for the short relay. I am quite sure that there are not seven people who can beat you.' Despite this temptation, Neugass held firm.[62]

The cases of Glickman and Stoller are rather different. Marty Glickman was from New York City and in 1936 was a freshman at Syracuse University. Sam Stoller was a student at the University of Michigan. Each of them chose to compete in the Olympic trials and they were both successful in gaining places on the Olympic squad as members of the sprint relay team, the only Jews on the US track-and-field team. They had proved their ability and had made the team – but should they go? Two ideologies now clashed with one another – religious and athletic. The latter prevailed and Glickman and Stoller made their way to Berlin. The former explained his decision in two ways. First, he admitted that he took part 'for purely selfish reasons ... it was my ambition. Any athlete wants to be at the top and make the Olympic team. Holy Gee! It was my goal.'[63] However, he added that

> I qualified my desire ... and my actual drive to be on the
> Olympic team in Nazi Germany by rationalizing that if a Jew
> could make the Olympic team and run in Germany and win, then
> he would help disprove this myth of Nazi Aryan supremacy.[64]

He could have also justified his visit by arguing that he wanted to see for himself what the situation was in Berlin. But it is clear that, as an 18 year old, Glickman never seriously considered boycotting the Games, seemingly having a naive sense of the extent of Nazism at the time.[65]

Harold Abrahams, the winner of the 100 metres at the 1924 Olympics, also felt that he was able to visit the Berlin Games as a BBC journalist. In McNeish's version of the weeks and months leading up the Berlin Games, Abrahams, an assimilated Jew, felt that most opposition to him attending the Games would come from London's Orthodox Jewish community; they would 'see it as a silent acceptance of everything the swastika stood for'.[66] For Abrahams, and others who were saturated with an ideology of sport, it was an impossible event to miss.

Moral dilemmas have faced runners when campaigns have taken place involving the possibility, for example, of boycotting the Moscow Games in 1980 as a response to Soviet military engagements in Afghanistan. But moral dilemmas also arise once athletes have made the decision to attend major sports events. Ethical questions might have faced the organisers of the NCAA championships in Indianapolis in June 1986. Should the meet continue, following the catastrophe of Kathy Ormsby? (See Chapter 5.) It did. The same dilemma must have faced the runners in the 5,000 meters race (for which Ormsby had been entered), which had been scheduled a day or so after the unforeseen tragedy in the 10,000 metres. Should they compete? One, Ellen Reynolds from Duke University, who had finished second to Ormsby in the record-breaking race at Philadelphia, withdrew. Given the circumstances, 'her heart was no longer in it'.[67] For the other entrants, the championships went on as scheduled. Stephanie Herbst, the winner of the 10,000 metres race (her time breaking Ormsby's collegiate record), also won the 5,000 metres. She said that although she first considered not running in the 5,000 metres, 'a lot of people who get deeply into distance running have problems. Running is their life ... You have to go out and get that run in *no matter what.*'[68]

Events at the Munich Olympic Games in 1972 had arguably provided even greater ethical dilemmas. During the Games, the Olympic village was the site of the massacre of 11 Israeli sportsmen by representatives of what was known as the 'Black September Movement'.[69] The murders at the Munich Olympic village clearly represented the polar opposite of what the Olympics were supposed to stand for. Having almost been witnesses to the massacres, what should athletes do in response? One option was to remain in Munich and participate as originally planned. The alternative was to demonstrate their opposition to the Games by refusing to take any further part in an event that had become a site for murder. The day after the murders was set aside for a memorial service in the Olympic stadium. The president of the IOC, Avery Brundage, insisted that the Games must go on, a day behind schedule. His announcement was met by resounding applause from the 80,000 spectators, leading Red Smith, the *New York Times* journalist, to describe it as being more like a pep rally than a memorial service.[70]

For some athletes the murders were so evil that further participation was out of the question. The entire Philippines track and field team immediately left Munich. So did six members of the Dutch team. Among them was Jos Hermans, who had qualified for the final of the 10,000 metres and was a potential medallist. He preferred to return home than to take part. His compatriot, the sprinter Wilma van Gool, observed that they were leaving in protest at the 'obscene' decision to continue with the 'Games'.[71] Such athletes seem to have displayed goodness born of an imagination that went beyond the banal. Esther Roth, an Israeli sprinter, left Munich accompanying her murdered friends and compatriots in their coffins.

Other runners may have been affected emotionally but stayed to take part in their races. US marathon runner Kenny Moore claimed that he

> ran the 1972 Olympic marathon expressly measuring my own suffering against that of my fellow Olympians. Every time I would get a stitch in my side, or a cramp running up a hamstring, I would ask myself if this passing ache were comparable to what they felt in that phosphorous conflagration. That settled, I would run on, chastened.[72]

Moore finished fourth, having treated the race as a personal memorial to the dead Israelis. His compatriot, Frank Shorter, the eventual winner, rationalized his position by stating that the murders 'should not distract us from our performance because that is what they [the terrorists] want'.[73]

For others, the massacre was seemingly little more than an inconvenient interruption to their plans. According to Steve Prefontaine's biographer,

> Pre's plans for the race were shattered by the terrorist attack upon Israeli athletes within the Olympic Village ... Knowing Steve would be upset, Dellinger [his coach] went to the village, vaulted a fence, and brought him out. They went to Austria, an hour away, and spent the day up in the mountains. Pre took a run and tried to forget ... Though still shaken, Pre looked good in the qualifying heats ... [b]ut beneath his surface calm, he was extremely upset, first by the tragedy itself, which stole all the

glamour of the Games for him, and also by the change in the time schedule caused by the memorial service for the slain athletes.[74]

It was the race plans that were shattered. The reasons for Prefontaine's distress hardly seem to have been the murders but their knock-on effects on the Olympic organization. It was as if it was just an ordinary unscheduled incident. Indeed, coach Dellinger identified the priority succinctly: 'I tried to counsel him that you can't let these types of thing (sic) bother you.'[75] Prefontaine was to finish fourth in the 5,000 metres final.

For Ron Hill, the British marathon runner and Munich Olympian, his autobiographical allusions to the massacre are entirely incidental to his concern for the correct diet in the days leading up to the marathon. Part of his diary for 5 September 1972 states:

> lunch at 12.15 p.m. [...] olives, lettuce and some meat or other, I can't remember with 'diet' getting to my mind ...there was a story of some shooting ... Arab guerillas (sic) had shot two Israelis and had about 20 hostages ... rumours flying of the Games being postponed 24 hours ... that would affect the diet ... back to the room and wrote some postcards... rumours still going ... a notice on our board said the Games may start again at 1.00 or 2.00 p.m. tomorrow ... we didn't know what to do about the 'diet'.[76]

The next day's entries included:

> ran 7 miles, felt OK in snatches but got tired towards the end ... as I turned a bloke in his pyjamas was telling someone else that a bomb had been thrown into the room with the Israeli hostages ... breakfast at 8.00 a.m., cornflakes, scrambled egg on toast and four sausages, coffees with fructose. 10.00 a.m., at the Memorial Service at the stadium Avery Brundage announced that there would be a day of mourning, everything would be put back for a day ... so we'll have to see how the diet works now.[77]

Hill finished sixth in the marathon, a result with which he was greatly disappointed.

Prefontaine and Hill, at the time of their participation in the 1972 Olympics, were, almost certainly, regarded by many as good people, perhaps moral people. They had committed no crime; they were athletes who felt that athletic results were their main aim in life. Each is still regarded by many as a hero. But for Prefontaine, his feeling after the Olympics was that he was devastated, 'disillusioned' and 'disheartened'.[78] Hill felt that 'Life would never be the same'.[79] In neither case, however, did their disappointment and distress result from the massacre (of their fellow Olympians) but from their perceptions of their poor performances in their respective races. The massacre was an inconvenience. The novelist Alan Sillitoe, writing shortly after the Munich Olympics, argued that the resumption of the Games in 'such indecent haste' revealed not only the unwillingness of the organizers to forsake their pride but also their financial investments. The athletes who continued to participate, he added, were 'in the grip of their physical investment at the expense of all human feeling'.[80]

The priorities displayed by the runners noted above are far from unique. A characteristic of most athletes' autobiographies (and their biographies) is the over-emphasis on the sporting aspects of their lives at the expense of social, economic and political happenings.[81] As James McNeish noted: 'how unpolitical and self-worshipping athletes are, even intellectuals like [Godfrey] Brown, how unaware they seem to be of events occurring beneath their noses.'[82]

Runners and Criminal Imagination

Tuan observes that moralists 'suspect imagination for its tendency to excess'.[83] One example of excess is greed that can, of course, be satisfied by cheating, rule-breaking, law-breaking, crime and evil. Consider first a rather ambiguous case of cheating, as demonstrated in Antipodean views of Bannister's four-minute mile. The Australian runner Ron Clarke referred to the result as having been achieved in 'artificial circumstances'. By this he meant the 'careful attention to pre-arranged pace-making'[84] by Chris Brasher and Chris Chataway, which, at the time bordered on the margins of 'good sportsmanship' and 'fair play'. It was certainly not a race in the conventional sense of the word. Soon after pace-making was banned by the English Amateur Athletics Association, and it appears unlikely that the four-minute mile would have been approved had the revised rules applied at the time.

Cheating can reflect a meanness of spirit as well as the formal breaking of rules. Marty Liquori avers that the serious runner is 'always seeking any advantage, no matter how tiny'.[85] Illustrating how an athlete may gain (unfair) advantage over another, he describes (in a light-hearted vein) a pair of 'strategies' used in cross-country races:

> The first is simple: If you are running along a narrow path that's lined with trees, you merely grab a limb and snap it back at the guy behind you, forcing him to duck or to throw his hands up

for protection. The second demands some planning: If you know you're coming to a sharp turn around a tree, you stay back until the right moment, then you increase your speed and cut in front of the guy and make the turn with an inch to spare and force him to stop or to run into the tree.[86]

These are examples of playfulness – unfair play at the expense of others.

The breaking of rules is widespread in sport and running is no exception. Consider, for the example, the rule operated by the NCAA that collegiate athletes in the United States should not receive payment for racing during their period of college eligibility. In his autobiography, Carl Lewis reveals how he accepted money while still a student at Houston University by competing on the European track circuit. This contravened NCAA regulations. He was fully aware of his rule-breaking so why did he do it? The answer was:

> As far as I was concerned, any college athlete who had been to Europe and been exposed to the opportunities for track athletics would be crazy not to think about the money. After all, the whole idea of a summer job is to put some money away for the school year.[87]

The Nike shoe corporation colluded in the rule-breaking. Having won the 1981 NCAA 100 metres (and long jump), Lewis told how

> The mighty Adidas athletes had been beaten by a college kid wearing Nikes [that is, Lewis]. The people from Nike certainly noticed because I was rooming with Don Coleman, the Nike rep. He was paying for everything, and we definitely ran up some bills. Don never minded spending money on a winner. Nike had plenty to spend, and part of Don's job was to keep the Nike athletes happy – even if that included breaking a whole bunch of NCAA rules.[88]

Evil exists in sport[89] but I suspect that there is less of it among runners than among those who participate in several other sports. Lewis's rule-breaking could hardly be called criminal and few would say it was evil. However, he was not necessarily moral. His growing wealth and imagination enabled numerous purchases but, as Tuan notes, 'a superfluity of material goods is a bane to moral life'.[90]

Now consider the example of some less well-known runners. Possibly the least known of those runners mentioned so far is Ernst Jokl. Born in Breslau, Germany (now Wrocław, Poland), in 1907, Jokl was a world-renowned sports scientist – popularly known as 'the father of American sports medicine'.[91] He was active in sports-medical research while living in Germany, South Africa and the United States. He died in 1998. As a young man in 1920s Germany he was a runner, sprinter and hurdler. He claimed that, as a 17 year old, he ran under 50 seconds for the 400 metres as a member of his university's 4 x 400 metres relay team.[92] His best result was in 1927 when, it is recorded, he ran 58.0 seconds for the 400 metres hurdles. From what data are available, it is reckoned that this result ranked him 44th fastest in the world for that year. He left Germany in 1933 as a result of the anti-Semitic policies of the Nazis and settled in South Africa where he continued his research and undertook studies that covered an astonishing range of subjects. After the Second World War he migrated to the USA and spent the remainder of his life writing and researching at the University of Kentucky. He is widely regarded as a polymath scholar who today might be better termed a workaholic. Many people in sports science remember Jokl as a major figure in his field.

Jokl also seems to have possessed a vivid imagination. In 1981, during an interview at Stellenbosch University on a return visit to South Africa, he claimed that he had won German national titles and run in the 1928 Olympics at Amsterdam, competing in the 400 metres hurdles. He also claimed that his wife had won an Olympic gymnastics medal.[93] Extensive searches of Olympic data have revealed that neither Jokl nor his wife ever competed in the Olympic Games. Nor does any record exist that he was a German champion. Assuming that the account of the interview was accurate, Jokl appears to have had an ill-disciplined imagination. Why should he have claimed that he and his wife were Olympians and champions? Was it a daydream, a joke, a slip of the tongue, a lie, or the result of some form of mental sickness? Provided that it is not taken too far, suggests Tuan, a 'good spinner of yarn, no matter how fantastic, is often appreciated as one may appreciate any other temporary form of excess innocently and skilfully performed'.[94] He cannot be termed a criminal. Like Lewis, he was not evil. Although a famous sports scientist, Jokl showed himself in this, and some other questionable aspects of his life, to be less than perfect – but no more flawed than humanity itself.[95]

The same might be said about Jeffrey Archer, a notorious British peer, former member of parliament, aspirant mayor of London, 'author' of numerous popular novels, and one-time Oxford University sprinter. With a relentlessness matched by few other biographers, Michael Crick has chronicled Archer's life and deeds which are, like Jokl's, not primarily focused on running but on acts of deception.[96] Those perpetrated by Archer seem to far exceed in seriousness anything undertaken by Jokl, though one can never be certain.

In the numerous tales told about him, Archer is often identified as having been an athlete in his younger days. To be sure, he did represent Oxford University as a sprinter and once ran for England in an end of season competition against Sweden. The record books show that his best performances were 9.8 seconds for the 100 yards, 21.5 for the 220 and 49.8 for the quarter-mile. In 1964 Archer competed for Oxford University in the annual track meet with Cambridge University. In those days this meeting took place at the White City Stadium in London and was considered one of the most important meetings of the early season. At that time, each of the 'ancient universities' usually included one or two international athletes in their teams. Archer represented Oxford in the 100 yards. The race was shown live on BBC (such was the significance of the Oxford–Cambridge meet at the time). The murky black-and-white videotape shows Archer at the start of the race. He false starts, beating the gun; he false starts a second time; and a third. Somehow he got away without incurring the normal disqualification for two false starts – and won the race. This was, more or less, the story of Jeffrey Archer's life – getting away with it.

Being a student at Oxford facilitated Archer's running career but his entry into that august institution was somewhat unconventional. He entered the groves of academe under the most devious of circumstances, passing himself off as a graduate of an American university that turned out to have been a Californian body-building school. He claimed to hold the Oxford University 100 yards record of 9.6 seconds, but that had been a wind-assisted result.[97] He got away with theft, forgery, writing highly successful novels, and womanising.[98] He was eventually found guilty of perjury and subsequently served a prison sentence. As Tuan puts it, 'an indifference to truth is incompatible with morality'.[99] And a wise man – and Archer isn't stupid – 'is uncomfortably close to a wizard whose magical powers may not be used for virtuous ends'.[100] Runners like Jokl and Archer recall the Tuanian warning: The good life 'has an air of lightness – even playfulness; but if it is truly good the playful thrust must be anchored in a respect for truth and in a reflexive awareness of one's own mortality'.[101]

Tuan accepts that 'play has a dark side that is too often forgotten'; 'Sadism', he reminds us, 'is a form of play'.[102] As far as I know, Ernst Jokl and Jeffrey Archer are not renowned for their sadism. But the playfulness that characterized much of their lives certainly has a dark side. In some ways, the wealth that they accumulated created a good life for them. However, it has been part of, what Tuan would term, 'the hypocritically good world' of the modern age.[103] Having been a runner and leading a life of crime are far from incompatible. Archer may not be a good person but many would argue that it would be unreasonable to label him as evil. And even if Archer could be termed cruel, Tuan reminds us that while cruelty is evil it is not one of the seven deadly sins.[104]

Rudolf Harbig was born in 1913. He is widely regarded as one of the greatest runners of all time. He competed for Germany in the 1936 Olympics, winning a bronze medal in the 4 x 400 metres relay. A year later, like many Germans, he joined the National Socialist (Nazi) party. He was trained by Waldamer Gerschler (see Chapter 4) and widely used the interval running method of training. He won the European 800 metres title in 1938 but it was in 1939 that Harbig was to become a dual world record holder. In July of that year, on a 500-metre track in Milan, he smashed the world 800 metres record with a staggering time of 1 minute 46.6 seconds. This surpassed by a large margin the previous record of 1 minute 48.4 seconds set by the British runner Sydney Wooderson a year earlier. On another 500-metre track in Frankfurt am Main in August he ran 400 metres in 46.0 seconds, breaking the world record of the American Archie Williams by one-tenth of a second. Given these fantastic performances Harbig was widely favoured as a gold medallist in the Tokyo Olympics that were planned for 1940 but cancelled due to the outbreak of war.

Harbig continued competing during the early years of the war, notably against his Italian track adversary Mario Lanzi. In the biography of his pupil, Gerschler notes that Harbig volunteered for the eastern front where he became a paratrooper. Gerschler continued:

'Which goal', we ask ourselves, 'is greater?' To become an Olympic champion? To continue the hard life of the German sportsman, or to accept the even harder life of the German soldier? … We need not speak the answer. It is in our blood. Let us be just, though, and acknowledge the sacrifice that Harbig, in particular has made … He would have become an Olympic champion … That is over now![105]

In the preface to the book, Karl Ritter von Halt (Hitler's last *Reichssportführer*, a rabid Nazi who was named as a war criminal),[106] praised Harbig's *athletic* motto, 'I go into battle for Germany'. Harbig was killed near Kiev in 1944 and was posthumously awarded the 'German Cross'.[107] Was being a member of the Nazi party in 1930s Germany a denotation of evil? Arguably not. Rather, it may typify human-ness – though hardly humane-ness. It can at least be read as an understandable human response to the *zeitgeist*.

Yet those with absolute power and those who run in the Olympics can each, it seems, be evil. Adolf Hitler, watching the 1936 Olympics, argued that black athletes should be excluded from the Olympics. He believed that they possessed natural athletic talent and – in his terms – animal-like speed. For these reasons he felt they had an unfair advantage. Such superior talent, he felt, should be banned from Olympic participation. Indeed, he explicitly stated that when the 1940 Olympic Games took place, black athletes would be excluded. If Adolf Hitler had had his way, the 1936 Olympic 100 and 200 metres champion would not have been Jesse Owens but the Dutchman Martinus Osendarp. The Dutch sprinter, arguably the best in Europe at the time, had won the 1935 English 220 yards and the 1936 100 yards championships. In 1936, Jesse Owens won the Olympic 100 metre dash with fellow African-American Ralph Metcalfe second. In the 200 metres, black Americans also took the first two places, Owens again winning with Matthew Robinson second. Third in each race was Osendarp, beaten both times by what Hitler called the 'Negro auxiliaries'. Following the Olympics, Osendarp continued competing and won English and European championship medals in 1938.

In 1940 Germany occupied The Netherlands. During wartime, track athletics did not come to a halt and in 1941 a track meet was held in Amsterdam for the SS and Police Sports associations. Osendarp, an Olympic hero, was a competitor. He had joined the Dutch Volunteer SS and in this capacity was able to collaborate with the Nazi occupiers of his country and inform on athletes with whom he had competed in Berlin.[108] After the war he received a prison sentence for informing on his fellow citizens.[109]

So runners are not necessarily people to be admired and, on conventional criteria, they are not necessarily moral or good. Questions of morality, however, do not quite end here. As Tuan points out, 'the ability to act effectively makes for the good life'.[110] People can be made happy through the witnessing of a great feat of running. Crowds are said to leave the stadium happy when a world record is broken. But this could be read as the provision (for many) of nothing more than a late modern version of the Roman bread and circuses. And a job well done by a runner of any level also gives satisfaction to the athlete; but is the satisfaction greater when running is a commercial transaction, driven by the desire for fortune as well as fame? Or when a runner defeats an opponent from a stigmatized nation? To the first question, I turn to Tuan for an answer. Over time, he notes 'good' for most humans has been physical survival and little else. From this comes the desire for things that can be purchased. So good is translated into goods; 'so much of life turns out to be a struggle not for good but for goods'.[111] Goods may be psychic (winning a race or breaking a record) but increasingly these become less significant than tangible rewards (winning $100,000 or a Mercedes car).

To the casual observer, the runner may be a model of the good life. Vitality and grace are admirable qualities that many would identify with Achilles, the fleet of foot. Olympic athletes are heroes; they may become celebrities; they appear to bring pleasure to people. But it is hard to be humble if you are an Olympic champion or world-record breaker. Celebrities feed on their own pride. Can they possibly be moral?

There is a danger, however, in focusing on morals. In so doing there is the possibility of falling into dualisms and polarizations: good versus bad.

Too much emphasis on the moral runs the risk of being moralistic.[112] But it does not take much excavation to discover that runners have the strengths and weaknesses of all of us. Indeed, looking closely at runners reveals their human-ness *in extremis*. As Tuan put it, the Greek hero Hercules may have been one of the founders of the Olympic games but he was also crude, brutal and obscene. Similarly, modern heroes are contradictory; they are ordinary mortals writ large.[113]

When I look at the world of sport, there can be little doubt that at one level (at least) there has been progress. At the global scale (though not necessarily at the local), times for all events, from the 100 metres to the marathon, have got faster. People in more and more countries are taking up running, to an extent that would have been almost unbelievable half-a-century earlier. As late as the 1940s a sporting encyclopaedia was confident that Africans would never make world-class athletes.[114] But in what sort of world has such progress occurred? Has there been moral progress? The answer seems to be ambiguous. There have been signs that some of the excesses of serious sport are being rejected, with fewer people seemingly taking up serious running in western Europe and north America. The message of the 1960s counter-culture, to replace 'sport' with 'play', may have been successful – but only partially.

In what sort of running should *homo currens* participate? The socialist economist Colin Leys wrote an essay on sport in which he indirectly addressed this question. In it he felt that the liberation of serious sport was unlikely and that the most that could be hoped for was the future de-sportization of play.[115] Is this a pessimistic conclusion? Yes, to an extent. After all, I have shown earlier that in England (at least) the opposite seems to have happened with the sportization of the National Curriculum. However, it must be admitted that such excesses are absent elsewhere and in some countries serious running has become neglected or de-emphasized.

Tuan would argue that through sustained effort we should become more moral *and* imaginative about the good life.[116] This can be applied to a body-cultural life, a life that might include running. This takes me back to my introduction and my comments on literature and sports writing. Lenk and Gebauer echo Tuan's stress on imagination. They plead for more imagination in our representations of sports. Art has long stopped trying to seek reality as one of its objectives. In writing sport we might also try to turn the world upside down by providing unexpected outcomes and bizarre scenarios (witness the work in previous chapters of Sillitoe and Lundberg – and perhaps Warren, McNeish and Heywood). This would cause us to stop and think about achievement sport's inadequacies as well as its possible positive contributions to late-modern life.

Notes

Series Editor's Foreword

1. G.C.F. Mead and Rupert C. Clift (eds.), *English Verse: Old and New An Anthology for Schools* (Cambridge: Cambridge University Press, 1947), pp.112–13. I still have it!
2. Ibid.
3. He was killed in the Great War fighting on the Western Front.
4. See J.A. Mangan, *Athleticism in the Victorian and Edwardian Public School: the emergence and consolidation of an educational ideology* (London: Frank Cass, 2000), pp.84–5, for a brief consideration of public school runs.
5. Mead and Clift, *English Verse*, pp.112–13.
6. John Bale, *Running Cultures: Racing in Time and Space* (London: Frank Cass, 2004), p.11.
7. Ibid., p.3.
8. Ibid.
9. Ibid., p.4.
10. Ibid.
11. Mead and Clift, *English Verse*, pp.112–13.

Introduction

1. The notion of a technology of the body draws on Marcal Mauss, 'Techniques of the body', in Jonathon Crary and Stanford Kwinter (eds), *Incorporations* (New York: Zone, [1934] 1992), pp.455–77.
2. Tuan has implied this in his writing but it is mainly associated with David Harvey, *The Condition of Postmodernity* (Oxford: Blackwell, 1989). See, however, earlier renditions by Donald Janelle, 'Central place development in a time-space context', *Professional Geographer*, 20, 1 (1968), pp.5–10 and Ronald Abler, 'Effects of space-adjusting technologies on the human geography of the future', in Ronald Abler, Donald Janelle, Allen Philbrick and John Sommer (eds), *Human Geography in a Shrinking World* (North Scituate: Duxbury Press, 1975), pp.36–56.
3. Among the many reviews of this film, see the Jungian reading by Steven Walker, www.cgjung page.org/films/runlola.html (accessed 20 Aug. 2001). Devouring time and space is, of course, a central feature of many thrillers and westerns.
4. Jeffrey Nash, 'The short and the long of it: legitimising motives for running', in Jeffrey Nash and James Spradley (eds), *Sociology: A Descriptive Approach* (New York: Rand McNally, 1976), p.162.
5. Examples of the few such studies that exist include those of Henning Eichberg, 'Race track and labyrinth: the space of physical culture in Berlin', *Journal of Sport History*, 17, 2 (1990), pp.245–60, and 'Stronger, funnier, deadlier: Track and field on its way to the ritual of the record', in John M. Carter and Arnd Krüger (eds), *Ritual and Record: Sports Records and Quantification in Pre-Modern Societies* (New York: Greenwood Press 1990), pp.123–34.

6. Nicholas Entrikin, 'Geographer as humanist', in Paul Adams, Steven Hoelscher and Karen Till (eds), *Textures of Place: Exploring Humanist Geographies* (Minneapolis: University of Minnesota Press, 2001), p.430. Entrikin notes that to the social scientist this 'method' may appear anecdotal but to the humanist it is a way of interpreting the particulars of experience in search of the universal, p.430. See also Douglas Pocock, 'Classics in human geography revisited', *Progress in Human Geography*, 18, 3 (1994), p.356.

7. Blurb by Simon Schama on the dust-jacket of Yi-Fu Tuan, *Passing Strange and Wonderful: Aesthetics, Nature and Culture* (Washington, DC: Island Press, 1993).

8. Robert Sack, *Homo Geographicus* (Baltimore: Johns Hopkins University Press, 1997), p.v.

9. Entrikin, 'Geographer as humanist', p.427.

10. See *Progress in Human Geography*, 18, 3 (1994), pp.355–9. Numerous appreciative allusions to Tuan's œuvre are found in Adams, Hoelscher and Till (eds), *Textures of Place*.

11. Peter Jackson and Susan Smith, *Exploring Social Geography* (London: Allen and Unwin, 1984), p.22. The 'maverick' tag alludes to Tuan's insistence on a humanistic approach at a time when human geography was dominantly positivistic and scientistic.

12. See, for example, Richard Giulianotti, *Football: A Sociology of the Global Game* (Cambridge: Polity, 1999), p.69.

13. On Tuan and theory see Entrikin, 'Geographer as humanist'.

14. Edward Relph, 'Classics in Human Geography revisited', *Progress in Human Geography*, 18, 3 (1994), pp.356–8.

15. Personal communication from Yi-Fu Tuan, 31 Jan. 1995.

16. Ibid.

17. Roger Bannister, *First Four Minutes* (London: Putnam, 1955); Tuan, *Passing Strange and Wonderful*, p.36 and *The Good Life* (Madison: University of Wisconsin Press, 1986), p.15. Bannister was an Oxford contemporary of Tuan's.

18. Yi-Fu Tuan, *Who am I? An Autobiography of Emotion, Mind and Spirit* (Madison: University of Wisconsin Press, 1999), pp.95–6.

19. Yi-Fu Tuan, 'Space and place: Humanistic perspectives', *Progress in Geography*, 6 (1974), pp.226–7; Yi-Fu Tuan, *Space and Place: The Prespective of Experience* (Minneapolis: University of Minnesota Press, 1977), p.52.

20. Yi-Fu Tuan, *Dear Colleague: Common and Uncommon Observations* (Minneapolis: University of Minnesota Press, 2002), pp.5; 62; 149.

21. Tuan, *Passing Strange and Wonderful*, p.37.

22. Tuan, *The Good Life*, p.18.

23. Tuan, quoting Joyce Carol Oates in 'Dear Colleague', 10, 9 (1995) (a bi-weekly letter distributed by Tuan to his colleagues and graduate students at the University of Wisconsin). In the published collection of letters in Tuan's book *Dear Colleague*, the allusion to Oates is omitted. However, Tuan does refer to the sexual symbolism in John Updike's description of the 'primordial poetry of a man and a woman ... together ... making a single species' during ice dancing (Tuan, *Dear Colleague*, pp.94–5). See also, Tuan, *Who am I?*, p.83. As I was completing this book, Tuan informed me of his awareness of even more sporting references – academic writings, novels and movies – with strong sporting allusions: Email communication from Yi-Fu Tuan, 14 Nov. 2002.

24. Tuan, *Who am I?*, p.71.

25. Ibid., p.84. See also Tuan, *Dear Colleague*, p.210.

26. Personal communication from Yi-Fu Tuan, 31 Jan. 1995.

27. Ibid.

28. Yi-Fu Tuan, 'A life of learning', *Occasional Paper*, 24, American Council of Learned Societies (1998), http://www.acls.org/op42tuan.htm (accessed 11 Jan. 2001). This is a broadly 'philosophical approach' and Tuan alludes to his work as 'philosophical' on several occasions. After all, 'the philosopher's job is to build perspectives' and, in the case of sports philosophy, to 'look below the surface of games and look at what surrounds them to find what is valuable to analyse and to discuss': Spencer Wertz, *Talking a Good Game: Inquiries into the Principles of Sport* (Dallas: Southern Methodist University Press, 1991), p.9.

29. John Pickles, *Geography and Humanism, Concepts and Techniques in Modern Geography*, 44 (Norwich: GeoAbstracts, 1986), p.17.

30. Yi-Fu Tuan, 'Life as a field trip', *The Geographical Review*, 2, 49 (2001), p.43.

31. Yi-Fu Tuan, 'Sign and metaphor', *Annals of the Association of American Geographers* 68, 3 (1978), p.363.

32. Ibid.

33. Douglas Pocock (ed.), *Humanistic Geography and Literature* (London: Croom Helm, 1981).

34. Yi-Fu Tuan 'Literature and geography: Implications for geographical research', in David Ley and Marwyn Samuels (eds), *Humanistic Geography: Prospects and Problems* (London: Croom Helm, 1978), p.200. There is a growing realization that 'text only inadequately commemorates ordinary lives since it values what is written or spoken over multisensual practices and experiences', one of which is running. It has to be added, however, that such 'non-representational theory' all too easily lapses into romanticism and essentialism. Running is not beyond the realm of language as it is always mediated by words: It is 'taught, scripted, performed and watched'. See Catherine Nash, 'Performativity in practice: Some recent work in cultural geography', *Progress in Human Geography*, 24, 4 (2000), pp.655–8.

35. Hans Lenk and Gunter Gebauer, 'Sport and sports literature from the perspective of methodological interpretation', *Aethlon*, 5, 2 (1988), p.81. On writing sport, see also Jim Denison, 'Sport narratives', *Qualitative Enquiry*, 2, 3 (1996), pp.351–62.

36. Lenk and Gebauer, 'Sport and sports literature', p.82.

37. Yi-Fu Tuan, 'Humanistic geography', *Annals of the Association of American Geographers,* 66, 2 (1976), p.276. Tuan's outlook would fit neatly enough with the views of sports sociologist Alan Ingham, who notes that 'in working with contradiction instead of normative functionalism, we can develop a different sense of determination. Instead of simplistic notions of cause and effect, we can become attuned to the notion of multiple determinations and to the idea that determinations are not one-dimensional'. Alan Ingham, 'Toward a department of physical cultural studies and an end to tribal warfare', in Juan–Miguel Fernández–Balboa (ed.), *Critical Postmodernism in Human Movement, Physical Education and Sport* (Albany: State University of New York Press, 1997), p.172.

38. See, for example, Derek Gregory, 'Humanistic geography' in R.J. Johnston, Derek Gregory, Geraldine Pratt and Michael Watts (eds), *Dictionary in Human Geography* (4th Edition) (Oxford: Blackwell, 2000), who notes that humanistic geography is an approach that can be 'distinguished by the central and active role it gives to human awareness and human agency, human consciousness and human creativity', p.361.

39. Stephen Daniels, 'Arguments for a humanistic geography' in R.J. Johnston (ed.), *The Future of Geography* (London: Methuen, 1985), pp.143–58; Paul Adams, Steven Hoelscher and Karen Till, 'Place in context: Rethinking humanist geographies', in Adams, Hoelscher and Till (eds) *Textures of Place*, p.xix.

40. I am grateful to Sigmund Loland for this point.

41. Jean-Marie Brohm, *Sport: A Prison of Measured Time* (London: Ink Links, 1978).

42. Jean Baudrillard, *America* (London: Verso, 1989), pp.38–9. Even so, I still occasionally manage to obtain a sense of freedom, release and élan in bursts of relatively fast striding, even sprinting.

43. Following Chataway's 8th place in the 1956 Olympic 5,000 metres at Melbourne: Quoted in *Track and Field News*, 9, 11 (1956), p.11.

44. Nicholas Entrikin, *The Betweenness of Place* (Cambridge: Cambridge University Press, 1991), p.58.

45. R.J. Johnston, *Philosophy and Human Geography* (London: Arnold, 1983), p.84.

46. Yi-Fu Tuan, 'Surface phenomena and aesthetic experience', *Annals of the Association of American Geographers*, 79, 2 (1989), p.240.

47. Edward Relph, *Place and Placelessness* (London: Pion, 1976), and *Rational Landscapes and Humanistic Geography* (London: Croom Helm, 1981); Robert Sack, *Human Territoriality* (Cambridge: Cambridge University Press, 1986), and *Homo Geographicus*.

48. Adams, Hoelscher and Till, 'Place in context', p.xxi.

Chapter 1

1. Lenk and Gebauer, 'Sport and sports literature', p.77.
2. Yi-Fu Tuan, 'Environment, behaviour and thought', in Frederick Boal and David Livingstone (eds), *The Behavioural Environment* (London: Routledge, 1989), p.77.
3. From W.H. Auden, 'Runner' in Gareth Battista (ed.), *The Runner's Literary Companion* (New York: Penguin, 1994), p.294.
4. C.L.R. James, *Beyond a Boundary* (London: Stanley Paul, 1986), p.viii.
5. Pirkko Markula and Jim Denison, 'See spot run: Movement as an object of textual analysis', *Qualitative Enquiry*, 6, 3 (2000), p.418.
6. For examples, see Jacques Gleyse, 'Instrumental rationalization of human movement', in Geneviève Rail (ed.), *Sport and Postmodern Times* (Albany: State University of New York Press, 1998), pp.239–60, and Nigel Thrift, 'The still point: Resistance, expressive embodiment and dance', in Steve Pile and Michael Keith (eds), *Geographies of Resistance* (London: Routledge, 1997), pp.124–51. I take configurations to mean 'the webs of interdependence which link and both constrain and enable the actions of individuals': Grant Jarvie and Joseph Maguire, *Sport and Leisure in Social Thought* (London: Routledge, 1994), p.133.
7. Henning Eichberg, *Body Cultures: Essays on Sport, Space and Identity* (London: Routledge, 1998).
8. Ronald Lutz, 'Careers in running: Individual needs and social organization', *International Review for the Sociology of Sport*, 26, 3 (1991), pp.153–73.
9. Yi-Fu Tuan, *Space and Place: The Prospective of Experience* (Minneapolis: University of Minnesota Press, 1977), p.35.
10. Tim Ingold, *The Perception of the Environment* (London: Routledge, 2000), p.375.
11. Yi-Fu Tuan, *The Good Life* (Madison: University of Wisconsin Press, 1986), p.15.
12. Roger Bannister, *First Four Minutes* (London: Putnam, 1955), p.1.
13. Catherine Bates, *Play in a Godless World* (London: Open Gates Press: 1999), p.186.
14. Ibid., p.75.
15. Roger Caillois, *Man, Play and Games* (London: Routledge, 1965).
16. Tuan, *Space and Place*, p.52.
17. Johan Huizinga, *Homo Ludens: A Study of the Play-element in Culture* (Boston: Houghton Mifflin, 1955), p.10. Huizinga's use of the word 'play' is much broader than mine.
18. Arthur Lydiard and Garth Gilmour, *Run to the Top* (London: Herbert Jenkins, 1962), p.143, emphasis added.
19. Mark Heprin, *Memoir from Antproof Case* (New York: Harcourt Brace, 1995), p.291
20. Tuan, *The Good Life*, p.157.
21. Ibid., p.13.
22. It has been suggested that boys and girls learn to run in different ways and that for some girls, the whole body is not put into fluid and directed motion and tends not to reach, extend and stretch. A restricted form of running may have resulted from girls having traditionally been less exposed to sports activities than have boys. They learned different protocols of body management and deportment: see Iris Young, *Throwing Like a Girl* (Bloomington: Indiana University Press, 1990), pp.141–59. This distinction is almost certainly of less significance today and the stereotype of girls as second-class athletes is being eroded.
23. Yi-Fu Tuan, *Passing Strange and Wonderful: Aesthetics, Nature and Culture* (Washington, DC: Island Press, 1993), p.36.
24. W.R. Loader, *Testament of a Runner* (London: Sportsmans Book Club, 1962), p.127.
25. Yi-Fu Tuan, *Dominance and Affection: The Making of Pets* (New Haven: Yale University Press, 1984), p.164.
26. Yi-Fu Tuan, *Escapism* (Baltimore: Johns Hopkins University Press, 1998). p.163.
27. Peter Kühnst, *Sport: A Cultural History in the Mirror of Art* (Dresden: Verlag der Kunst, 1996), p.262.
28. Taylor Downing, *Olympia* (London: British Film Institute, 1992), p.71.
29. Graham McFee and Alan Tomlinson, 'Riefenstahl's *Olympia*: Ideology and aesthetics in the shaping

of the Aryan athletic body', in J.A. Mangan (ed.), *Shaping the Superman: Fascist Body as Political Icon – Aryan Fascism* (London: Frank Cass, 1999), p.100.
30. Fred Rohé, *The Zen of Running* (New York: Random House, 1974) (unpaginated).
31. Susan Jackson and Mihaly Csikszentmihalyi, *Flow in Sports* (Champaign, Ill: Human Kineitics, 1999).
32. J.A. Mangan, *Athleticism in the Victorian and Edwardian Public School* (London: Frank Cass, [1981] 2000), p.84.
33. F.A.M. Webster, *Athletics* (London: Allen and Unwin, 1925), pp.24–5.
34. Quoted in Norbert Müller (ed.), *Olympism: Pierre de Coubertin 1863–1937: Selected Writings* (Lausanne: International Olympic Committee, 2000), p.55. Coubertin did not favour female participation in serious sports.
35. From Rudyard Kipling, 'If', in Battista, *The Runners' Literary Companion*, p.301.
36. Elspeth Huxley, *White Man's Country: Lord Delamere and the Making of Kenya* (vol. 1) (London: Macmillan, 1935), p.239.
37. For an excellent review that takes in the relationship between exercise and landscape, see David Matless, *Landscape and Englishness* (London: Reaktion Books, 1998).
38. Quoted in Fred Wilt, *How they Train* (Los Altos: Track and Field News, 1959), p.66.
39. Jean Baudrillard, *The Transparency of Evil* (London: Verso, 1993), p.48.
40. Ibid., p.47.
41. J.B. Jackson, 'The abstract world of the hot-rodder', *Landscape*, 7, 1 (1957–58), pp.22–7.
42. Milan Kundera, *Slowness* (London: Faber, 1996), p.4.
43. Derek McCormack, 'Body shopping: Reconfiguring geographies of fitness', *Gender, Space and Culture*, 6, 2 (1999), pp.155–77.
44. Chris Shilling, *The Body and Social Theory* (London: Sage, 1993), p.203.
45. Department for Education and Employment, *The National Curriculum for Physical Education* (London: DFEE, 1995).
46. Jean-Marie Brohm, *Sport: A Prison of Measured Time* (London: Ink Links, 1978), p.41.
47. Quoted in Kühnst, *Sport*, p.292.
48. Claudio Tamburrini, 'What's wrong with doping?' in Torbjörn Tännsjö and Claudio Tamburrini (eds), *Values in Sport* (London: Spon, 2000), p.216.
49. Department of Environment, Transport and Regions, *Sport: Raising the Game* (London: Department of National Heritage, 1995), p.8.
50. David Kirk, 'Schooling bodies in new times: The reform of school physical education in high modernity', in Juan-Miguel Fernández-Balboa (ed.), *Critical Postmodernism in Human Movement, Physical Education and Sport* (Albany: State University of New York Press, 1997), pp.39–63.
51. Yi-Fu Tuan, *Dear Colleague: Common and Uncommon Observations* (Minneapolis: University of Minnesota Press, 2002), p.137.
52. Yi-Fu Tuan, 'Space and Place: A humanistic perspective', *Progress in Geography*, 6 (1974), pp.211–52.
53. Ibid., p.227.
54. Henning Eichberg, 'Forward race and the laughter of pygmies: On Olympic sport', in Mikulás Teich and Roy Porter (eds), *Fin de siècle and its Legacy* (Cambridge: Cambridge University Press, 1990), p.119; Kurt Weis, 'Concepts of time and concepts of man: Does the case of sport show how man both creates and falls victim to his image of time?', in Otmar Weiss and Wolfgang Schultz (eds), *Sport in Space and Time* (Vienna: Vienna University Press, 1995), pp.306-7; Otto Penz, 'Sport and speed', *International Review for the Sociology of Sport*, 25, 2 (1990), p.157.
55. Paul Weiss, *Sport: A Philosophic Enquiry* (Carbondale: University of Southern Illinois Press, 1969), p.101.
56. Ibid., p.111.
57. James Gleick, *Faster: The Acceleration of Just About Everything* (New York: Pantheon, 1999), p.108.
58. A.V. Hill, *Living Machines* (London: Bell, 1945), p.220.
59. Weiss, *Sport: A Philosophic Enquiry*, p.107.
60. Tuan, *Space and Place*, p.37.
61. Ibid, p.40.

62. Niels Kayser Nielsen, 'Sport, landscape and horizon', in John Bale (ed.), *Community, Landscape and Identity: Horizons in a Geography of Sports* (Keele: Occasional Paper 20, Department of Geography, Keele University, 1994), pp.54–70.

63. Eric Dunning, *Sport Matters: Sociological Studies of Sport, Violence and Civilization* (London: Routledge, 1999), pp.67–9.

64. Quoted in Tovio Kaila, *Boken om Nurmi* (Porvoo: Söderström, 1925), p.165.

65. Eichberg, 'Forward race and the laughter of pygmies', p.115. The late-nineteenth-century obsession with speed, and the ways in which it is represented, is thoroughly dealt with by Stephen Kern, *The Culture of Time and Space: 1800–1919* (Cambridge: Harvard University Press, 1983).

66. Henning Eichberg, 'Stronger, funnier, deadlier: Track and field on its way to the ritual of the record', in John M. Carter and Arnd Krüger (eds), *Ritual and Record: Sports Records and Quantification in Pre-Modern Societies* (New York: Greenwood Press, 1990), p.129.

67. Ibid., p.123.

68. Ibid., p.131.

69. The 1900 times were recorded to one-fifth of a second. Ekkehard zur Megede and Richard Hymans, *Progression of World Best Performances and Official IAAF World Records* (Monaco: IAAF, 1995). See also www.iaaf.org

70. Juha Heikkala, 'Discipline and excel: Techniques of the self and body in the logic of competing', *Sociology of Sport Journal*, 10, 4 (1993), pp.402–3.

71. Adam Phillips, *Houdini's Box: On the Arts of Escape* (London: Faber, 2001), p.73.

72. Quoted in *Runners World*, '2:04 marathon predicted for the year 2000'. More ambitious predictions suggest that by the end of 2100 the world records in, for example, the 100 metres will be 9.61s., the 800 metres in 35.92s., and the 5,000 metres 11m. 44.89s. See Alphonse Juilland, *Rethinking Track and Field: the Future of the World's Oldest Sport* (Milan: SEP Editrice, 2002), p.119.

73. Sigmund Loland, 'Record sports: an ecological critique and a reconstruction', *Journal of the Philosophy of Sport*, 28, 2 (2001), p.129.

74. For example, David Harvey, *The Condition of Postmodernity* (Oxford: Blackwell, 1989), pp.240–3 and David Harvey, *Justice, Nature and the Geography of Difference* (Oxford: Blackwell, 1996), pp.242–7.

75. On the alleged differences in performances on cinder and synthetic tracks see Juilland, *Rethinking Track and Field*, pp.138–41.

76. Coubertin, quoted in Müller, *Olympism*, p.200. See also Ted Butryn, 'Cyborg horizons: Sport and the ethics of self-technologization', in Andy Miah and Simon Eassom (eds), *Sport and Technology: History, Philosophy and Policy* (Amsterdam: Elsevier, 2002), pp.111–33.

77. Jeremy Stein, 'Reflections on time, time-space compression and technology in the nineteenth century', in Jon May and Nigel Thrift (eds), *Timespace: Geographies of Temporality* (London: Routledge, 2001), pp.106–19; Coubertin, quoted in Müller, *Olympism*, p.107.

78. Juilland, *Rethinking Track and Field*, p.132.

79. James McNeish, *Lovelock* (Auckland: Godwit, [1986] 1994), pp.165–6 (brackets added). McNeish's book caused something of a controversy when it was published in New Zealand in 1986. It is part biography, part novel. McNeish notes: 'Fiction is tidier than real life and there are inherent dangers in a fictional diary approach such as I have adopted, but there is one advantage: the view from inside the subject's head is restricted and this has forced me to curb the novelist's tendency to embroider. I have tried not to indulge in myth-making. [...] unless my interpretation is badly astray, the narrative essentially corresponds to Jack Lovelock's real life.' Ibid., pp.12–13.

80. Marty Liquori and Skip Myslenski, *On the Run: In Search of the Perfect Race* (New York: Morrow, 1979), p.101.

81. Norris McWhirter, 'Unusual facts and fallacies', in H.A. Meyer (ed.), *Athletics* (London: Oxford University Press, 1958), p.200.

82. Gunner Olsson, *Birds in Egg/Eggs in Bird* (London: Pion, 1980), p.198.

83. Mark Seltzer, *Bodies and Machines* (New York: Routledge, 1992).

84. Tuan, *The Good Life*, p.15, italics added. What sort of time is he referring to here? It seems that he has in mind a Heideggerian view of time that carries connotations of death – something that all

people surely wish to forget. The time recorded by the stopwatch, therefore, is just another way of forgetting the promise of death in time: Yi-Fu Tuan, email communication, 14 Nov. 2002.

85. Montague Shearman, *Athletics and Football* (London: Longmans, Green, 1888), p.205.
86. Cited in Müller, *Olympism*, p.160.
87. Shearman, *Athletics and Football*, p.213.
88. Sigmund Loland, 'The logic of progress and the art of moderation in competitive sports', in Torbjörn Tännsjö and Claudio Tamburrini (eds), *Values in Sport* (London: Spon, 2000), pp.39–56.
89. May and Thrift, *Timespace*, 'Introduction', p.19.
90. Kundera, *Slowness*, pp.4–5.
91. F.A.M. Webster, *Athletes in Action* (London: John F. Shaw, 1931), p.7.
92. Quoted in Harry Gordon, *Young Men in a Hurry* (Melbourne: Lansdowne Press, 1962), p.106.
93. Duncan Mackay, *The Guardian Unlimited*, 7 Sept. 2001, http:www.guardian.co.uk/o,6961,,oo.html (accessed 10 Jan. 2002).
94. Reported in *Athletics World*, 2, 11 (1954), p.93.
95. Marcus Doel, *Poststructuralist Geographies* (Edinburgh: Edinburgh University Press, 1999), p.14. See also Gleick, *Faster*, pp.277–8.
96. These data are taken from Mark Butler (ed.), *Statistics Handbook 1995* (Monaco: IAAF, 1995).
97. Edward Ullman, 'Space and/or time: Opportunities for substitution and prediction', *Transactions of the Institute of British Geographers*, 64 (1974), p.133.
98. Anson Rabinbach, *The Human Motor* (Berkeley: University of California Press, 1990), p.300.
99. John Bale and Joe Sang, *Kenyan Running: Movement Culture, Geography and Global Change* (London: Frank Cass, 1996), p.163.
100. Ibid., p.34.
101. I am aware that aesthetic pleasure can be obtained by an appreciation of number patterns and even from lists of results. My contrast here is mainly with the assumed objectivity of numbers and the frequently acknowledged subjectivity of writing, painting and sculpture.
102. Eldon Snyder, 'Sociology of nostalgia: Sports halls of fame and museums in America', *Sociology of Sport Journal*, 10, 2 (1991), pp.228–38.
103. Gerald Redmond, 'A plethora of shrines: Sport in the museum and hall of fame', *Quest*, 1, 9 (1973), p.2. See also Snyder, 'Sociology of nostalgia'.
104. A third statue of Nurmi was erected near the Sports Science department in the campus of the University of Jyväskylä, but I have been unable to establish its current whereabouts.
105. David Smith, *Moral Geographies: Ethics in a World of Difference* (Edinburgh: Edinburgh University Press, 2000), pp.46–7.
106. This is in marked contrast to the case of the statue of Michael Jordan in Chicago. See Synthia Sydnor; 'Sport, celebrity and liminality', in Noel Dyck (ed.), *Sports Games and Cultures* (Oxford: Berg, 2000), pp.221–41.
107. See Nuala Johnson, 'Sculpting heroic histories', *Transactions of the Institute of British Geographers*, 19, 1 (1994), p.79.
108. David Wiggins, '"Great speed but little stamina": The historical debate over black athletic supremacy', *Journal of Sport History*, 16, 2 (1989), pp.158–85.
109. http://www.prefontainerun.com/memorial.html (accessed 17 Dec. 2001).
110. Tom Jordan, *Pre: The Story of America's Greatest Running Legend* (Emmaus, PA: Rodale Press, [1977] 1997).
111. Theresa Walton, 'Steve Prefontaine – From rebel with a cause to bourgeoise hero', paper presented at symposium on 'Sport and Cultural Distinctiveness', Iowa City (1999).
112. Miles Richardson, 'The gift of presence: The act of leaving artefacts at shrines, memorials and other tragedies', in Paul Adams, Steven Hoelscher and Karen Till (eds), *Textures of Place: Exploring Humanist Geographies* (Minneapolis: University of Minnesota Press, 2001), p.263. Richardson draws on Yi-Fu Tuan, 'The significance of the artefact', *The Geographical Review*, 70, 1 (1980), pp.462–72.
113. John Gibson, *Performance Versus Results: A Critique of Values in Contemporary Sport* (Albany: State University of New York Press, 1993).
114. Tuan, *Escapism*, pp.140–1.

115. Quoted in *Track and Field News*, 10, 7 (1957), p.2.
116. Allen Guttmann, 'The road all runners run', unpublished paper (1988). Guttmann's reading tends to assume that runners 'ponder the mark that they will leave in time'. On athletes' concern with the presentation of themselves in history, see Raymond Schmidt and Wilbert Leonard, 'Immortalizing the self through sport', *American Journal of Sociology*, 91, 5 (1986), pp.1088–111.
117. W. Umminger, *Supermen, Heroes and Gods: The Story of Sport through the Ages* (New York: McGraw Hill, 1963), p.195.
118. Quoted in Bale and Sang, *Kenyan Running*, pp.51–2.
119. http://news.bbc.co.uk/sport/hi/english/athletics/newsid_1434000/1434664.stm (accessed 7 Nov. 2001).
120. Quoted in Don Parkes and Nigel Thrift, *Times, Spaces and Places: A Chronogeographic Perspective* (Chichester: Wiley, 1980), p.20.
121. McNeish, *Lovelock*, p.113.
122. Gunter Gebauer, 'Citius-Altius-Fortius and the problem of sport ethics: A philosopher's viewpoint', in Fernand Landry, Marc Landry and Magdeleine Yerlès (eds), *Sport: the Third Millennium* (Sainte–Foy: Les presses de L'Université Laval, 1991), p.468.
123. Tuan, *Escapism*, p.xii.
124. Caillois, *Man, Play and Games*.
125. Bates, *Play in a Godless World*, p.22. See also Huizinga, *Homo Ludens*, pp.197–8.
126. My view here is contrary to that of the philosopher, Drew Hyland (*Philosophy of Sport* (New York: Paragon House, 1990), p.120). I am not suggesting here that there is an association between play and mistakes.
127. Raymond Krise and Bill Squires, *Fast Tracks: The History of Distance Running* (Battleboro, VT: Stephen Greene Press, 1982), pp.205–6.

Chapter 2

1. For example, Arne Naess, *Ecology, Community and Lifestyle* (Cambridge: Cambridge University Press, 1989), p.178.
2. Phillip Wagner, 'Sport: Culture and geography', in Allan Pred (ed.), *Time and Space in Geography* (Lund: Gleerup, 1981), p.92.
3. See Edward Relph, *Place and Placelessness* (London: Pion, 1976) and Marc Augé, *Non-Places* (London: Verso, 1995).
4. Henning Eichberg, 'Stronger, funnier, deadlier: Track and field on its way to the ritual of the record', in John M. Carter and Arnd Krüger (eds), *Ritual and Record: Sports Records and Quantification in Pre-Modern Societies* (New York: Greenwood Press, 1990), pp.123–34. Eichberg's other papers on running include 'Race track and labyrinth: The space of physical culture in Berlin', *Journal of Sport History*, 17, 2 (1990), pp.245–60, and 'Forward race and the laughter of pygmies: On Olympic sport', in Mikulás Teich and Roy Porter (eds), *Fin de siècle and its Legacy* (Cambridge: Cambridge University Press, 1990), pp.115–31.
5. There are a large number of unfair advantages that are tolerated in sports. Why they are tolerated is not entirely clear but perhaps it is because of their inevitability. See Roger Gardner, 'On performance enhancing substances and the unfair advantage argument', *Journal of the Philosophy of Sport*, 16, 1 (1989), pp.59–73.
6. See John Bale, 'A geographical theory of sport', in John Nauright and Verner Møller (eds), *The Essence of Sport* (Odense: University of South Jutland Press, 2003), pp.81–91.
7. Paul Weiss, *Sport: A Philosophic Enquiry* (Carbondale: University of Southern Illinois Press, 1969), p.105.
8. Irit Rogoff, *Terra Infirma: Geography's Visual Culture* (London: Routledge, 2000), p.21.
9. Relph, *Place and Placelessness*; Augé, *Non-Places*.
10. Kenneth Frampton, 'Towards a critical regionalism', in Hal Foster (ed.), *Postmodern Culture* (London: Verso, 1985), pp.16–30.
11. John Bale, *Landscapes of Modern Sport* (London: Leicester University Press, 1994).

12. Allen Guttmann, *From Ritual to Record* (New York: Columbia University Press, 1978), p.43.
13. Stewart Culin, *Games of the North American Indians* (New York: Dover, [1907] 1975).
14. Bale, *Landscapes of Modern Sport*, p.23. See also Peter Nabokov, *Indian Running* (Santa Fe: Ancient City Press, 1981), pp.84 and 91, and J. Oxendine, *American Indian Sports Heritage* (Champaign: Human Kinetics, 1988), p.81.
15. Montague Shearman, *Athletics and Football* (London: Longmans, Green, 1888), pp.17–18.
16. This is not to say that professionals did not engage in track races. On the contrary; for many years during the nineteenth century, the best times for many distances were achieved by professionals in times considerably superior to those of the amateurs. In 1886 the British runner Walter George, the best miler of his day, recorded 4 minutes 12.75 seconds for the classic distance. It was not until 1915 that it was bettered by an amateur, Norman Taber of the USA.
17. Yi-Fu Tuan, *Dominance and Affection: The Making of Pets* (New Haven: Yale University Press, 1984), p.173.
18. Yi-Fu Tuan, 'Discrepancies between environmental attitude and behavior: examples from Europe and China', *Canadian Geographer*, 15, 2 (1971), p.178.
19. L. Tarasti, 'The significance of the environment for sport', *Sport Science Review* (1988), p.41.
20. Tuan, *Dominance and Affection*, p.176.
21. Ibid., p.ix.
22. Ibid., p.2. Tuan's interest in metaphor is illustrated in one of his first published articles. See Yi-Fu Tuan, 'Use of simile and metaphor in geographical descriptions', *The Professional Geographer*, 9, 1 (1957), pp.9–11, and 'Sign and metaphor', *Annals of the Association of American Geographers* 68, 3 (1978), pp.363–72. The importance of metaphors in written work is that they not only structure the way we think about the world, they also suggest new ways of thinking about things.
23. Tuan, *Dominance and Affection*, p.5.
24. Shearman, *Athletics and Football*, p.187.
25. Ibid., pp.183–4.
26. A.R. Downer, *Running Recollections and How to Train* (Tarland: Balgownie Books, [1902] 1982), p.41. Of the 26 races between Downer and his rival Charles Bradley between 1893 and 1896, 14 were on grass.
27. Ingo Pyker, 'Sport and ecology', in Søren Riiskjær (ed.), *Sport and Space* (Copenhagen: Council of Europe, 1993), p.73.
28. Gordon Pirie, *Running Wild* (London: W.H. Allen, 1961), p.213.
29. Peter Lovesey, *The Official Centenary History of the Amateur Athletics Association* (London: Guniness Superlatives, 1979), p.15, emphasis added.
30. F.A.M. Webster, *Sports Grounds and Buildings* (London: Pitman, 1940), pp.111–18.
31. Yi-Fu Tuan, *Segmented Worlds and Self* (Minneapolis: University of Minnesota Press, 1982), p.8.
32. Roberto Quercetani, *Athletics* (Milan: Vallardi, 1990), p.41.
33. 'The Fenner's [Cambridge] track was built with the intention of making competitors run with their left hand to the inside of the track, the contrary being the practice at all other running grounds'; Shearman, *Athletics and Football*, pp.185–6
34. Tuan, *Dominance and Affection*.
35. W.R. Loader, *Testament of a Runner* (London: Sportsmans Book Club, 1962), p.11.
36. Roger Bannister, *First Four Minutes* (London: Putnam, 1955), pp.39–40.
37. Gunner Olsson, 'Toward a sermon of modernity', in Mark Billinge, Derek Gregory and Ron Martin (eds), *Recollections of a Revolution* (London: Macmillan, 1984), p.83.
38. Pauli Karjalainen, 'Earth writing as humane art', in Kaia Lehri and Virve Searpik (eds), *Place and Location* (Tallin: Proceedings of the Estonian Academy of Arts, 8, 2000), p.24, parentheses and emphasis added.
39. Eichberg, 'Race track and labyrinth', p.259.
40. Zygmunt Bauman, *Globalization* (Cambridge: Polity Press, 1998), pp.41–2.
41. Ronald Rees, *Interior Landscapes: Gardens and the Domestic Environment* (Baltimore: Johns Hopkins University Press, 1993).
42. Quercetani, *Athletics*, p.vi; Lovesey, *The Official Centenary History*, p.86.

43. Ross McWhirter and Norris McWhirter, *Get to Your Marks!* (London: Kaye, 1951), p.87.
44. Quoted in John Hoberman, *The Olympic Crisis: Sport, Politics and the Moral Order* (New Rochelle: Astride D. Caratzas, 1986), p.111.
45. Arnd Krüger, 'Strength through joy: The culture of consent under fascism, Nazism and Francoism', in Jim Riordan and Arnd Krüger (eds), *The International Politics of Sport in the Twentieth Century* (London: Spon, 1999), p.68.
46. Ibid; see also Hoberman, *The Olympic Crisis*, p.111.
47. Shearman, *Athletics and Football*, p.184, emphasis added.
48. Ibid., p.185.
49. Ibid., p.186.
50. McWhirter and McWhirter, *Get to your Marks*, p.54. On the varying size of running tracks and the case for and against the standardized 400-metre track, see Alphonse Juilland, *Rethinking Track and Field: The Future of the World's Oldest Sport* (Milan: SEP Editrice, 2002), pp.160–5.
51. Shearman noted that the AAA accepted performances where competitors 'covered more than a full lap, and so run uphill and downhill. Even this, however, can hardly be considered strictly fair, as experience shows that more time is gained running down and long and steady decline than is lost by coming up a short stiff incline'; Shearman, *Athletics and Football*, p.186.
52. Ibid., p.87.
53. Quoted in Norbert Müller (ed.), *Olympism: Pierre de Coubertin 1863–1937: Selected Writings* (Lausanne: International Olympic Committee, 2000), p.418.
54. Robert Sack, *Human Territoriality* (Cambridge: Cambridge University Press, 1986).
55. Guy Butler, *Modern Athletics* (Cambridge: Cambridge University Press, 1929), p.74.
56. Sack, *Human Territoriality*.
57. Ibid.
58. Tuan, *Segmented Worlds and Self*, p.11.
59. Yi-Fu Tuan, *Landscapes of Fear* (Oxford: Blackwell, 1979), p.6.
60. Yi-Fu Tuan, 'Attention: Moral-cognitive geography', *Journal of Geography*, 86, 1 (1987), pp.11–13.
61. Ibid.
62. Ibid.
63. Yi-Fu Tuan, *The Good Life* (Madison: University of Wisconsin Press, 1986), p.93.
64. Yi-Fu Tuan, *Morality and Imagination* (Madison: University of Wisconsin Press, 1989), p.167.
65. David Seamon, *A Geography of the Lifeworld* (London: Croom Helm, 1979).
66. Ibid., p.59.
67. Yi-Fu Tuan, *Topophilia: A Study of Environmental Perception, Attitudes and Values* (Englewood Cliffs: Prentice Hall, 1974), p.4.
68. Ibid., p.93.
69. James McNeish, *Lovelock* (Auckland: Godwit, [1986] 1994), p.354.
70. Loader, *Testament of a Runner*, p.137.
71. On the idea of a stadium 'landscape ensemble', see Karl Raitz (ed.), *The Theater of Sport* (Baltimore: Johns Hopkins University Press, 1998).
72. Quoted in Müller, *Olympism*, p.262.
73. Micael Ekberg, 'Stockholms olympiastadion', in Jan Lindroth and Ann Katrin Atmer (eds), 'Idrotten Platser', *Bebyggelsehistorisk Tidskrift*, 40 (2002), p.102.
74. Quoted in Douglas Brown, *Theories of Beauty and Modern Sport: Pierre de Coubertin's Aesthetic Imperative for the Modern Olympic Movement, 1884–1914* (doctoral thesis, University of Western Ontario, 1997), p.267.
75. Ibid., p.268.
76. Sigmund Loland, *Fair Play: A Moral Norm System* (London: Routledge, 2002), pp.118–21.
77. See Daniel Wann, Merrill Melnick, Gordon Russell and Dale Pearse, *Sports Fans: The Psychology and Social Impact of Spectators* (London: Routledge, 2001).
78. Yi-Fu Tuan, *Dear Colleague: Common and Uncommon Observations* (Minneapolis: University of Minnesota Press, 2002), p.35. Contrast this with the Foucauldian view of 'docile bodies'.
79. Brown, *Theories of Beauty and Modern Sport*, p.264.
80. Tuan, *Dear Colleague*, p.119.

81. Patricia Nell Warren, *The Front Runner* (New York: Bantam, 1975), p.15.

82. Loader, *Testament of a Runner*, pp.154–5.

83. Kirsten Roessler, email communication, 14 Sept. 2001.

84. Adam Phillips, *Houdini's Box: On the Arts of Escape* (London: Faber, 2001), p.88. Phillips's work on Houdini's exhibitions of escape seems to be relevant to the study of sports in a variety of contexts.

85. Torbjörn Tännsjö, 'Is it fascistoid to admire sports heroes?', in Torbjörn Tännsjö and Claudio Tamburrini (eds), *Values in Sport* (London: Spon, 2000), pp.9–23.

86. For example, see James Coleman, 'Athletics in high school', *Annals of the American Academy of Political and Social Science*, 338, 1 (1961), pp.3–43.

87. Tuan, *Topophilia*, p.101.

88. Ibid., p.100. On patriotism in sport see Nicholas Dixon, 'A justification for moderate patriotism in sport', in Tännsjö and Tamburrini (eds), *Values in Sport*, pp.74–86, and Paul Gomberg, 'Patriotism in sports and war', in Tännsjö and Tamburrini (eds), *Values in Sport*, pp.87–98.

89. Quoted in Müller, *Olympism*, pp.589–90. De Coubertin alluded to an 'athletic geography' that may differ at times from political geography: Ibid., p.590.

90. P. Jain, 'On a discrepancy in track races', *Research Quarterly for Exercise and Sport*, 51, 4 (1980), p.432.

91. K.F. Dyer and T. Dwyer, *Running out of Time: An Examination of the Improvement in Running Records* (Kensington, NSW: New South Wales University Press, 1984), p.142.

92. Tadeusz Łobożewicz, *Meteorologie im Sport* (Berlin: Sportverlag, 1981).

93. Weiss, *Sport: A Philosophic Enquiry*, p.164.

94. Bannister, *First Four Minutes*, p.110.

95. Tom Jordan, *Pre: The Story of America's Greatest Running Legend* (Emmaus, PA: Rodale Press, [1977] 1997), p.22.

96. See Bale, 'A geographical theory of sport'.

97. See Reinhard Rürup, *1936: Die Olympischen Spiele und der Nationalsozialismus* (Berlin: Stiftung Topographie des Terrors, 1999), p.177.

98. Sigmund Loland, 'The logic of progress and the art of moderation in competitive sports', in Torbjörn Tännsjö and Claudio Tamburrini (eds), *Values in Sport* (London: Spon, 2000), p.43.

99. Sigmund Loland, 'Record sports: An ecological critique and a reconstruction', *Journal of the Philosophy of Sport*, 28, 2 (2001), p.136.

Chapter 3

1. Yi-Fu Tuan, *Topophilia: A Study of Environmental Perception, Attitudes and Values* (Englewood Cliffs: Prentice Hall, 1974), pp.102–6.

2. Raymond Williams, *The Country and the City* (London: Hogarth Press, 1985).

3. W.R. Loader, *Testament of a Runner* (London: Sportsmans Book Club, 1962), p.55.

4. Quoted in Amby Burfoot, *The Runner's Guide to the Meaning of Life* (New York: Rodale, 2000), p.101.

5. Ross McWhirter and Norris McWhirter, *Get to Your Marks!* (London: Kaye, 1951), p.82.

6. Amby Burfoot, *The Evolution of Training Systems*, http://www.runnersworld.com/training/evolution1,html (accessed 23 Feb. 2001).

7. Mike Spino and Jeffrey Warren, *Mike Spino's Mind/Body Running Program* (New York: Bantam, 1979), pp.4–5. I am grateful to Olav Ballisager (Aarhus University) for alerting me to this reference.

8. Ibid., p.5.

9. Quoted in Lennart Persson and Thomas Pettersson, *Svensk Friidrott 100 År* (Stockholm: Sellin, 1995), p.345. I am grateful to Niels Kayser Nielsen (Aarhus University) for translating this from the Swedish.

10. Loader, *Testament of a Runner*, p.22.

11. Herb Elliott, *The Golden Mile* (London: Cassell, 1961), p.98.

12. Gordon Pirie, *Running Fast and Injury Free*, http://www.geocities.com/Colosseum/Pressbox/2204/gordmw2a.doc (accessed 31 Oct. 2002).

13. Roger Bannister, *First Four Minutes* (London: Putnam, 1955), p.146.
14. Ibid., p.116.
15. Ibid., p.146.
16. Ibid., p.117.
17. Ibid., p.118.
18. Yi-Fu Tuan, *Landscapes of Fear* (Oxford: Blackwell, 1979), p.15.
19. Spino and Warren, *Mike Spino's Mind/Body Running Program*, p.4.
20. Quoted in Ross McWhirter, 'The long climb', *Athletics World*, 2, 5 (1954), p.35.
21. Burfoot, *The Evolution of Training Systems*.
22. Elliott, *The Golden Mile*, p.32.
23. Quoted in Murray Phillips and Frank Hicks, 'Conflict, tensions and complexities: Athletic training in Australia in the 1950s', *International Journal of the History of Sport*, 17, 7/8 (2000), p.218.
24. Elliott, *The Golden Mile*, p.44.
25. Percy Cerutty, *Middle-Distance Running* (London: Pelham, 1964), p.42.
26. Phillips and Hicks, 'Conflict, tensions and complexities', p.211.
27. Loader, *Testament of a Runner*, p.68.
28. Patricia Nell Warren, *The Front Runner* (New York: Bantam, 1975), p.107.
29. Martyn Bowden, 'Jerusalem, Dover Beach and King's Cross: Imagined places as metaphors for the British class struggle in *Chariots of Fire* and *The Loneliness of the Long-Distance Runner*', in Stuart Aitken and Leo Zonn (eds), *Place, Power and Spectacle: A Geography of Film* (Lanham: Rowman and Littlefield, 1994), p.77. The forename Colin appears in the film but not in the novella.
30. Alan Sillitoe, *The Loneliness of the Long-Distance Runner* (London: W.H. Allen, 1959), pp.18–19. On the poetics of Sillitoe's writing in this book see Serge Fenoulière, 'The loneliness of the long-distance runner', http://www.discip.crdp.ac-caen.fr/anglais/documents/sill5AA0.htm (accessed 29 Nov. 2001).
31. Bowden, 'Jerusalem, Dover Beach and King's Cross', p.78.
32. Ibid.
33. Roberto Quercetani and Rooney Magnusson, *Track and Field Performances through the Ages 1929–1936* (Florence: Association of Track and Field Statisticians, 1986).
34. Jack Schumacher, *Die Finnen, das grosse Sportvolk* (Berlin: Wilhelm Limpert Verlag, 1936), pp.83–4. I am grateful to Tuija Kilpelainen for the reference and to Ruth Bale for the translation into English.
35. Mervi Tervo, 'Nationalism, sports and gender in Finnish sports journalism in the early twentieth century', *Gender, Place and Culture*, 18, 2 (2001), pp.357–73.
36. On sport and environmental determinism, see John Bale, 'Lassitude and latitude: Observations on sport and environmental determinism', *International Review for the Sociology of Sport*, 37, 2 (2002), pp.147–58. On other forms of determinism in sport, notably Appleton's 'prospect-refuge theory' and Balint's psychoanalytic approach, see John Bale, *Landscapes of Modern Sport* (London: Leicester University Press, 1994), pp.122–5.
37. Peter Pirie, quoted in Dick Booth, *The Impossible Hero* (London: Corsica Press, 2000), p.100.
38. Yi–Fu Tuan, *Escapim* (Baltimore: Johns Hopkins University Press, 1998), p.19.
39. Tuan, *Landscapes of Fear*, p.144.
40. Gillian Rose, *Feminism and Geography: The Limits of Geographical Knowledge* (London: Verso, 1993), p.34; Marie-Luise Klein, 'Social-spatial conditions affecting women's sport. The case of the Ruhr area', *International Review for the Sociology of Sport*, 28, 2/3 (1993), pp.145–59; Tuan, *Landscapes of Fear*.
41. Peter Lovesey, *The Official Centenary History of the Amateur Athletics Association* (London: Guinness Superlatives, 1979), pp.14–15.
42. Dave Martin and Roger Gynn, *The Marathon Footrace* (Springfield, MA: Thomas, 1979), p.205.
43. Jean Baudrillard, *America* (London: Verso, 1989), p.19.
44. H. Berking and S. Neckel, 'Urban marathon: The staging of individuality as an urban event', *Theory, Culture and Society*, 20, 4 (1993), p.68.
45. Baudrillard, *America*, p.20.

46. Ibid.
47. Ibid., pp.20–1.
48. Christopher Winters, 'Running', *Landscape*, 24, 2 (1980), p.19.
49. Berking and Neckel, 'Urban marathon', p.71.
50. I am grateful to Tiffany Muller (University of Wisconsin) for this information.
51. Berking and Neckel, 'Urban marathon', pp.67–8.
52. David Harvey, *The Condition of Postmodernity* (Oxford: Blackwell, 1989), pp.177–9.
53. Bero Rigauer, *Sport and Work* (New York: Columbia University Press, 1981), p.39.
54. J.A. Mangan, *Athleticism in the Victorian and Edwardian Public School* (London: Frank Cass, [1981] 2000), pp.19–20.
55. Montague Shearman, *Athletics and Football* (London: Longmans, Green, 1888), p.377.
56. F.A.M. Webster, *Athletics* (London: Allen and Unwin, 1925), p.25.
57. Jay Appleton, *The Experience of Landscape* (Chichester: Wiley, 1975), p.179.
58. Yi-Fu Tuan, *The Good Life* (Madison: University of Wisconsin Press, 1986), p.25.
59. Alberto Salazar, *Alberto Salazar's Guide to Running* (Camden, ME: Ragged Island Press, 2001), p.41.
60. Tuan, *The Good Life*, p.114.
61. Winters, 'Running', p.22.
62. Tuan, *The Good Life*, p.114.
63. T.O. Beechcroft, 'The half-miler', in John Foster (ed.), *The Experience of Sport* (London: Longman, 1975), p.53.
64. Sillitoe, *The Loneliness of the Long Distance Runner*, pp.43 and 49.
65. D.G.A. Lowe, *Track and Field Athletics* (London: Pitman, 1935), p.5.
66. Yi-Fu Tuan, *Passing Strange and Wonderful: Aesthetics, Nature and Culture* (Washington, DC: Island Press, 1993), p.41.
67. Ibid.
68. Ibid.
69. See http://www.canadiandeathrace.com.
70. Tuan, *Passing Strange and Wonderful*, p.159.
71. Paul Adams, 'Peripatetic imagery and peripatetic sense of place', in Paul Adams, Steven Hoelscher and Karen Till (eds), *Textures of Place: Exploring Humanist Geographies* (Minneapolis: University of Minnesota Press, 2001), p.193.
72. Steven Connor, 'Slow going' (1998), http://www.bbk.ac.uk/eh/eng/skc/slow.htm (accessed 1 Dec. 2002).
73. Rebecca Solnit, *Wanderlust: A History of Walking* (New York: Bantam, 1979), p.128.
74. Burfoot, *The Runner's Guide to the Meaning of Life*, p.133.
75. Carl Sauer, 'The education of a geographer', *Annals of the Association of American Geographers*, 46, 3 (1956), p.299.

Chapter 4

1. Yi-Fu Tuan, *Dominance and Affection: The Making of Pets* (New Haven: Yale University Press, 1984), p.167.
2. Ibid., p.139.
3. Juha Heikkala, 'Discipline and excel: Techniques of the self and body in the logic of competing', *Sociology of Sport Journal*, 10, 4 (1993), p.401.
4. Ibid.
5. Gordon Pirie, *Running Wild* (London: W.H. Allen, 1961), p.18.
6. Heikkala, 'Discipline and excel', p.403.
7. Ibid., p.408.
8. Tuan, *Dominance and Affection*, p.118.
9. F.A.M. Webster, *Why? The Science of Athletics* (London: John F. Shaw, 1937), p.287.
10. Powerful investigative journalism and careful academic research show that sexual and other abuse of young athletes is widely prevalent in a variety of sports. For example, see respectively, Joan

Ryan, *Little Girls in Pretty Boxes* (London: Women's Press, 1996), and Celia Brackenridge, *Spoilsports* (London: Spon, 2000).

11. Leslie Heywood, *Pretty Good for a Girl: A Memoir* (New York: The Free Press, 1998), p.129.
12. Yi-Fu Tuan, *Who am I? An Autobiography of Emotion, Mind and Spirit* (Madison: University of Wisconsin Press, 1999), p.102.
13. Patricia Nell Warren, *The Front Runner* (New York: Bantam, 1975), p.6.
14. W.R. Loader, *Testament of a Runner* (London: Sportsmans Book Club, 1962), p.70.
15. Tuan, *Dominance and Affection*, p.108.
16. Ibid., p.174.
17. Ibid., p.175.
18. Alan Sillitoe, *The Loneliness of the Long-Distance Runner* (London: W.H. Allen, 1959), p.12.
19. The extent of sexual abuse in sport is outlined in Brackenridge, *Spoilsports*, but as studies of this subject tend to aggregate sports into various macro-groups, the extent to which runners are subject to abuse is not clearly known. It is not, however, negligible: see Heywood, *Pretty Good for a Girl*.
20. Yi-Fu Tuan, *Escapism* (Baltimore: Johns Hopkins University Press, 1998), p.125.
21. On apprenticeship in sport see Ejgil Jespersen, 'Modeling in sporting apprenticeship', *Nordisk Pedagogik*, 7, 3 (1997), pp.78–85.
22. Brackenridge, *Spoilsports*, p.84.
23. Robert Sands, *Instant Acceleration: Living in the fast Lane: The Cultural Identity of Speed* (Lanham, MY: University Press of America, 1995), p.110.
24. Ibid., p.30.
25. Yi-Fu Tuan, *Morality and Imagination* (Madison: University of Wisconsin Press, 1989), p.110.
26. Pirie, *Running Wild*, p.18.
27. Quoted in Dick Booth, *The Impossible Hero* (London: Corsica Press, 2000), p.100n.
28. Michael Burke, 'Obeying until it hurts: Coach-athlete relationships', *Journal of the Philosophy of Sport*, 28, 3 (2001), pp.227–40.
29. Jack Scott, *The Athletic Revolution* (New York: The Free Press, 1971), pp.38–9.
30. Ibid., p.44.
31. John Bale, *The Brawn Drain: Foreign Student-Athletes in American Universities* (Urbana: University of Illinois Press, 1991).
32. Murray Phillips and Frank Hicks, 'Conflict, tensions and complexities: Athletic training in Australia in the 1950s', *International Journal of the History of Sport*, 17, 7/8 (2000), p.219.
33. Quoted in Fred Wilt, *How they Train* (Los Altos: Track and Field News, 1959), pp.23–4.
34. Ron Clarke and Alan Trengrove, *The Unforgiving Minute* (London: Pelham, 1966), p.29.
35. Quoted in Herb Elliott, *The Golden Mile* (London: Cassell, 1961), pp.38–9.
36. Percy Cerutty, *Middle-Distance Running* (London: Pelham, 1964), p.174.
37. George Kneller, *The Educational Philosophy of National Socialism* (New Haven: Yale University Press, 1941), Chs. 5–6.
38. George Mosse, *The Image of Man* (New York: Oxford University Press, 1996), pp.96–7.
39. Phillips and Hicks, 'Conflict, tensions and complexities', p.211.
40. John Hoberman, *Sport and Political Ideology* (London: Heinemann, 1984), p.211.
41. Quoted in Dirk Lund Christensen, *Washindi: Løbere fra Kenya* (Copenhagen: Frydenlund, 2000), p.182.
42. Tuan, *Dominance and Affection*, p.15.
43. Bill Mallon, *The 1904 Olympic Games* (Jefferson, NC: McFarland, 1999).
44. The circumstances surrounding this event are discussed in William Baker, *Jesse Owens: An American Life* (New York: The Free Press, 1986), p.142.
45. Ibid., p.155.
46. Ibid., p.144.
47. Ibid.
48. Booth, *The Impossible Hero*, p.189.
49. Tuan, *Dominance and Affection*, p.134.
50. The revival of interest in 'racial science' is exemplified in academic and popular works. See, respectively, John Hoberman, *Darwin's Athletes: How Sport has Damaged Black America and*

Preserved the Myth of Race (Boston: Houghton Mifflin, 1997), and John Entine, *Taboo: Why Black Americans Dominate Sports and Why we're Afraid to Talk About it* (New York: Public Affairs, 2000). For another approach, see John Bale and Joe Sang, *Kenyan Running: Movement Culture, Geography and Global Change* (London: Frank Cass, 1996).

51. Ernest Cashmore, *Black Sportsmen* (London: Routledge, 1984).
52. Frantz Fanon, *Black Skin, White Masks* (London: Pluto Press, 1986).
53. Ben Carrington, 'Double-consciousness and the black British athlete', in K. Owusu (ed.), *Black British Culture and Society* (London: Routledge, 1999), pp.136–7.
54. Frank Murphy, *The Silence of Great Distance: Women Running Long* (Kansas City: WindSprint Press, 2000), p.149.
55. Quoted in Bernadette Deville-Danthu, *Le Sport en Noir et Blanc* (Paris: L'Harmattan, 1997), pp.121 and 316.
56. Elliott, *The Golden Mile*, p.121.
57. Steven Jackson, 'A twist of race: Ben Johnson and the Canadian crisis of racial and national identity', *Sociology of Sport Journal*, 15, 1 (1998), p.31.
58. Gunter Gebauer, 'On the role of everyday physical-fitness sports in our time', in Karin Volkwein (ed.), *Fitness as Cultural Phenomenon* (Münster: Waxman, 1998), p.85.
59. Chris Shilling, *The Body and Social Theory* (London: Sage, 1993), p.37.
60. Quoted in Booth, *The Impossible Hero*, p.98.
61. Roger Bannister, *First Four Minutes* (London: Putnam, 1955), p.74.
62. Ibid.
63. Booth, *The Impossible Hero*, p.40.
64. Heywood, *Pretty Good for a Girl*, p.147.
65. Tuan, *Dominance and Affection*, p.15.
66. Yi-Fu Tuan, *Passing Strange and Wonderful: Aesthetics, Nature and Culture* (Washington, DC: Island Press, 1993), p.38.
67. For example, Jean-Marie Brohm, *Sport: A Prison of Measured Time* (London: Ink Links, 1978), and Bero Rigauer, *Sport and Work* (New York: Columbia University Press, 1981).
68. Tuan, *Passing Strange and Wonderful*, p.38.
69. D.G.A. Lowe, *Track and Field Athletics* (London: Pitman, 1935), p.17.
70. John Hoberman, *Mortal Engines: The Science of Performance and the Dehumanization of Sports* (New York: The Free Press, 1992), p.68. Note also Mark Seltzer, *Bodies and Machines* (New York: Routledge, 1992).
71. Anson Rabinbach, *The Human Motor* (Berkeley: University of California Press, 1990); note also the title of physiologist A.V. Hill's *Living Machines* (London: Bell, 1945).
72. Hoberman, *Mortal Engines*, p.114.
73. Phillips and Hicks, 'Conflict, tensions and complexities', p.215. This view is contradicted by Roger Bannister, who observed that Stampfl, 'a friend with [an] attractive cheerful personality', had 'no wish to turn the athlete into a machine working at his dictation': Bannister, *First Four Minutes*, p.160.
74. See, for example, Anne Maxwell, *Colonial Photography and Exhibitions* (London: Leicester University Press, 1999).
75. A succinct review of Marey's work is found in Hoberman, *Mortal Engines*, pp.76–80.
76. Brohm, *Sport: A Prison of Measured Time*, p.55. See also William Hutchings, 'The work of play: Anger and the expropriated athletes of Alan Sillitoe and David Storey', *Modern Fiction Studies*, 33, 1 (1987), p.35.
77. Quoted in Susan Buck-Morss, *The Dialectics of Seeing* (Boston: MIT Press, 1997), p.326.
78. Lowe, *Track and Field Athletics*, p.11.
79. Howard Slusher, *Man, Sport and Existence* (London: Henry Kimpton, 1967), pp.112–13.
80. F.A.M. Webster, *Great Moments in Athletics* (London: Country Life, 1947), p.74.
81. Ibid.
82. F.A.M. Webster, *Olympic Cavalcade* (London: Hutchinson, 1948), p.114.
83. Martti Jukola, *Athletics in Finland* (Porvoo: Söderström, 1932), p.45, emphasis added.
84. See Hannu Itkonen and Seppo Knuuttila, 'Aika voi sun ainoastaan', *Suomen Urheiluhistoriallisen Seuran Vuosikirja* (1998), pp.197–218.

Notes   181

85. Veli-Matti Autio, 'Paavo Nurmi (1897–1973)', in *National Biography of Finland* (1993), http://www.kansallisbiografia.fi/english.html (accessed 11 May 2002).

86. Quoted from the writings of the German sociologist Heinz Risse, in Peter Kühnst, *Sport: A Cultural History in the Mirror of Art* (Dresden: Verlag der Kunst, 1996), p.298.

87. Kneller, *The Educational Philosophy of National Socialism*.

88. Rigauer, *Sport and Work*, p.34.

89. Reported in Wilt, *How they Train*, pp.84 and 87.

90. The French architect Le Corbusier rendered the house as 'machine for living in': see, for example, Michael Jones, *Living Machines* (San Francisco: Ignatius Press, 1995).

91. David Seamon, *A Geography of the Lifeworld* (London: Croom Helm, 1979), p.56.

92. Marty Liquori and Skip Myslenski, *On the Run: In Search of the Perfect Race* (New York: Morrow, 1979), p.211.

93. Heywood, *Pretty Good for a Girl*, p.150.

94. Cheryl Cole, 'Addiction, exercise and cyborgs: Technologies of deviant bodies', in Geneviève Rail (ed.), *Sport and Postmodern Times* (Albany: State University of New York Press, 1998), p.272.
See also Derek McCormack, 'Body shopping: Reconfiguring geographies of fitness', *Gender, Space and Culture*, 6, 2 (1999), pp.155–77.

95. Geneviève Rail, 'The dissolution of polarities as a megatrend in postmodern sport', in Fernand Landry, Marc Landry and Magdeleine Yerlès (eds), *Sport: the Third Millennium* (Sainte-Foy: Les presses de L'Université Laval, 1991), p.746.

96. Geneviève Rail, 'Seismography of the postmodern condition', in Geneviève Rail (ed.), *Sport and Postmodern Times* (Albany: State University of New York Press, 1998), p.148.

97. James McNeish, *Lovelock* (Auckland: Godwit, [1986] 1994), p.215. In 1969 Gordon Pirie was asked by a doctor what stimulants he took. When Pirie said that he took none, the doctor replied, 'Well, you must be one of the few mugs left who doesn't.' Pirie, *Running Wild*, p.29.

98. Knud Lundberg, *The Olympic Hope* (London: Stanley Paul, 1958), pp.50–1.

99. Ibid., p.51.

100. Ibid., p.29.

101. Ibid., pp.69–70.

102. Ibid., pp.77–8.

103. Quoted in Reinhard Rürup, *1936: Die Olympischen Spiele und der Nationalsozialismus* (Berlin: Stiftung Topographie des Terrors, 1999), p.201.

104. See Hoberman, *Mortal Engines*. The widespread use of doping is also stressed in Stephen Downes and Duncan Mackay, *Running Scared* (Edinburgh: Mainstream Publishing, 1996). For a thought-provoking essay on doping see Claudio Tamburrini, 'What's wrong with doping?', in Torbjörn Tännsjö and Claudio Tamburrini (eds), *Values in Sport* (London: Spon, 2000), pp.200–216.

105. Quoted in Murphy, *The Silence of Great Distance*, p.271.

106. Heywood, *Not Bad for a Girl*, pp.145–6.

107. Ibid., p.146; Murphy, *The Silence of Great Distance*, pp.270–1; Tamburrini, 'What's wrong with doping', p.216.

108. Kalevi Heinilä, 'Notes on inter-group conflicts in international sport', in Eric Dunning (ed.), *The Sociology of Sport* (London: Frank Cass, 1971), pp.343–51.

109. Tuan, *Dominance and Affection*, p.169.

110. Hoberman, *Mortal Engines*, p.27.

111. Brohm, *Sport: A Prison of Measured Time*, p.85. Brohm's source is the French newspaper, *Le Nouvel Observateur*.

112. Hoberman, *Mortal Engines*, pp.282–4.

113. Ibid., p.234.

114. Heywood, *Pretty Good for a Girl*.

115. Liquori and Myslenski, *On the Run*, p.120.

116. Bannister, *First Four Minutes*, p.31.

117. Ibid., p.107. The extent to which Bannister's claim of self-coaching was part of the Oxbridge habit of understating the seriousness with which he took running is not known. Some observers

do claim that Bannister obtained much more advice from Stampfl than he admitted. See Chapter 5.

118. Ibid., p.56.
119. Jespersen, 'Modeling in sporting apprenticeship', p.178.
120. Tuan, *Dominance and Affection*, p.176.
121. David Lowenthal, 'Making a pet of nature', in Paul Adams, Steven Hoelscher and Karen Till (eds), *Textures of Place: Exploring Humanist Geographies* (Minneapolis: University of Minnesota Press, 2001), pp.90–1. On the problem of 'trust' in coach-athlete relationships, see Debra Shogan, *The Making of High-Performance Athletes: Discipline, Diversity and Ethics* (Toronto: University of Toronto Press, 1999).
122. Tuan, *Dominance and Affection*, p.164.
123. Gebauer, 'On the role of everyday physical-fitness sports in our times', p.85.
124. Sands, *Instant Acceleration*, p.25.
125. Quoted in Brohm, *Sport: A Prison of Measured Time*, p.24.
126. Heywood, *Pretty Good for a Girl*, p.186.
127. Ibid., p.141.
128. Norbert Müller (ed.), *Olympism: Pierre de Coubertin 1863–1937: Selected Writings* (Lausanne: International Olympic Committee, 2000), pp.417–18.
129. Richard Lazarus, 'Cognitive-Motivational-Relational theory of emotion', in Yuri Hanin (ed.), *Emotions in Sport* (Champaign, Ill: Human Kinetics, 2000), p.44.
130. Robert Zeller, 'Running addiction and masculinity in David Foster's "Eye of the Bull"', unpublished paper.
131. Kevin Lewis, 'The lonely marathoner', *Theology Today*, 39, 1 (1982), http://theologytoday.ptsem .edu/apr1982/v–article4.htm (accessed 29 Nov. 2001).
132. Zeller, 'Running addiction and masculinity'.
133. Jeffrey Segrave, 'Sport as escape', *Journal of Sport and Social Issues*, 24, 1 (2000), p.76.
134. Quoted in Phillips and Hicks, 'Conflict, tensions and complexities', p.219.
135. McNeish, *Lovelock*, pp.340–1.
136. Ibid., p.69.
137. Elliott, *The Golden Mile*, p.39.
138. Pirie, *Running Wild*, p.27.
139. Bannister, *First Four Minutes*, p.165, emphasis added.
140. Ibid.
141. Tuan, *Escapism*, pp.126–9; *Who am I?*, p.101; and Yi-Fu Tuan, 'Geography and evil: A Sketch', in James Proctor and David Smith (eds), *Geography and Ethics: Journeys in a Moral Terrain* (London: Routledge, 1999) pp.113–15.
142. Quoted in Sally Magnusson, *The Flying Scotsman* (London: Quartet Books, 1981), p.45.
143. Cerutty, *Middle-Distance Running*, pp.81 and 159. Was Cerutty here thinking about Jesus on the cross?
144. Allen Guttmann, *The Erotic in Sports* (New York: Columbia University Press, 1996), p.108. I cannot say that I ever felt like this myself; afraid, yes, but not sexualized.
145. This subject is dealt with in the context of football (soccer) in Gerhard Vinnai, *Football Mania* (London: Ocean Books, 1973).
146. Murphy, *The Silence of Great Distance*, p.348.
147. Jim Denison,'An elephant's trunk', *Sport Literate*, 2, 3 (1998), pp.64–85.
148. Heywood, *Pretty Good for a Girl*, p.143.
149. Jim Denison, 'Boxed in', in Andrew Sparkes and Martti Silvenoinen (eds), *Talking Bodies: Men's Narratives of the Body and Sport* (Jyväskylä: SoPhi, 1999), pp.33–4.
150. Ibid., p.36.
151. Heywood, *Pretty Good for a Girl*, p.186–9.
152. Michael Messner, *Power at Play: Sports and the Problem of Masculinity* (Boston: Beacon Press, 1992).
153. Ibid, 147. On stopping running see also Murphy, *The Silence of Great Distance*.
154. Heywood, *Pretty Good for a Girl*, p.188.

155. Ron Hill, *The Long, Hard Road* (Hyde: Ron Hill Sports, 1982), Vol.2, p.423.
156. Pirkko Markula and Jim Denison, 'See spot run: Movement as an object of textual analysis', *Qualitative Enquiry*, 6, 3 (2000), pp.413–14.
157. Guttmann, *The Erotic in Sports*, p.94.
158. Ibid., p.93.
159. Ibid.
160. Sara Maitland, 'The loveliness of the long distance runner', in Joli Sandoz (ed.), *A Whole Other Ball Game: Women's Literature on Women's Sports* (New York: Noonday Press, 1997), p.165.
161. Warren, *The Front Runner*, p.17.
162. Quoted in Pronger, *The Arena of Masculinity* (London: GMP Publishers, 1990), p.30.
163. Warren, *The Front Runner*, p.16.
164. Norman Harris, *The Legend of Lovelock* (Wellington: Reed, 1964), p.80.
165. Michael Kane, *Modern Men: Mapping Masculinity in English and German Literature* (London: Cassell, 1999), pp.180–1.
166. Tuan, *Passing Strange and Wonderful*, p.37.
167. Pirie, *Running Wild*, p.19.
168. Quoted in Susan Bandy, 'The female athlete as protagonist: From Cynisca to Butcher', *Aethlon*, 15, 1 (1997), p.93.
169. Ibid.
170. McNeish, *Lovelock*, p.99.
171. Quoted in Mike Spino and Jeffrey Warren, *Mike Spino's Mind/Body Running Program* (New York: Bantam, 1979), p.21.
172. Amby Burfoot, *The Runner's Guide to the Meaning of Life* (New York: Rodale, 2000), p.80.
173. Nigel Thrift, 'The still point: Resistance, expressive embodiment and dance', in Steve Pile and Michael Keith (eds), *Geographies of Resistance* (London: Routledge, 1997), p.149.
174. Nigel Thrift, 'Entanglements of power', in Joanne Sharp, Chris Philo, Ronan Pattison and Paul Routledge (eds), *Entanglements of Power* (London: Routledge, 2000), p.274.
175. Quoted on BBC2 TV programme 'Reputations', screened 24 July 2001.
176. Quoted in Burfoot, *The Runner's Guide to the Meaning of Life*, p.66.
177. Pirie, *Running Wild*, p.19.
178. Susan Jackson and Mihaly Csikszentmihalyi, *Flow in Sports* (Champaign, Ill: Human Kineitics, 1999), p.36.
179. Ibid., p.128.
180. F.A.M. Webster, *Athletes in Action* (London: John F. Shaw, 1931), p.7.
181. Lewis, 'The lonely marathoner'.
182. Loader, *Testament of a Runner*, p.48.
183. Lewis, 'The lonely marathoner'.
184. Heywood, *Pretty Good for a Girl*, p.193.

Chapter 5

1. Michael Messner, *Power at Play: Sports and the Problem of Masculinity* (Boston: Beacon Press, 1992), p.13. It will be well known to pet owners that they can, on many occasions, display various forms of resistance to acts of domination.
2. Joanne Sharp, Chris Philo, Ronan Pattison and Paul Routledge, 'Introduction', in Joanne Sharp, Chris Philo, Ronan Pattison and Paul Routledge (eds), *Entanglements of Power* (London: Routledge, 2000), pp.1–43.
3. Tim Cresswell, *In Place/Out of Place: Geography, Ideology and Transgression* (Minneapolis: University of Minnesota Press, 1996), pp.22–3.
4. Ibid.
5. C.L.R. James, *Beyond a Boundary* (London: Stanley Paul, 1986). For a discussion of the 'boundary' as used by James, see Grant Farred, 'The Maple man: How cricket made a postcolonial intellectual', in Grant Farred (ed.), *Rethinking C.L.R. James* (Oxford: Blackwell, 1996), p.180.

6. Messner, *Power at Play*, p.13.
7. Quoted in Susan Buck-Morss, *The Dialectics of Seeing* (Boston: MIT Press, 1997), p.326.
8. Jean-Marie Brohm, *Sport: A Prison of Measured Time* (London: Ink Links, 1978), p.178.
9. James, *Beyond a Boundary*. On ways of 'reading' the boundary, see, for example, Ian Baucom, *Out of Place: Englishness, Empire and the Locations of Identity* (Princeton: Princeton University Press, 1999), and Farred, 'The Maple man'.
10. Kenneth Surin, 'C.L.R. James' materialist aesthetic of cricket', in Hilary Beckles and Brian Stoddart (eds), *Liberation Cricket* (Manchester: Manchester University Press, 1995), pp.318–19.
11. James McNeish, *The Man from Nowhere* (Auckland: Godwit, 1991), p.39.
12. As was customary at the time, no intermediate time was taken at 800 metres. However, the existing world record for 800 metres was 1:51.9, so Peltzer had broken two world records in a single race.
13. McNeish, *The Man from Nowhere*, p.39.
14. Ibid., p.42.
15. Ibid., p.39.
16. For example, in Roberto Quercetani, *Athletics* (Milan: Vallardi, 1990), and 'German Federation honour "Odd Otto"', http://www.athletics-online.co.uk/000311otto.htm (accessed 25 July 2001). Several allusions to Peltzer are made in James McNeish, *Lovelock* (Auckland: Godwit, [1986] 1994).
17. George Mosse, *The Image of Man* (New York: Oxford University Press, 1996).
18. Ibid.
19. Arnd Krüger, 'The homosexual and homoerotic in sport', in Jim Riordan and Arnd Krüger (eds), *The International Politics of Sport in the Twentieth Century* (London: Spon, 1999), p.206.
20. Dick Booth, *The Impossible Hero* (London: Corsica Press, 2000).
21. Gordon Pirie, 'Answers the questionnaire'. Pirie made this response to a questionnaire published in *Athletics Weekly* in the mid 1950s. I have been unable to track down the precise bibliographic details.
22. Booth, *The Impossible Hero*.
23. Roger Bannister, *First Four Minutes* (London: Putnam, 1955), p.190.
24. Bannister quoted in Booth, *The Impossible Hero*, p.95.
25. Bannister, *First Four Minutes*, p.55.
26. Quoted in Booth, *The Impossible Hero*, p.96.
27. Bannister, *First Four Minutes*, p.102.
28. Ibid., p.162.
29. Ibid., p.159.
30. Bernadette Deville-Danthu, *Le Sport en Noir et Blanc* (Paris: L'Harmattan, 1997).
31. John Bale and Joe Sang, *Kenyan Running: Movement Culture, Geography and Global Change* (London: Frank Cass, 1996).
32. David Wiggins, '"Great speed but little stamina": The historical debate over black athletic supremacy', *Journal of Sport History*, 16, 2 (1989), pp.158–85.
33. Roberto Quercetani and Fulvio Regli (eds), *International Athletics Annual* (London: World Sports, 1953), pp.30–1.
34. Quoted in Bale and Sang, *Kenyan Running*, p.6.
35. Quercetani and Regli, *International Athletics Annual*, pp.55–7.
36. Cresswell, *In Place/Out of Place*, p.26.
37. Carl Lewis with Jeffrey Marx, *Inside Track: My Professional Life in Amateur Track and Field* (New York: Simon and Schuster, 1992).
38. Ibid.
39. Stuart Hall, 'The spectacle of the "other"', in Stuart Hall (ed.), *Representation: Cultural Representations and Signifying Practices* (London: Sage, 1997), p.233.
40. Theresa Walton, 'Steve Prefontaine – From rebel with a cause to bourgeois hero', paper presented at symposium on 'Sport and Cultural Distinctiveness', Iowa City (1999).
41. Ibid.
42. Ibid.
43. Tom Jordan, *Pre: The Story of America's Greatest Running Legend* (Emmaus, PA: Rodale Press, [1977] 1997).

44. Theresa Walton, 'Steve Prefontaine'.
45. Ibid.
46. Ron Hill, *The Long, Hard Road* (Hyde: Ron Hill Sports, 1981), Vol.1, p.6.
47. Ibid., p.7.
48. 'Wizard' Wilson and the 'Tough of the Track', http://members.tripod.com/waterford.ac/new_page_5htm (accessed 23 Nov. 2001).
49. David Young, *The Modern Olympics: A Struggle for Revival* (Baltimore: Johns Hopkins University Press, 1996), pp.35–6.
50. Martyn Bowden, 'Jerusalem, Dover Beach and King's Cross: Imagined places as metaphors for the British class struggle in *Chariots of Fire* and *The Loneliness of the Long-Distance Runner*', in Stuart Aitken and Leo Zonn (eds), *Place, Power and Spectacle: A Geography of Film* (Lanham: Rowman and Littlefield, 1994), pp.69–100; Alan Sillitoe, *The Loneliness of the Long-Distance Runner* (London: W.H. Allen, 1959). In the novel the runner is known only as Smith. The forename Colin is introduced in the movie version of the story.
51. Hans Lenk and Gunter Gebauer, 'Sport and sports literature from the perspective of methodological interpretation', *Aethlon*, 5, 2 (1988), p.83.
52. Robert Zeller, 'Running away: "The Loneliness of the Long–Distance Runner" revisited', *Aethlon*, 13, 1 (1995), p.49.
53. Sillitoe, *Loneliness of the Long-Distance Runner*, pp.51–2.
54. Ibid., p.53.
55. Bowden, 'Jerusalem, Dover Beach, and King's Cross', p.85.
56. Ibid., p.85.
57. Lenk and Gebauer, 'Sport and sports literature', p.83.
58. Allen Guttmann, 'Faustian athletes? Sports as a theme in Modern German literature', *Modern Fiction Studies*, 33, 1 (1987), p.22.
59. William Hutchings, 'The work of play: Anger and the expropriated athletes of Alan Sillitoe and David Storey', *Modern Fiction Studies*, 33, 1 (1987), p.39, italics added.
60. Zeller, 'Running away'.
61. Frank Murphy, *The Silence of Great Distance: Women Running Long* (Kansas City: WindSprint Press, 2000), p.303. Murphy's book – an idiosyncratic history of women's distance running – provides a more detailed account of Ormsby's running history. See also Sharon Robb, 'Runner's story: Why did Kathy Ormsby jump off that bridge?' in Ron Rappoport (ed.), *A Kind of Grace* (Berkeley: Zenobia Press, 1994), pp.107–13; Zeller, 'Running away'; and Phil Richards, 'A spirited recovery' (1996), www://suffering.net/ormsby.htm (accessed 17 June 2002).
62. Murphy, *The Silence of Great Distance*, p.328.
63. Ibid., p.342.
64. Ibid., p.350.
65. Zeller, 'Running away', p.49. Zeller also alludes to the example of distance runner Gerry Lindgren as an athlete who 'ran away' from track – but not literally as in the cases of Smith and Ormsby.
66. Murphy, *The Silence of Great Distance*, p.345.
67. Zeller, 'Running away', p.46.
68. Richards, 'A spirited recovery'.
69. Murphy, *The Silence of Great Distance*.
70. Eugene Levitt, quoted in Murphy, *The Silence of Great Distance*, p.367.
71. Zeller, 'Running away', p.46. Zeller argues that the relationship between Smith and Ormsby lies in the nature of serious competitive running and the way in which it forms runners as subjects. Both Smith and Ormsby found themselves in situations where they were expected to train on their own in the service of an institution. Their self-identities clash with those imposed on them by the institution; ibid.
72. Christopher Winters, 'Running', *Landscape*, 24, 2 (1980), p.19.
73. Annemarie Jutel, 'Thou dost run as in flotation: Femininity and the emergence of the women's marathon', unpublished paper.
74. William Morgan, 'Hassiba Boulmerka and Islamic Green: International sports, cultural differences,

and their postmodern interpretation', in Geneviève Rail (ed.), *Sport and Postmodern Times* (Albany: State University of New York Press, 1998), p.347.
75. Ibid., pp.348–9.

Chapter 6

1. Yi-Fu Tuan, *Escapism* (Baltimore: Johns Hopkins University Press, 1998), p.i.
2. Ibid., p.31.
3. In my case, the dreams were converted into a sort of reality: I did run in Sweden (in fact, in the Olympic Stadium) and at White City, but my results were pale imitations of those of my heroes.
4. Jeffrey Segrave, 'Sport as escape', *Journal of Sport and Social Issues*, 24, 1 (2000), p.61. On the other hand, sport may be attractive because of its similarity to everyday life, rather than because it is different.
5. John Rooney, *The Recruiting Game* (Lincoln: University of Nebraska Press, 1980), and John Bale, *The Brawn Drain: Foreign Student-Athletes in American Universities* (Urbana: University of Illinois Press, 1991).
6. See, for example, Harold McConnell, 'Recruiting patterns in Midwestern major college football', *Geographical Perspectives*, 53, 1 (1984), pp.27–43.
7. David Ley, 'Cultural-humanistic geography', *Progress in Human Geography*, 9, 3 (1985), p.417.
8. Tim Cresswell, 'The production of mobilities', *New Formations*, 43 (2001), p.15.
9. Yi-Fu Tuan, *Cosmos and Hearth: A Cosmopolite's Viewpoint* (Minneapolis: University of Minnesota Press, 1996).
10. Ibid., p.2.
11. A.R. Downer, *Running Recollections and How to Train* (Tarland: Balgownie Books, [1902] 1982), p.31.
12. Marty Liquori and Skip Myslenski, *On the Run: In Search of the Perfect Race* (New York: Morrow, 1979), p.51.
13. Zygmunt Bauman, *Postmodern Ethics* (Oxford: Blackwell, 1994), p.240.
14. Tuan, *Escapism*, p.9.
15. Roger Bannister, *First Four Minutes* (London: Putnam, 1955), p.97.
16. Liquori and Myslenski, *On the Run*, p.167.
17. Tuan, *Cosmos and Hearth*, p.134.
18. Ibid., p.157.
19. Gordon Pirie, *Running Wild* (London: W.H. Allen, 1961), p.129.
20. Cited in František Kožík, *Zátopek the Marathon Victor* (Prague: Artia, 1954), p.102.
21. Pirie, *Running Wild*, p.191.
22. Liquori and Myslenski, *On the Run*, pp.228–9.
23. Yi-Fu Tuan, *Topophilia: A Study of Environmental Perception, Attitudes and Values* (Englewood Cliffs: Prentice Hall, 1974), p.63.
24. Quoted in Norbert Müller (ed.), *Olympism: Pierre de Coubertin 1863–1937: Selected Writings* (Lausanne: International Olympic Committee, 2000), p.187.
25. Patricia Nell Warren, *The Front Runner* (New York: Bantam, 1975), p.126.
26. James McNeish, *Lovelock* (Auckland: Godwit, [1986] 1994). On the 1936 Olympics see Richard Mandell, *The Nazi Olympics* (New York: Ballantyne, 1971), and the stunning book edited by Reinhard Rürup, *1936: Die Olympischen Spiele und der Nationalsozialismus* (Berlin: Stiftung Topographie des Terrors, 1999).
27. Yi-Fu Tuan, *Space and Place: The Perspective of Experience* (Minniapolis: University of Minnesota Press, 1977), p.183.
28. Ibid.
29. Tuan, *Cosmos and Hearth*, p.2.
30. Tuan, *Escapism*, p.5.
31. Cresswell, 'The production of mobilities', p.16
32. The language in this paragraph is suggested by Sarah Whatmore, *Hybrid Geographies* (London: Routledge, 2002), p.31.

33. Ibid., p.57.
34. Jon Entine, *Taboo: Why Black Americans Dominate Sports and Why we're Afraid to Talk About it* (New York: Public Affairs, 2000), p.56.
35. Ibid., emphasis added.
36. Bale, *The Brawn Drain*.
37. Ibid.
38. Ibid., p.141.
39. Ibid.
40. Ibid., pp.141–2.
41. Tuan, *Escapism*, p.9.
42. Jim Peters, *In the Long Run* (London: Cassell, 1955), p.44.
43. Kalevi Heinilä, 'Notes on inter-group conflicts in international sport', in Eric Dunning (ed.), *The Sociology of Sport* (London: Frank Cass, 1971), pp.343–51.
44. Wilbur Zelinsky, 'The world and its identity crisis', in Paul Adams, Steven Hoelscher and Karen Till (eds), *Textures of Place: Exploring Humanist Geographies* (Minneapolis: University of Minnesota Press, 2001), p.133.
45. Ibid., p.124.
46. Peter Taylor, 'The state as a container: Territoriality in the modern world-system', *Progress in Human Geography*, 18, 2 (1994), pp.151–62.
47. Don Mitchell, *Cultural Geography* (Oxford: Blackwell, 2000), p.262.
48. Ibid., p.141.
49. Zelinsky, 'The world and its identity crisis', p.142.
50. Cresswell, 'The production of mobilities', p.16.
51. Brian Vine, *Zola* (London: Stanley Paul, 1994).
52. Zygmunt Bauman, 'Morality in an age of contingency', in Paul Heelas, Scott Lash and Paul Morris (eds), *Detraditionalization* (Oxford: Blackwell, 1996), p.52.
53. Budd and Maree were not the only South African runners to change nationality during the 1980s. Others included the steeplechaser Jon da Sliva who represented Portugal, 800 metres runner Mark Handelsman who migrated to Israel, Cornelia Burki became a Swiss 1,500 metres and 3,000 metres champion, and Matthew Moshweratu selected Botswana as a nation to represent in the Olympics.
54. Quoted in John Bale and Joe Sang, *Kenyan Running: Movement Culture, Geography and Global Change* (London: Frank Cass, 1996), p.184.
55. Quoted in Ben Carrington, 'Double consciousness and the black British athlete', in K. Owusu (ed.), *Black British Culture and Society* (London: Routledge, 1999), pp.135–6.
56. Ibid., p.136.
57. Stephen Downes and Duncan Mackay, *Running Scared* (Edinburgh: Mainstream Publishing, 1996), p.35.
58. Stuart Hall, 'The spectacle of the "other"', in Stuart Hall (ed.), *Representation: Cultural Representations and Signifying Practices* (London: Sage, 1997), pp.228–9.
59. Carrington, 'Double consciousness and the black British athlete', p.152.
60. Billy Ehn, 'National feeling in sport: The case of Sweden', *Ethnologia Europea*, 19, 1 (1988), pp.57–66.
61. Toni Bruce and Christopher Hallinan, 'Cathy Freeman: The Quest for Australian Identity', in David Andrews and Steven Jackson (eds), *Sports Stars: The Cultural Politics of Sporting Celebrity* (London: Routledge, 2001), p.262.
62. Ibid., p.267.
63. This reading of Johnson is based on Steven Jackson, 'A twist of race: Ben Johnson and the Canadian crisis of racial and national identity', *Sociology of Sport Journal*, 15, 1 (1998), pp.21–40.
64. Ibid., p.27.
65. Ibid., p.28.
66. For a brief biography of Katz see Martti Hannus, 'The life story of Elias Katz', *Track Stats*, 39, 3 (2001), pp.35–8.
67. Cresswell, 'The production of mobilities'.

Chapter 7

1. Yi-Fu Tuan, *The Good Life* (Madison: University of Wisconsin Press, 1986), p.157.
2. Yi-Fu Tuan, *Passing Strange and Wonderful: Aesthetics, Nature and Culture* (Washington, DC: Island Press, 1993), p.19.
3. Robert Sack, *Homo Geographicus* (Baltimore: Johns Hopkins University Press, 1997), p.212.
4. Ibid.
5. F.A.M. Webster, *Athletics* (London: Allen and Unwin, 1925), p.61.
6. D.G.A. Lowe, *Track and Field Athletics* (London: Pitman, 1935), p.17.
7. Yi-Fu Tuan, email communication, 14 Nov. 2002.
8. Sack, *Homo Geographicus*, p.212.
9. Cited in František Kožík, *Zátopek the Marathon Victor* (Prague: Artia, 1954), p.84.
10. Gunter Gebauer, 'On the role of physical-fitness sports in our time', in Karin Volkwein (ed.), *Fitness as Cultural Phenomenon* (Münster: Waxman, 1998), p.85.
11. Drew Hyland, *Philosophy of Sport* (New York: Paragon House, 1990), p.24.
12. F.A.M. Webster, *Athletes in Action* (London: John F. Shaw, 1931), p.7.
13. Reported in Amanda Smith, 'Herb Elliott and Percy Cerutty', *The Sports Factor* (broadcast 5 Jan. 2001), http://www.abc.net.au/rn/talks/8.30/sportsf/.
14. Quoted in Murray Phillips and Frank Hicks, 'Conflict, tensions and complexities: Athletic training in Australia in the 1950s', *International Journal of the History of Sport*, 17, 7/8 (2000), p.219.
15. Gunter Gebauer, 'Citius-Altius-Fortius and the problem of sport ethics: A philosopher's viewpoint', in Fernand Landry, Marc Landry and Magdeleine Yerlès (eds), *Sport: the Third Millennium* (Sainte-Foy: Les presses de L'Université Laval, 1991), p.468.
16. F.A.M. Webster, *Why? The Science of Athletics* London: John F. Shaw, 1937), p.55.
17. Donald Hall, 'Introduction: Muscular Christianity', in Donald Hall (ed.), *Muscular Christianity: Embodying the Victorian Age* (Cambridge: Cambridge University Press, 1994), p.7.
18. Ibid., pp.7–8.
19. Norman Vance, *The Sinews of the Spirit: The Ideal of Christian Manliness in Victorian Literature and Religious Thought* (Cambridge: Cambridge University Press, 1985), p.172.
20. Guy Butler, *Modern Athletics* (Cambridge: Cambridge University Press, 1929), p.6.
21. Ibid., pp.5–6.
22. Yi-Fu Tuan, *Morality and Imagination* (Madison: University of Wisconsin Press, 1989), p.3.
23. Vance, *The Sinews of the Spirit*, p.192.
24. Ibid., p.26.
25. Ibid., pp.47–8.
26. Thomas Hughes, *Tom Brown's Schooldays* (London: Dent, [1857] 1949), part 1, Ch.6, p.115.
27. Quoted in Sally Magnusson, *The Flying Scotsman* (London: Quartet Books, 1981), p.67.
28. Mike Spino and Jeffrey Warren, *Mike Spino's Mind/Body Running Program* (New York: Bantam, 1979), p.14.
29. Frank Murphy, *The Silence of Great Distance: Women Running Long* (Kansas City: WindSprint Press, 2000), p.303.
30. Quoted in Ove Korsgaard, 'Sport as a practice of religion', in John Carter and Arnd Krüger (eds), *Ritual and Record: Sports Records and Quantification in Pre-Modern Societies* (New York: Greenwood Press, 1990), p.115.
31. Ibid., p.121.
32. Ibid., p.117. The view that serious sport can be read as a religion is supported by R. Coles, 'Football as a "surrogate" religion', in M. Hill (ed.), *Sociological Yearbook of Religions in Britain*, 3 (1975), pp.61–77.
33. On the 'ritual and record debate' see John Carter and Arnd Krüger, *Ritual and Record: Sports Records and Quantification in Pre–Modern Societies* (New York: Greenwood Press, 1990).
34. Alan Cairns, *Prelude to Imperialism* (London: Routledge, 1965), p.78.
35. See http://www.chepkero.com/history.html, emphasis added (accessed 17 Jan. 2002).
36. See http://www.ryunrunning.com/.

37. Department of Environment, Transport and Regions, *Sport: Raising the Game* (London: Department of National Heritage, 1995), p.40.
38. Ibid., p.iii.
39. Vance, *The Sinews of the Spirit*, p.192.
40. Michael Novak, *The Joy of Sports* (Lanham: Hamilton Press, 1988), p.209.
41. J.A. Mangan, *Athleticism in the Victorian and Edwardian Public School* (London: Frank Cass, [1981] 2000), p.84.
42. Jim Ryun with Mike Phillips, *In Quest of Gold: The Jim Ryun Story* (San Francisco: Harper and Row, 1984), pp.152–3.
43. Yi-Fu Tuan, *Escapism* (Baltimore: Johns Hopkins University Press, 1998), p.202.
44. Quoted in Ron Clarke and Alan Trengrove, *The Unforgiving Minute* (London: Pelham, 1966), p.54.
45. Gebauer, 'Citius-Altius-Fortius', p.470.
46. Tuan, *Morality and Imagination*, p.3.
47. Ibid., p.4.
48. Ibid.
49. Ibid., p.3.
50. Allen Guttmann, 'Faustian athletes? Sports as a theme in Modern German literature', *Modern Fiction Studies*, 33, 1 (1987), p.22.
51. Tuan, *The Good Life*, p.3.
52. Tuan, *Morality and Imagination*, p.97.
53. Quoted in Kožík, *Zátopek the Marathon Victor*, p.84.
54. Wilbur Zelinsky, 'When every place is above average: Welcoming signs along America's highways', *Landscape*, 30, 1 (1988), pp.1–10.
55. D.P. Thomson, *Scotland's Greatest Athlete*, quoted in Vance, *The Sinews of the Spirit*, p.45.
56. Magnusson, *The Flying Scotsman*, p.40.
57. Ibid.
58. Ibid., p.100.
59. Roberto Quercetani, *Athletics* (Milan: Vallardi, 1990), p.48.
60. Magnusson, *The Flying Scotsman*.
61. Susan Bachrach, *The Nazi Olympics Berlin 1936* (Boston: Little, Brown, 2000), p.63.
62. Ibid.
63. Quoted in Peter Levine, *From Ellis Island to Ebberts Field: Sport and the American Jewish Experience* (New York: Oxford University Press, 1992), p.222.
64. Ibid.
65. Having made the trip to Berlin, Glickman and Stoller were not included in the 4 x 100 metres relay team. It could have been an act of anti-Semitism; alternatively, the coaches could have favoured an athlete from their own university. See Allen Guttmann, *The Olympics* (Urbana: University of Illinois Press, 1992), p.69. Protests by Glickman and Stoller were not necessarily met with sympathy by the Jewish press in the USA. One journalist observed that they had the chance to protest by not taking the trip to Germany: 'By sacrificing their honor for a free boat ride, they have sacrificed all right to sympathy.' Quoted in Levine, *From Ellis Island to Ebberts Field*, p.228.
66. James McNeish, *Lovelock* (Auckland: Godwit, [1986] 1994), p.207.
67. Email communication from Frank Murphy, 16 July 2002.
68. Murphy, *The Silence of Great Distance*, pp.358 and 362, emphasis added. However, the impact of Ormsby's tragedy affected Herbst for the rest of her running career; Ibid.
69. The definitive work on the massacre at Munich is Simon Reeve, *One Day in September* (London: Faber, 2000).
70. Guttmann, *The Olympics*, p.140.
71. Quoted in Reeve, *One Day in September*, p.123.
72. Ibid., p.125.
73. Ibid., p.124.
74. Tom Jordan, *Pre: The Story of America's Greatest Running Legend* (Emmaus, PA: Rodale Press, [1977] 1997), p.56.
75. Ibid., p.57.

76. Ron Hill, *The Long, Hard Road* (Hyde: Ron Hill Sports, 1981, 1982), Vol.2, p.208.
77. Ibid., pp.208–10.
78. Jordan, *Pre*, pp.58–9.
79. Hill, *The Long, Hard Road,* Vol.2, p.239.
80. Alan Sillitoe, *Mountains and Caverns* (London: W.H. Allen, 1975), p.88.
81. Gyöngi Földesi, 'The use of autobiographies in sport sociology: A pilot study', in Otmar Weiss and Wolfgang Schultz (eds), *Sport in Space and Time* (Vienna: Vienna University Press, 1995), pp.147–56.
82. James McNeish, *The Man from Nowhere* (Auckland: Godwit, 1991), p.27. Godfrey Brown was the UK 400 metres silver medallist at the 1936 Berlin Olympics. My selection of athletes used to exemplify humanness (in this and other chapters) is rather arbitrary. Those who are regarded widely as more notorious ex-runners – like O.J. Simpson and Ben Johnson, for example – are not mentioned. Such runners' indiscretions are already over-documented and researched. There are too many cheats and tricksters in running to record here – and that is not my aim anyway. For some examples, see Stephen Downes and Duncan Mackay, *Running Scared* (Edinburgh: Mainstream Publishing, 1996).
83. Tuan, *Morality and Imagination*, p.11.
84. Clarke and Trengrove, *The Unforgiving Minute*, p.41. The Bannister race was described by an Australian journalist as 'highly organized' – in other words, not a truly run *race*: Harry Gordon, *Young Men in a Hurry* (Melbourne: Lansdowne Press, 1962), p.105.
85. Marty Liquori and Skip Myslenski, *On the Run: In Search of the Perfect Race* (New York: Morrow, 1979), p.196.
86. Ibid.
87. Carl Lewis with Jeffrey Marx, *Inside Track: My Professional Life in Amateur Track and Field* (New York: Simon and Schuster, 1992), p.43.
88. Ibid., p.47.
89. Spencer Wertz, *Talking a Good Game: Inquiries into the Principles of Sport* (Dallas: Southern Methodist University Press, 1991), p.69.
90. Tuan, *Morality and Imagination*, p.11.
91. See Steve Bailey, *Science in the Service of Physical Education and Sport* (Chichester: Wiley, 1996); note also John Bale, 'Geography and the Olympics: An evaluation of the work of Ernst Jokl', *Journal of Science and Medicine in Sport*, 3, 3 (2000), pp.223–9.
92. Ernst Jokl, 'Indisposition after running', in E. Jokl and E. Simon (eds), *International Research in Sport and Physical Education* (Springfield: Thomas, 1960), p.682.
93. A.L. Boshoff, *Die geskienis van die Departement van Liggaamlike Opvoedkunde aan die Universiteit van Stellenbosch (1936–1975)*, (master's dissertation, Stellenbosch University, 1981), p.36. The truth of this story depends entirely on Boshoff's honesty and accuracy in recording Jokl's words.
94. Tuan, *Morality and Imagination*, p.151.
95. See John Bale, 'The mysterious Professor Jokl', paper read at the annual conference of the British Society of Sports History, Leicester (2002).
96. Michael Crick, *Stranger than Fiction* (London: Penguin, 1995).
97. Ibid., p.106.
98. Ibid.
99. Tuan, *Morality and Imagination*, p.4.
100. Ibid., p.132.
101. Tuan, *The Good Life*, p.11.
102. Yi-Fu Tuan, 'Geography and evil: A sketch', in James Proctor and David Smith (eds), *Geography and Ethics: Journeys in a Moral Terrain* (London: Routledge, 1999), p.113.
103. Tuan, *Morality and Imagination*, p.154.
104. Tuan, 'Geography and evil', p.109.
105. Quoted in Reinhard Rürup, *1936: Die Olympischen Spiele und der Nationalsozialismus* (Berlin: Stiftung Topographie des Terrors, 1999), p.210.
106. Arnd Krüger, 'The homosexual and homoerotic in sport', in Jim Riordan and Arnd Krüger (eds), *The International Politics of Sport in the Twentieth Century* (London: Spon, 1999), p.206.

107. Rürup, *1936: Die Olympischen Spiele*, p.210.
108. Ibid., p.204.
109. Roberto Quercetani, *Athletics: A History of Modern Track and Field Athletics* (Milan: Vallardi, 1990) p.87.
110. Tuan, *The Good Life*, p.23.
111. Tuan, *Escapism*, p.114.
112. Tuan, 'Geography and evil', p.117.
113. Tuan, *The Good Life*, p.32.
114. Quoted in Matti Goksøyr, '"One certainly expected a great deal more from the savages". The Anthropology days at St. Louis and their aftermaths', *International Journal of the History of Sport*, 7, 2 (1990), pp.297–86.
115. Colin Leys, 'Sport, the state and dependency theory', in Hart Cantelon and Richard Gruneau (eds), *Sport, Culture and the Modern State* (Toronto: Toronto University Press, 1982), p.310.
116. Tuan, *Morality and Imagination*, p.176.

Bibliography

Abler, Ronald, 'Effects of space-adjusting techniques on the human geography of the future', in Ronald Abler, Donald Janelle, Allen Philbrick and John Sommer (eds), *Human Geography in a Shrinking World* (North Scituate, MA: Duxbury Press, 1975), pp.36–56.

Adams, Paul, 'Peripatetic imagery and peripatetic sense of place', in Paul Adams, Steven Hoelscher and Karen Till (eds), *Textures of Place: Exploring Humanist Geographies* (Minneapolis: University of Minnesota Press, 2001), pp.186–206.

Adams, Paul, Steven Hoelscher and Karen Till, 'Place in context: Rethinking humanist geographies', in Paul Adams, Steven Hoelscher and Karen Till (eds), *Textures of Place: Exploring Humanist Geographies* (Minneapolis: University of Minnesota Press, 2001), pp.xiii–xxxiii.

Adams, Paul, Steven Hoelscher and Karen Till (eds), *Textures of Place: Exploring Humanist Geographies* (Minneapolis: University of Minnesota Press, 2001).

Appleton, Jay, *The Experience of Landscape* (Chichester: Wiley, 1975).

Augé, Marc, *Non-Places* (London: Verso, 1995).

Autio, Veli-Matti, 'Paavo Nurmi (1897–1973)', in *National Biography of Finland* (1993), http://www.kansallisbiografia.fi/english.html (accessed 11 May 2002).

Bachrach, Susan, *The Nazi Olympics Berlin 1936* (Boston: Little, Brown, 2000).

Bailey, Steve, *Science in the Service of Physical Education and Sport* (Chichester: Wiley, 1996).

Baker, William, *Jesse Owens: An American Life* (New York: The Free Press, 1986).

Bale, John, *The Brawn Drain: Foreign Student-Athletes in American Universities* (Urbana: University of Illinois Press, 1991).

Bale, John, *Landscapes of Modern Sport* (London: Leicester University Press, 1994).

Bale, John, 'Geography and the Olympics: An evaluation of the work of Ernst Jokl', *Journal of Science and Medicine in Sport*, 3, 3 (2000), pp.223–9.

Bale, John, 'Nyandika Maiyoro and Kipchoge Keino: Transgression, colonial rhetoric and the postcolonial athlete', in David Andrews and Steven Jackson (eds), *Sports Stars: The Cultural Politics of Sporting Celebrity* (London: Routledge, 2001), pp.218–30.

Bale, John, 'Lassitude and latitude: Observations on sport and environmental determinism', *International Review for the Sociology of Sport*, 37, 2 (2002), pp.147–58.

Bale, John, 'The mysterious Professor Jokl', paper read at the annual conference of the British Society of Sports History, Leicester (2002).

Bale, John, 'A geographical theory of sport', in John Nauright and Verner Møller (eds), *The Essence of Sport* (Odense: University Press of Southern Denmark, 2003), pp.81–91.

Bale, John and Joe Sang, *Kenyan Running: Movement Culture, Geography and Global Change* (London: Frank Cass, 1996).

Bandy, Susan, 'The female athlete as protagonist: From Cynisca to Butcher', *Aethlon*, 15, 1 (1997), pp.89–97.

Bannister, Roger, *First Four Minutes* (London: Putnam, 1955).

Bates, Catherine, *Play in a Godless World* (London: Open Gates Press, 1999).

Battistia, Gareth (ed.), *The Runner's Literary Companion* (New York: Penguin, 1994).

Baucom, Ian, *Out of Place: Englishness, Empire and the Locations of Identity* (Princeton: Princeton University Press, 1999).

Baudrillard, Jean, *America* (London: Verso, 1989).

Baudrillard, Jean, *The Transparency of Evil* (London: Verso, 1993).

Bauman, Zygmunt, *Postmodern Ethics* (Oxford: Blackwell, 1994).

Bauman, Zygmunt, 'Morality in an age of contingency', in Paul Heelas, Scott Lash and Paul Morris (eds), *Detraditionalization* (Oxford: Blackwell, 1996), pp.49–58.

Bauman, Zygmunt, *Globalization* (Cambridge: Polity Press, 1998).

Beechcroft, T.O., 'The half-miler', in John Foster (ed.), *The Experience of Sport* (London: Longman, 1975), pp.48–60.

Berking, H. and S. Neckel, 'Urban marathon: The staging of individuality as an urban event', *Theory, Culture and Society*, 20, 4 (1993), pp.63–78.

Booth, Dick, *The Impossible Hero* (London: Corsica Press, 2000).

Boshoff, A.L., *Die geskienis van die Departement van Liggaamlike Opvoedkunde aan die Universiteit van Stellenbosch (1936–1975)* (master's dissertation, Stellenbosch University, 1981).

Bowden, Martyn, 'Jerusalem, Dover Beach and King's Cross: Imagined places as metaphors for the British class struggle in *Chariots of Fire* and *The Loneliness of the Long-Distance Runner*', in Stuart Aitken and Leo Zonn (eds), *Place, Power and Spectacle: A Geography of Film* (Lanham: Rowman and Littlefield, 1994), pp.69–100.

Brackenridge, Celia, *Spoilsports* (London: Spon, 2000).

Brohm, Jean-Marie, *Sport: A Prison of Measured Time* (London: Ink Links, 1978).

Brown, Douglas, *Theories of Beauty in Modern Sport: Pierre de Coubertin's Aesthetic Imperative for the Modern Olympic Movement, 1884–1914* (doctoral thesis, University of Western Ontario, 1997).

Bruce, Toni and Christopher Hallinan, 'Kathy Freeman: The Quest for Australian Identity', in David Andrews and Steven Jackson (eds), *Sports Stars: The Cultural Politics of Sporting Celebrity* (London: Routledge, 2001), pp.257–70.

Buck-Morss, Susan, *The Dialectics of Seeing* (Boston: MIT Press, 1997).

Burfoot, Amby, *The Runner's Guide to the Meaning of Life* (New York: Rodale, 2000).

Burfoot, Amby, *The Evolution of Training Systems*, http://www.runnersworld.com/training/evolution1,html (accessed 23 Feb. 2001).

Burke, Michael, 'Obeying until it hurts: Coach-athlete relationships', *Journal of the Philosophy of Sport*, 28, 3 (2001), pp.227–40.

Butler, Guy, *Modern Athletics* (Cambridge: Cambridge University Press, 1929).

Butler, Mark (ed.), *Statistics Handbook* (Monaco: IAAF, 1995).

Butryn, Ted, 'Cyborg horizons: Sport and the ethics of self-technologization', in Andy Miah and Simon Eassom (eds), *Sport and Technology: History, Philosophy and Policy* (Amsterdam: Elsevier, 2002), pp.111–33.

Cairns, Alan, *Prelude to Imperialism* (London: Routledge, 1965).

Callois, Roger, *Man, Play and Games* (London, Routledge, 1965).

Carrington, Ben, 'Double consciousness and the black British athlete', in K. Owusu (ed.), *Black British Culture and Society* (London: Routledge, 1999), pp.133–56.

Carter, John and Arnd Krüger (eds), *Ritual and Record: Sports Records and Quantification in Pre-Modern Societies* (New York: Greenwood Press, 1990).

Cashmore, Ernest, *Black Sportsmen* (London: Routledge, 1984).

Cerutty, Percy, *Middle-Distance Running* (London: Pelham, 1964).

Christensen, Dirk Lund, *Washindi: Løbere fra Kenya* (Copenhagen: Frydenlund, 2000).

Clarke, Ron and Alan Trengrove, *The Unforgiving Minute* (London: Pelham, 1966).

Cole, Cheryl, 'Addiction, exercise and cyborgs: Technologies of deviant bodies', in Geneviève Rail (ed.), *Sport and Postmodern Times* (Albany: State University of New York Press, 1998), pp.261–76.

Coleman, James, 'Athletics in high school', *Annals of the American Academy of Political and Social Science*, 338, 1 (1961), pp.3–43.

Coles, R., 'Football as a "surrogate" religion', in M. Hill (ed.), *Sociological Yearbook of Religions in Britain*, 3 (1975), pp.61–77.

Connor, Steven, 'Slow going' (1998), http://www.bbk.ac.uk/eh/eng/skc/slow .htm (accessed 1 Dec. 2002).

Cresswell, Tim, *In Place/Out of Place: Geography, Ideology and Transgression* (Minneapolis: University of Minnesota Press, 1996).

Cresswell, Tim, 'The production of mobilities', *New Formations*, 43 (2001), pp.11–25.

Crick, Michael, *Stranger than Fiction* (London: Penguin, 1995).

Culin, Stewart, *Games of the North American Indians* (New York: Dover, [1907] 1975).

Daniels, Stephen, 'Arguments for a humanistic geography', in R.J. Johnston (ed.), *The Future of Geography* (London: Methuen, 1985), pp.143–58.

Denison, Jim, 'Sport narratives', *Qualitative Enquiry*, 2, 3 (1996), pp.351–62.

Denison, Jim, 'An elephant's trunk', *Sport Literate*, 2, 3 (1998), pp.64–85.

Denison, Jim, 'Boxed in', in Andrew Sparkes and Martti Silvenoinen (eds), *Talking Bodies: Men's Narratives of the Body and Sport* (Jyväskylä: SoPhi, 1999), pp.29–36.

Department for Education and Employment, *The National Curriculum for Physical Education* (London: DFEE, 1995).

Department of Environment, Transport and Regions, *Sport: Raising the Game* (London: Department of National Heritage, 1995).

Deville-Danthu, Bernadette, *Le Sport en Noire et Blanc* (Paris: L'Harmattan, 1997).

Dixon, Nicholas, 'A justification for moderate patriotism in sport', in Torbjörn Tännsjö and Claudio Tamburrini (eds), *Values in Sport* (London: Spon, 2000), pp.74–86.

Doel, Marcus, *Poststructuralist Geographies* (Edinburgh: Edinburgh University Press, 1999).

Downer, A.R., *Running Recollections and How to Train* (Tarland: Balgownie Books, [1902] 1982).

Downes, Stephen and Duncan Mackay, *Running Scared* (Edinburgh: Mainstream Publishing, 1996).

Downing, Taylor, *Olympia* (London: British Film Institute, 1992).

Dunning, Eric, *Sport Matters: Sociological Studies of Sport, Violence and Civilization* (London: Routledge, 1999).

Dyer, K.F. and T. Dwyer, *Running out of Time: An Examination of the Improvement in Running Records* (Kensington, NSW: New South Wales University Press, 1984).

Ehn, Billy, 'National feeling in sport: The case of Sweden', *Ethnologia Europea*, 19, 1 (1988), pp.57–66.

Eichberg, Henning, *Body Cultures: Essays on Sport, Space and Identity* (London: Routledge, 1998).

Eichberg, Henning, 'Forward race and the laughter of pygmies: On Olympic sport', in Mikulás Teich and Roy Porter (eds), *Fin de siècle and its Legacy* (Cambridge: Cambridge University Press, 1990), pp.115–31.

Eichberg, Henning, 'Race track and labyrinth: The space of physical culture in Berlin', *Journal of Sport History*, 17, 2 (1990), pp.245–60.

Eichberg, Henning, 'Stronger, funnier, deadlier: Track and field on its way to the ritual of the record', in John M. Carter and Arnd Krüger (eds), *Ritual and Record: Sports Records and Quantification in Pre-Modern Societies* (New York: Greenwood Press, 1990), pp.123–34.

Ekberg, Micael, 'Stockholms olympiastadion', in Jan Lindroth and Ann Katrin Atmer (eds), 'Idrotten Platser', *Bebyggelsehistorisk Tidskrift*, 40 (2002), pp.87–102.

Elliott, Herb, *The Golden Mile* (London: Cassell, 1961).

Enriken, Nicholas, *The Betweenness of Place* (Cambridge: Cambridge University Press, 1991).

Enriken, Nicholas, 'Geographer as humanist', in Paul Adams, Steven Hoelscher and Karen Till (eds), *Textures of Place: Exploring Humanist Geographies* (Minneapolis: University of Minnesota Press, 2001), pp.426–40.

Entine, Jon, *Taboo: Why Black Americans Dominate Sports and Why we're Afraid to Talk About it* (New York: Public Affairs, 2000).

Fanon, Frantz, *Black Skin, White Masks* (London: Pluto Press, 1986).

Farred, Grant, 'The Maple man: How cricket made a postcolonial intellectual', in Grant Farred (ed.), *Rethinking C.L.R. James* (Oxford: Blackwell, 1996), pp.165–85.

Fenoulière, Serge, 'The loneliness of the long-distance runner', http://www. discip.crdp.ac-caen.fr/anglais/documents/sill5AA0.htm (accessed 29 Nov. 2001).

Földesi, Gyöngi, 'The use of autobiographies in sport sociology: A pilot study', in Otmar Weiss and Wolfgang Schultz (eds), *Sport in Space and Time* (Vienna: Vienna University Press, 1995), pp.147–56.

Frampton, Kenneth, 'Towards a critical regionalism', in Hal Foster (ed.), *Postmodern Culture* (London: Verso, 1985), pp.16–30.

Gardner, Roger, 'On performance enhancing substances and the unfair advantage argument', *Journal of the Philosophy of Sport*, 16, 1 (1989), pp.59–73.

Gebauer, Gunter, 'Citius-Altius-Fortius and the problem of sport ethics: A philosopher's viewpoint', in Fernand Landry, Marc Landry and Magdeleine Yerlès (eds), *Sport: the Third Millennium* (Sainte-Foy: Les presses de L'Université Laval, 1991), pp.467–73.

Gebauer, Gunter, 'On the role of everyday physical-fitness sports in our time', in Karin Volkwein (ed.), *Fitness as Cultural Phenomenon* (Münster: Waxman, 1998), pp.83–91.

Gibson, John, *Performance Versus Results: A Critique of Values in Contemporary Sport* (Albany: State University of New York Press, 1993).

Giulianotti, Richard, *Football: A Sociology of the Global Game* (Cambridge: Polity, 1999).

Gleick, James, *Faster: The Acceleration of Just About Everything* (New York: Pantheon, 1999).

Gleyse, Jacques, 'Instrumental rationalization of human movement', in Geneviève Rail (ed.), *Sport and Postmodern Times* (Albany: State University of New York Press, 1998), pp.239–60.

Goksøyr, Matti, '"One certainly expected a great deal more from the savages". The Anthropology days at St. Louis and their aftermaths', *International Journal of the History of Sport*, 7, 2 (1990), pp.297–86.

Gomberg, Paul, 'Patriotism in sports and war', in *Values in Sport* (London: Spon, 2000), pp.87–98.

Gordon, Harry, *Young Men in a Hurry* (Melbourne: Lansdowne Press, 1962).

Gregory, Derek, 'Humanistic geography', in R.J. Johnston, Derek Gregory, Geraldine Pratt and Michael Watts (eds), *Dictionary in Human Geography* (4th Edition) (Oxford: Blackwell, 2000), pp.361–4.

Guttmann, Allen, *From Ritual to Record* (New York: Columbia University Press, 1978).

Guttmann, Allen, 'Faustian athletes? Sports as a theme in Modern German literature', *Modern Fiction Studies*, 33, 1 (1987), pp.21–33.

Guttmann, Allen, 'The road all runners run', unpublished paper (1988).

Guttmann, Allen, *The Olympics* (Urbana: University of Illinois Press, 1992).

Guttmann, Allen, *The Erotic in Sports* (New York: Columbia University Press, 1996).

Hall, Donald, 'Introduction: Muscular Christianity', in Donald Hall (ed.), *Muscular Christianity: Embodying the Victorian Age* (Cambridge: Cambridge University Press, 1994), pp.1–25.

Hall, Stuart, 'The spectacle of the "other"', in Stuart Hall (ed.), *Representation: Cultural Representations and Signifying Practices* (London: Sage, 1997), pp.223–90.

Hannus, Martti, 'The life story of Elias Katz', *Track Stats*, 39, 3 (2001), pp.35–8.

Harris, Norman, *The Legend of Lovelock* (Wellington: Reed, 1964).

Harvey, David, *The Condition of Postmodernity* (Oxford: Blackwell, 1989).

Harvey, David, *Justice, Nature and the Geography of Difference* (Oxford: Blackwell, 1996).

Heikkala, Juha, 'Discipline and excel: Techniques of the self and body in the logic of competing', *Sociology of Sport Journal*, 10, 4 (1993), pp.397–412.

Heinilä, Kalevi, 'Notes on inter-group conflicts in international sport', in Eric Dunning (ed.), *The Sociology of Sport* (London: Frank Cass, 1971), pp.343–51.

Helprin, Mark, *Memoir from Antproof Case* (New York: Harcourt Brace, 1995).

Heywood, Leslie, *Pretty Good for a Girl: A Memoir* (New York: The Free Press, 1998).

Hill, A.V., *Living Machines* (London: Bell, 1945).

Hill, Ron, *The Long, Hard Road* (2 vols) (Hyde: Ron Hill Sports, 1981, 1982).

Hoberman, John, *Sport and Political Ideology* (London: Heinemann, 1984).

Hoberman, John, *The Olympic Crisis: Sport, Politics and the Moral Order* (New Rochelle: Astride D. Caratzas, 1986).

Hoberman, John, *Mortal Engines: The Science of Performance and the Dehumanization of Sports* (New York: The Free Press, 1992).

Hoberman, John, *Darwin's Athletes: How Sport has Damaged Black America and Preserved the Myth of Race* (Boston: Houghton Mifflin, 1997).

Hughes, Thomas, *Tom Brown's Schooldays* (London: Dent, [1857] 1949).

Huizinga, Johan, *Homo Ludens: A Study of the Play-element in Culture* (Boston: Houghton Mifflin, 1955).

Hutchings, William, 'The work of play: Anger and the expropriated athletes of Alan Sillitoe and David Storey', *Modern Fiction Studies*, 33, (1987), pp.35–47.

Huxley, Elspeth, *White Man's Country: Lord Delamere and the Making of Kenya* (vol. 1) (London: Macmillan, 1935).

Hyland, Drew, *Philosophy of Sport* (New York: Paragon House, 1990).

Ingham, Alan, 'Toward a department of physical culture studies and an end to tribal warfare', in Juan-Miguel Fernández-Balboa (ed.), *Critical Postmodernism in Human Movement, Physical Education and Sport* (Albany: State University of New York Press, 1997), pp.157–80.

Ingold, Tim, *The Perception of the Environment* (London: Routledge, 2000).

Itkonen, Hannu and Seppo Knuuttila, 'Aika voi sun ainoastaan', *Suomen Urheiluhistoriallisen Seuran Vuosikirja* (1998), pp.197–218.

Jackson, J.B., 'The abstract world of the hot-rodder', *Landscape*, 7 (1957–58), pp.22–7.

Jackson, Peter and Susan Smith, *Exploring Human Geography* (London: Allen and Unwin, 1984).

Jackson, Steven, 'A twist of race: Ben Johnson and the Canadian crisis of racial and national identity', *Sociology of Sport Journal*, 15, 1 (1998), pp.21–40.

Jackson, Susan and Mihaly Csikszentmihaly, *Flow in Sports* (Champaign, Ill: Human Kineitics, 1999).

Jain, P., 'On a discrepancy in track races', *Research Quarterly for Exercise and Sport*, 51, 4 (1980), pp.432–6.

James, C.L.R., *Beyond a Boundary* (London: Stanley Paul, 1986).

Janelle, Donald, 'Central place development in a time-place framework', *Professional Geographer*, 20, 1 (1968), pp.5–10.

Jarvie, Grant and Joseph Maguire, *Sport and Leisure in Social Thought* (London: Routledge, 1994).

Jespersen, Ejgil, 'Modeling in sporting apprenticeship', *Nordisk Pedagogik*, 7, 3 (1997), pp.78–85.

Johnson, Nuala, 'Sculpting heroic histories', *Transactions of the Institute of British Geographers*, 19, 1 (1994), pp.78–93.

Johnston, R.J., *Philosophy and Human Geography* (London: Arnold, 1983).

Jokl, Ernst, 'Indisposition after running', in E. Jokl and E. Simon (eds), *International Research in Sport and Physical Education* (Springfield: Thomas, 1960), pp.682–92.

Jones, Michael, *Living Machines* (San Francisco: Ignatius Press, 1995).

Jordan, Tom, *Pre: The Story of America's Greatest Running Legend* (Emmaus, PA: Rodale Press, [1977] 1997).

Juilland, Alphonse, *Rethinking Track and Field: The Future of the World's Oldest Sport* (Milan: SEP Editrice, 2002).

Jukola, Martti, *Athletics in Finland* (Porvoo: Söderström, 1932).

Jutel, Annemarie, 'Thou dost run as in flotation: Femininity and the emergence of the women's marathon', unpublished paper.

Kaila, Tovio, *Boken om Nurmi* (Porvoo: Söderström, 1925).

Kane, Michael, *Modern Men: Mapping Masculinity in English and German Literature* (London: Cassell, 1999).

Karjalainen, Pauli, 'Earth writing as humane art', in Kaia Lehri and Virve Searpik (eds), *Place and Location* (Tallin: Proceedings of the Estonian Academy of Arts, 8, 2000), pp.22–7.

Kern, Stephen, *The Culture of Time and Space: 1800–1919* (Cambridge: Harvard University Press, 1983).

Kirk, David, 'Schooling bodies in new times: The reform of school physical education in high modernity', in Juan-Miguel Fernández-Balboa (ed.), *Critical Postmodernism in Human Movement, Physical Education and Sport* (Albany: State University of New York Press, 1997), pp.39–63.

Klein, Marie-Luise, 'Social-spatial conditions affecting women's sport. The case of the Ruhr area', *International Review for the Sociology of Sport*, 28, 2/3 (1993), pp.145–59.

Kneller, George, *The Educational Philosophy of National Socialism* (New Haven: Yale University Press, 1941).

Korsgaard, Ove, 'Sport as a practice of religion', in John Carter and Arnd Krüger (eds), *Ritual and Record: Sports Records and Quantification in Pre-Modern Societies* (New York: Greenwood Press, 1990).

Kožík, František, *Zátopek the Marathon Victor* (Prague: Artia, 1954).

Krise, Raymond and Bill Squires, *Fast Tracks: the History of Distance Running* (Battleboro, VT: Stephen Greene Press, 1982).

Krüger, Arnd, 'Strength through joy: The culture of consent under fascism, Nazism and Francoism', in Jim Riordan and Arnd Krüger (eds), *The International Politics of Sport in the Twentieth Century* (London: Spon, 1999), pp.67–89.

Krüger, Arnd, 'The homosexual and homoerotic in sport', in Jim Riordan and Arnd Krüger (eds), *The International Politics of Sport in the Twentieth Century* (London: Spon, 1999), pp.191–216.

Kühnst, Peter, *Sport: A Cultural History in the Mirror of Art* (Dresden: Verlag der Kunst, 1996).

Kundera, Milan, *Slowness* (London: Faber, 1996).

Lazarus, Richard, 'Cognitive-Motivational-Relational Theory of emotion', in Yuri Hanin (ed.), *Emotions in Sport* (Champaign, Ill: Human Kinetics, 2000), pp.39–64.

Lenk, Hans and Gunter Gebauer, 'Sport and sports literature from the perspective of methodolological interpretation', *Aethlon*, 5, 2 (1988), pp.73–86.

Levine, Peter, *From Ellis Island to Ebberts Field: Sport and the American Jewish Experience* (New York: Oxford University Press, 1992).

Lewis, Carl with Jeffrey Marx, *Inside Track: My Professional Life in Amateur Track and Field* (New York: Simon and Schuster, 1992).

Lewis, Kevin, 'The lonely marathoner', *Theology Today*, 39, 1 (1982), http://theologytoday.ptsem.edu/apr1982/v-article4.htm (accessed 29 Nov. 2001).

Ley, David, 'Cultural/humanistic geography', *Progress in Human Geography*, 9, 3 (1985), pp.415–23.

Leys, Colin, 'Sport, the state and dependency theory', in Hart Cantelon and Richard Gruneau (eds), *Sport, Culture and the Modern State* (Toronto: Toronto University Press, 1982), pp.308–12.

Liquori, Marty and Skip Myslenski, *On the Run: In Search of the Perfect Race* (New York: Morrow, 1979).

Loader, W.R., *Testament of a Runner* (London: Sportsmans Book Club, 1962).

Łobożewicz, Tadeusz, *Meteorologie im Sport* (Berlin: Sportverlag, 1981).

Loland, Sigmund, 'The logic of progress and the art of moderation in competitive sports', in Torbjörn Tännsjö and Claudio Tamburrini (eds), *Values in Sport* (London: Spon, 2000), pp.39–56.

Loland, Sigmund, 'Record sports: An ecological critique and a reconstruction', *Journal of the Philosophy of Sport*, 28, 2 (2001), pp.127–39.

Loland, Sigmund, *Fair Play: A Moral Norm System* (London: Routledge, 2002).

Lovesey, Peter, *The Official Centenary History of the Amateur Athletics Association* (London: Guinness Superlatives, 1979).

Lowe, D.G.A., *Track and Field Athletics* (London: Pitman, 1935).

Lowenthal, David, 'Making a pet of nature', in Paul Adams, Steven Hoelscher and Karen Till (eds), *Textures of Place: Exploring Humanist Geographies* (Minneapolis: University of Minnesota Press, 2001), pp.84–92.

Lundberg, Knud, *The Olympic Hope* (London: Stanley Paul, 1958).

Lutz, Ronald, 'Careers in running: Individual needs and social organization', *International Review for the Sociology of Sport*, 26, 3 (1991), pp.153–73.

Lydiard, Arthur and Garth Gilmour, *Run to the Top* (London: Herbert Jenkins, 1962).

McConnell, Harold, 'Recruiting patterns in Midwestern major college football', *Geographical Perspectives*, 53, 1 (1984), pp.27–43.

McCormack, Derek, 'Body shopping: Reconfiguring geographies of fitness', *Gender, Space and Culture*, 6, 2 (1999), pp.155–77.

McFee, Graham and Alan Tomlinson, 'Riefenstahl's Olympia: Ideology and aesthetics in the shaping of the Aryan athletic body', in J.A. Mangan (ed.), *Shaping the Superman: Fascist Body as Political Icon – Aryan Fascism* (London: Frank Cass, 1999), pp.86–106.

McNeish, James, *Lovelock* (Auckland: Godwit, [1986] 1994).

McNeish, James, *The Man from Nowhere* (Auckland: Godwit, 1991).

McWhirter, Norris, 'Unusual facts and fallacies', in H.A. Meyer (ed.), *Athletics* (London: Oxford University Press, 1958), pp.186–203.

McWhirter, Ross, 'The long climb', *Athletics World*, 2, 5 (1954), p.35.

McWhirter, Ross and Norris McWhirter, *Get to Your Marks!* (London: Kaye, 1951).

Mackay, Duncan, The Guardian Unlimited, 7 Sept. 2001, http:www.guardian .co.uk/o,6961,,oo.html (accessed 10 Jan. 2002).

Magnusson, Sally, *The Flying Scotsman* (London: Quartet Books, 1981).

Maitland, Sara, 'The loveliness of the long distance runner', in Joli Sandoz (ed.), *A Whole Other Ball Game: Women's Literature on Women's Sports* (New York: Noonday Press, 1997), pp.161–71.

Mallon, Bill, *The 1904 Olympic Games* (Jefferson, NC: McFarland, 1999).

Mandell, Richard, *The Nazi Olympics* (New York: Ballantyne, 1971).

Mangan, J.A., *Athleticism in the Victorian and Edwardian Public School* (London: Frank Cass, [1981] 2000).

Markula, Pirkko and Jim Denison, 'See spot run: Movement as an object of textual analysis', *Qualitative Enquiry*, 6, 3 (2000), pp.406–31.

Martin, Dave and Roger Gynn, *The Marathon Footrace* (Springfield, MA: Thomas, 1979).

Massey, Doreen, 'Power geometry and a progressive sense of place', in Jon Bird, Barry Curtis, Tim Putnam, George Robertson and Lisa Tickner (eds), *Mapping the Futures: Local Cultures, Global Change* (London: Routledge, 1993), pp.59–69.

Matless, David, *Landscapes and Englishness* (London: Reaktion Books, 1998).

Mauss, Marcal, 'Techniques of the Body', in Jonathon Crary and Stanford Kwinter (eds), *Incorporations* (New York: Zone, [1934] 1992), pp.455–77.

Maxwell, Anne, *Colonial Photography and Exhibitions* (London: Leicester University Press, 1999).

May, Jon and Nigel Thrift, 'Introduction', in John May and Nigel Thrift (eds), *Timespace: Geographies of Temporality* (London: Routledge, 2001), pp.1–46.

Messner, Michael, *Power at Play: Sports and the Problem of Masculinity* (Boston: Beacon Press, 1992).

Mitchell, Don, *Cultural Geography* (Oxford: Blackwell, 2000).

Morgan, William, 'Hassiba Boulmerka and Islamic Green: International sports, cultural differences, and their postmodern interpretation', in Geneviève Rail (ed.), *Sport and Postmodern Times* (Albany: State University of New York Press, 1998), pp.345–66.

Mosse, George, *The Image of Man* (New York: Oxford University Press, 1996).

Müller, Norbert (ed.), *Olympism: Pierre de Coubertin 1863–1937: Selected Writings* (Lausanne: International Olympic Committee, 2000).

Murphy, Frank, *The Silence of Great Distance: Women Running Long* (Kansas City: WindSprint Press, 2000).

Nabakov, Peter, *Indian Running* (Santa Fe: Ancient City Press, 1981).

Naess, Arne, *Ecology, Community and Lifestyle* (Cambridge: Cambridge University Press, 1989).

Nash, Catherine, 'Performativity in practice: Some recent work in cultural geography', *Progress in Human Geography*, 24, 4 (2000), pp.653–64.

Nash, Jeffrey, 'The short and the long of it: Legitimising motives for running', in Jeffrey Nash and James Spradley (eds), *Sociology: A Descriptive Approach* (New York: Rand McNally, 1976).

Nielsen, Niels Kayser, 'Sport, landscape and horizon', in John Bale (ed.), *Community, Landscape and Identity: Horizons in a Geography of Sports* (Keele: Occasional Paper 20, Department of Geography, Keele University, 1994), pp.54–70.

Novak, Michael, *The Joy of Sports* (Lanham: Hamilton Press, 1988).

Olsson, Gunner, *Birds in Egg/Eggs in Bird* (London: Pion, 1980).

Olsson, Gunner, 'Towards a sermon of modernity', in Mark Billinge, Derek Gregory and Ron Martin (eds), *Recollections of a Revolution* (London: Macmillan, 1984), pp.73–85.

Oxendine, J., *American Indian Sports Heritage* (Champaign: Human Kinetics, 1988).

Parkes, Don and Nigel Thrift, *Times, Spaces and Places: A Chronogeographic Perspective* (Chichester: Wiley, 1980).

Penz, Otto, 'Sport and speed', *International Review for the Sociology of Sport*, 25, 2 (1990), pp.157–66.

Persson, Lennart and Thomas Pettersson, *Svensk Friidrott 100 År* (Stockholm: Sellin, 1995).

Peters, Jim, *In the Long Run* (London: Cassell, 1955).

Phillips, Adam, *Houdini's Box: On the Arts of Escape* (London: Faber, 2001).

Phillips, Murray and Frank Hicks, 'Conflict, tensions and complexities: Athletic training in Australia in the 1950s', *International Journal of the History of Sport*, 17, 7/8 (2000), pp.206–24.

Pickles, John, *Geography and Humanism, Concepts and Techniques in Modern Geography*, 44 (Norwich: GeoAbstracts, 1986).

Pirie, Gordon, *Running Wild* (London: W.H. Allen, 1961).

Pirie, Gordon, *Running Fast and Injury Free*, http://www.geocities.com/ Colosseum/Pressbox/2204/gordmw2a.doc (accessed 31 Oct. 2002).

Pocock, Douglas (ed.), *Humanistic Geography and Literature* (London: Croom Helm, 1981).

Pocock, Douglas, 'Classics in human geography revisited', *Progress in Human Geography*, 18, 3 (1994), pp.355–6.

Pronger, Brian, *The Arena of Masulinity* (London: GMP Publishers, 1990).

Pyker, Ingo, 'Sport and Ecology', in Søren Riiskjær (ed.), *Sport and Space* (Copenhagen: Council of Europe, 1993), pp.71–7.

Quercetani, Roberto, *Athletics* (Milan: Vallardi, 1990).

Quercetani, Roberto and Fulvio Regli (eds), *International Athletics Annual* (London: World Sports, 1953).

Quercetani, Roberto and Rooney Magnusson, *Track and Field Performances through the Ages, 1929–1936* (Florence: Association of Track and Field Statisticians, 1986).

Rabinbach, Anson, *The Human Motor* (Berkeley: University of California Press, 1990).

Raevuori, Antero, *Paavo Nurmi: Juoksijain Kuningas* (Poorvo: Werner Söderström, 1997).

Rail, Geneviève, 'The dissolution of polarities as a megatrend in postmodern sport', in Fernand Landry, Marc Landry and Magdeleine Yerlès (eds), *Sport: the Third Millennium* (Sainte-Foy: Les presses de L'Université Laval, 1991), pp.746–51.

Rail, Geneviève, 'Seismography of the postmodern condition', in Geneviève Rail (ed.), *Sport and Postmodern Times* (Albany: State University of New York Press, 1998), pp.143–62.

Raitz, Karl (ed.), *The Theater of Sport* (Baltimore: Johns Hopkins University Press, 1998).

Redmond, Gerald, 'A plethora of shrines: Sport in the museum and hall of fame', *Quest*, 1, 9 (1973), pp.41–8.

Rees, Ronald, *Interior Landscapes: Gardens and the Domestic Environment* (Baltimore: Johns Hopkins University Press, 1993).

Reeve, Simon, *One Day in September* (London: Faber, 2000).

Relph, Edward, *Place and Placelessness* (London: Pion, 1976).

Relph, Edward, *Rational Landscapes and Humanistic Geography* (London: Croom Helm, 1981).

Relph, Edward, 'Classics in human geography revisited', *Progress in Human Geography*, 18, 3 (1994), pp.356–8.

Richards, Phil, 'A spirited recovery' (1996), www://suffering.net/ormsby.htm (accessed 17 June 2002).

Richardson, Miles, 'The gift of presence: The act of leaving artefacts at shrines, memorials and other tragedies', in Paul Adams, Steven Hoelscher and Karen Till (eds), *Textures of Place: Exploring Humanist Geographies* (Minneapolis: University of Minnesota Press, 2001), pp.257–72.

Rigauer, Bero, *Sport and Work* (New York: Columbia University Press, 1981).

Robb, Sharon, 'Runner's story: Why did Kathy Ormsby jump off that bridge?', in Ron Rappoport (ed.), *A Kind of Grace* (Berkeley: Zenobia Press, 1994), pp.107–13.

Rodaway, Paul, *Sensuous Geographies: Body, Sense and Place* (London: Routledge, 1994).

Rogoff, Irit, *Terra Infirma: Geography's Visual Culture* (London: Routledge, 2000).

Rohé, Fred, *The Zen of Running* (New York: Random House, 1974).

Rooney, John, *The Recruiting Game* (Lincoln: University of Nebraska Press, 1980).

Rose, Gillian, *Feminism and Geography: The Limits of Geographical Knowledge* (London: Verso, 1993).

Rürup, Reinhard, *1936: Die Olympischen Spiele und der Nationalsozialismus* (Berlin: Stiftung Topgraphie des Terrors, 1999).

Ryan, Joan, *Little Girls in Pretty Boxes* (London: Women's Press, 1996).

Ryun, Jim with Mike Phillips, *In Quest of Gold: The Jim Ryun Story* (San Francisco: Harper and Row, 1984).

Sack, Robert, *Human Territoriality* (Cambridge: Cambridge University Press, 1986).

Sack, Robert, *Homo Geographicus* (Baltimore: Johns Hopkins University Press, 1997).

Salazar, Alberto, *Alberto Salazar's Guide to Running* (Camden, ME: Ragged Island Press, 2001).

Sands, Robert, *Instant Acceleration: Living in the fast Lane: The Cultural Identity of Speed* (Lanham, MY: University Press of America, 1995).

Sauer, Carl, 'The education of a geographer', *Annals of the Association of American Geographers*, 46, 3 (1956), pp.287–99.

Schmidt, Raymond and Wilbert Leonard, 'Immortalizing the self through sport', *American Journal of Sociology*, 91, 5 (1986), pp.1088–111.

Schumacher, Jack, *Die Finnen, das grosse Sportvolk* (Berlin: Wilhelm Limpert Verlag, 1936).

Scott, Jack, *The Athletic Revolution* (New York: The Free Press, 1971).

Seamon, David, *A Geography of the Lifeworld* (London: Croom Helm, 1979).

Segrave, Jeffrey, 'Sport as escape', *Journal of Sport and Social Issues*, 24, 1 (2000), pp.61–77.

Seltzer, Mark, *Bodies and Machines* (New York: Routledge, 1992).

Sharp, Joanne, Chris Philo, Ronan Pattison and Paul Routledge, 'Introduction' in Joanne Sharp, Chris Philo, Ronan Pattison and Paul Routledge (eds), *Entanglements of Power* (London: Routledge, 2000), pp.1–43.

Shearman, Montague, *Athletics and Football* (London: Longmans, Green, 1888).

Shilling, Chris, *The Body and Social Theory* (London: Sage, 1993).

Shogan, Debra, *The Making of High Performance Athletes: Discipline, Diversity and Ethics* (Toronto: University of Toronto Press, 1999).

Sillitoe, Alan, *The Loneliness of the Long-Distance Runner* (London: W.H. Allen, 1959).

Sillitoe, Alan, *Mountains and Caverns* (London: W.H. Allen, 1975).

Slusher, Howard, *Man, Sport and Existence* (London: Henry Kimpton, 1967).

Smith, Amanda, 'Herb Elliott and Percy Cerutty', *The Sports Factor* (broadcast 5 Jan. 2001), http://www.abc.net.au/rn/talks/8.30/sportsf/.

Smith, David, *Moral Geographies: Ethics in a World of Difference* (Edinburgh: Edinburgh University Press, 2000).

Snyder, Eldon, 'Sociology of nostalgia: Sports halls of fame and museums in America', *Sociology of Sport Journal*, 10, 2 (1991), pp.228–38.

Solnit, Rebecca, *Wanderlust: A History of Walking* (New York: Bantam, 1979).

Spino, Mike and Jeffrey Warren, *Mike Spino's Mind/Body Running Program* (New York: Bantam, 1979).

Stein, Jeremy, 'Reflections on time, time-space compression and technology in the nineteenth century', in Jon May and Nigel Thrift (eds), *Timespace: Geographies of Temporality* (London: Routledge, 2001), pp.106–19.

Surin, Kenneth, 'C.L.R. James's aesthetic of cricket', in Hilary Beckles and Brian Stoddart (eds), *Liberation Cricket* (Manchester: Manchester University Press, 1995), pp.313–41.

Sydnor, Synthia, 'Sport, celebrity and liminality', in Noel Dyck (ed.), *Sports Games and Cultures* (Oxford: Berg, 2000), pp.221–41.

Tamburrini, Claudio, 'What's wrong with doping?', in Torbjörn Tännsjö and Claudio Tamburrini (eds), *Values in Sport* (London: Spon, 2000), pp.200–16.

Tännsjö, Torbjörn, 'Is it fascistoid to admire sports heroes?', in Torbjörn Tännsjö and Claudio Tamburrini (eds), *Values in Sport* (London: Spon, 2000), pp.9–23.

Tarasti, L., 'The significance of the environment for sport', *Sport Science Review* (1988), pp.40–1.

Taylor, Peter, 'The state as a container: Territoriality in the modern world-system', *Progress in Human Geography*, 18, 2 (1994), pp.151–62.

Tervo, Mervi, 'Nationalism, sports and gender in Finnish sports journalism in the early twentieth century', *Gender, Place and Culture*, 18, 2 (2001), pp.357–73.

Thrift, Nigel, 'The still point: Resistance, expressive embodiment and dance', in Steve Pile and Michael Keith (eds), *Geographies of Resistance* (London: Routledge, 1997) pp.124–51.

Thrift, Nigel, 'Entanglements of power', in Joanne Sharp, Chris Philo, Ronan Pattison and Paul Routledge (eds), *Entanglements of Power* (London: Routledge, 2000), pp.267–78.

Tuan, Yi-Fu, 'Use of simile and metaphor in geographical descriptions', *The Professional Geographer*, 9, 1 (1957), pp.9–11.

Tuan, Yi-Fu, 'Discrepancies between environmental attitude and behavior: examples from Europe and China', *Canadian Geographer*, 15, 2 (1971), pp.176–91.

Tuan, Yi-Fu, *Topophilia: A Study of Environmental Perception, Attitudes and Values* (Englewood Cliffs: Prentice Hall, 1974).

Tuan, Yi-Fu, 'Space and place: A humanistic perspective', *Progress in Geography*, 6 (1974), pp.211–52.

Tuan, Yi-Fu, 'Humanistic geography', *Annals of the Association of American Geographers*, 66, 2 (1976), pp.266–76.

Tuan, Yi-Fu, *Space and Place: The Perspective of Experience* (Minneapolis: University of Minnesota Press, 1977).

Tuan, Yi-Fu, 'Sign and metaphor', *Annals of the Association of American Geographers* 68, 3 (1978), pp.363–72.

Tuan, Yi-Fu, 'Literature and geography: Implications for geographical research', in David Ley and Marwyn Samuels (eds), *Humanistic Geography: Prospects and Problems* (London: Croom Helm, 1978), pp.194–206.

Tuan, Yi-Fu, *Landscapes of Fear* (Oxford: Blackwell, 1979).

Tuan, Yi-Fu, 'The significance of the artifact', *The Geographical Review*, 70, 4 (1980), pp.462–72.

Tuan, Yi-Fu, *Segmented Worlds and Self* (Minneapolis: University of Minnesota Press, 1982).

Tuan, Yi-Fu, *Dominance and Affection: The Making of Pets* (New Haven: Yale University Press, 1984).

Tuan, Yi-Fu, *The Good Life* (Madison: University of Wisconsin Press, 1986).

Tuan, Yi-Fu, 'Attention: Moral-cognitive geography', *Journal of Geography*, 86, 1 (1987), pp.11–13.

Tuan, Yi-Fu, 'Environment, behaviour and thought', in Frederick Boal and David Livingstone (eds), *The Behavioural Environment* (London: Routledge, 1989), pp.77–81.

Tuan, Yi-Fu, *Morality and Imagination* (Madison: University of Wisconsin Press, 1989).

Tuan, Yi-Fu, 'Surface phenomena and aesthetic experience', *Annals of the Association of American Geographers*, 79, 2 (1989), pp.233–41.

Tuan, Yi-Fu, *Passing Strange and Wonderful: Aesthetics, Nature and Culture* (Washington, DC: Island Press, 1993).

Tuan, Yi-Fu, *Cosmos and Hearth: A Cosmopolite's Viewpoint* (Minneapolis: University of Minnesota Press, 1996).

Tuan, Yi-Fu, *Escapism* (Baltimore: Johns Hopkins University Press, 1998).

Tuan, Yi-Fu, 'A life of learning', *Occasional Paper*, 24, American Council of Learned Societies (1998), http://www.acls.org/op42tuan.htm (accessed 11 Jan. 2001).

Tuan, Yi-Fu, *Who am I? An Autobiography of Emotion, Mind and Spirit* (Madison: University of Wisconsin Press, 1999).

Tuan, Yi-Fu, 'Geography and evil: A sketch', in James Proctor and David Smith (eds), *Geography and Ethics: Journeys in a Moral Terrain* (London: Routledge, 1999), pp.106–19.

Tuan, Yi-Fu, 'Life as a field trip', *The Geographical Review*, 2, 49 (2001), pp.42–5.

Tuan, Yi-Fu, *Dear Colleague: Common and Uncommon Observations* (Minneapolis: University of Minnesota Press, 2002).

Ullman, Edward, 'Space and/or time: Opportunities for substitution and prediction', *Transactions of the Institute of British Geographers*, 64 (1974), pp.125–39.

Umminger, W., *Supermen, Heroes and Gods: The Story of Sport through the Ages* (New York: McGraw Hill, 1963).

Vance, Norman, *The Sinews of the Spirit: The Ideal of Christian Manliness in Victorian Literature and Religious Thought* (Cambridge: Cambridge University Press, 1985).

Vine, Brian, *Zola* (London: Stanley Paul, 1994).

Vinnai, Gerhard, *Football Mania* (London: Ocean Books, 1973).

Wagner, Phillip, 'Sport: Culture and geography', in Allan Pred (ed.), *Time and Space in Geography* (Lund: Gleerup, 1981), pp.85–108.

Walton, Theresa, 'Steve Prefontaine – From rebel with a cause to bourgeoise hero', paper presented at symposium on 'Sport and Cultural Distinctiveness', Iowa City (1999).

Wann, Daniel, Merrill Melnick, Gordon Russell and Dale Pearse, *Sports Fans: The Psychology and Social Impact of Spectators* (London: Routledge, 2001).

Warren, Patricia Nell, *The Front Runner* (New York: Bantam, 1975).

Webster, F.A.M., *Athletics* (London: Allen and Unwin, 1925).

Webster, F.A.M., *Athletes of Today: History, Development and Training* (London: Warne, 1929).

Webster, F.A.M., *Athletes in Action* (London: John F. Shaw, 1931).

Webster, F.A.M., *Why? The Science of Athletics* (London: John F. Shaw, 1937).

Webster, F.A.M., *Sports Grounds and Buildings* (London: Pitman, 1940).

Webster, F.A.M., *Great Moments in Athletics* (London: Country Life, 1947).

Webster, F.A.M., *Olympic Cavalcade* (London: Hutchinson, 1948).

Weis, Kurt, 'Concepts of time and concepts of man: Does the case of sport show how man both creates and falls victim to his image of time?', in Otmar Weiss and Wolfgang Schultz (eds), *Sport in Space and Time* (Vienna: Vienna University Press, 1995), pp.299–310.

Weiss, Paul, *Sport: A Philosophic Enquiry* (Carbondale: University of Southern Illinois Press, 1969).

Werge, Lars, *Wilson Kipketer* (Århus: Klim, 1998).

Wertz, Spencer, *Talking a Good Game: Inquiries into the Principles of Sport* (Dallas: Southern Methodist University Press, 1991).

Whatmore, Sarah, *Hybrid Geographies* (London: Routledge, 2002).

Wiggins, David, '"Great speed but little stamina": The historical debate over black athletic supremacy', *Journal of Sport History*, 16, 2 (1989), pp.158–85.

Williams, Raymond, *The Country and the City* (London: Hogarth Press, 1985).

Wilt, Fred, *How they Train* (Los Altos: Track and Field News, 1959).

Winters, Christopher, 'Running', *Landscape*, 24, 2 (1980), pp.19–22.

Young, David, *The Modern Olympics: A Struggle for Revival* (Baltimore: Johns Hopkins University Press, 1996).

Young, Iris, *Throwing Like a Girl* (Bloomington: Indiana University Press, 1990).

Zelinsky, Wilbur, 'Where every town is above average: Welcoming signs along America's highways', *Landscape*, 30, 1 (1988), pp.1–10.

Zelinsky, Wilbur, 'The world and its identity crisis', in Paul Adams, Steven Hoelscher and Karen Till (eds), *Textures of Place: Exploring Humanist Geographies* (Minneapolis: University of Minnesota Press, 2001), pp.129–49.

Zeller, Robert, 'Running away: "The Loneliness of the Long-Distance Runner" revisited', *Aethlon*, 13, 1 (1995), pp.46–52.

Zeller, Robert, 'Running addiction and masculinity in David Foster's "Eye of the Bull"', unpublished paper.

zur Megede, Ekkehard and Richard Hymans, *Progression in World Best Performances and Official IAAF World Records* (Monaco: IAAF, 1995).

Index

Abrahams, Harold 68, 69, 123, 147, 149–50, 156
abuse 78, 80, 99
Achilles 164
achievement running 18–25, 37–8, 43, 57, 92
acceleration, *see* speed
Adams, Paul 75
addiction to running 97–8; *see also* runner's high
Adidas 160
aesthetics 73, 74, 75, 86, 147
affection 40–4, 50, 52, 77–8
Africa 116–18
agony, *see* pain
amateur 114
Amateur Athletic Association (AAA) 40, 117
ancient Greek athletics, 39, 78
Andersson, Arne 27, 61, 62
Anthropology Days 83
Appleton, Jay 72
Archer, Jeffrey 161–2
Auden, W.H. 9
Augé, Marc 38

Bailey, Donovan 45
Baker, William 84
Bannister, Roger 2, 10–11, 27, 44, 58, 62, 63–5, 74, 86, 95–6, 99, 101, 105, 113, 114–16, 123, 130, 131, 134, 152, 159
Barnum, P.T. 83
Baudrillard, Jean 17, 70–1
Bauman, Zygmunt 44
Beccali, Luigi 103–4
Beechcroft, T.O. 74
Benjamin, Walter 87, 110
Bikila, Abebe 29
Bislett Stadium 29, 52
Bitok, Paul 27
Black Power 110
Black September Movement 156
Blake, William 67

Booth, Dick 84
Boulmerka, Hassiba 129–30
boundaries 49, 109, 110–11
Bowden, Martyn 67–8, 126
Bowerman, Bill 121
Brackenridge, Celia 80
Bradley, Bill 3
Brasher, Chris 115, 123, 159
Brecht, Berthold 18
Brohm, Jean-Marie 18, 87, 95, 110
Brown, Douglas 54
Browne, St John Orde 34, 49
Brundage, Avery 157
Budd, Zola 100, 141–2
bulimia 93
Burfoot, Amby 76, 105
Burghley, Lord 123
Butler, Guy 49, 150
Byers, Tom 35

Caillois, Roger 12, 36
Cambridge University 51, 123
Campbell, Darren 136
Canadian Death Race 75
Carlos, John 110
Carrington, Ben 85, 144
Carroll, Lewis 46
Cerutty, Percy 65–6, 81–2, 99, 149
Chariots of Fire 65, 68
Chataway, Chris 6, 53, 99, 115, 116, 118, 123, 159
children 10–11
chivalry 152
Christian view 100, 127, 149-150, 151
Christie, Linford 85, 144–5
Chumbawumba 141–2
cinder tracks 42–3
Clarke, Ron 81, 152, 159
class 123–5, 126
coaching 78–83
Coe, Sebastian 27
Colbeck, Edward 48
Coleman, Don 160

colonialism 116–17
commercializaion 48, 55
Compton, Denis 114
cosmopolitanism 131, 136–9
cosmos 132, 137
Coubertin, Pierre de 15, 23, 25, 48, 52, 54, 56, 135, 129, 150, 152
Cresswell, Tim 109, 132
Cretzmeyer, Francis X. 31
Crick, Michael 161
cricket 2, 41
cross-country running 71–2
Culin, Stewart 39
Cunningham, Glen 28
cyborg 91

darkness 64–5
Decker, Mary 85, 100, 141
Delaney, Ron 138
Dellinger, Bill 157–8
Denison, Jim 100–1
Deutschen Stadion 46
dominance 41, 50, 96
Dorando, Pietri 97
Downer, A.P. 41, 133
Downing, Taylor 14
Dunning, Eric 2
Edwards, Harry 110
Ehn, Billy 145
Eichberg, Henning 9, 10, 19, 21, 38, 44
El Moutawakel, Nawal 138
Elias, Norbert 2
Elliott, 'Jumbo' 138
Elliott, Herb 63, 65, 98, 149
Empire Games 42
endorphins 97
Entine, Jon 137
environmental determinism 69
envy 54–5
eroticism 78, 102–4
escape 98, 131–46
evil 160–3
exhaustion 17, 98–9

fair play 40
Fanon, Frantz 85
fartlek 62–3, 65
fascistoid 55–6
Finland 29, 68–9, 87–8
fitness 15–17
flow 106–7
foreplay 67
four-minute mile 21, 32, 123
France 116–17
Francis, Charlie 82
Freeman, Kathy 145

Gärderud, Anders 62

Gebauer, Gunther 4, 35, 85, 148, 149, 165
Gebrisalasse, Haile 29
Geography 1–2
Gerschler, Waldemar 65, 69, 78, 80, 85, 163
Girouard, Percy 16
Glickman, Martin 155–6
globalization 140
Goodwill Games 26
Gordon, Harry 153
Grace, W.G. 125
grass tracks 41–2
Green, Fred 117
Green, Milton 153
Greene, Maurice 35
Gretzky, Wayne 145
Grut, Torben 52
Guttmann, Allen 2, 34, 39, 100, 102, 151, 153

Hägg, Gunder 27, 61, 62, 117, 130
Hall, Stuart 119, 144
Halt, Carl Ritter von, *see* von Halt, Carl Ritter
Hampson, Shirley 114
Hampson, Tom 123
Harbig, Rudolf 85, 163
Hardy, Fred 137
Harvard University 86
Heartfield, John 89–90
hearth 132, 142
Heikkala, Juha 21
Heinilä, Kalevi 93, 140
Helprin, Mark 12
Hemery, David 138, 150
Herbst, Stephanie 156
Hercules 165
Hermans, Jos 157
Heywood, Leslie 78, 90, 93, 97, 101, 165
Hill, A.V. 20
Hill, Ron 102, 123, 158–9
Hitler, Adolph 163, 164
Hoberman, John 82, 87, 95
Holmér, Gösta 62, 65
homoeroticism, *see* eroticism
homosexuality 112, 135
horizon 21–2
Houdini, Harry 55
Housman, A.E. 33–4
Hughes, Thomas 72, 149, 150–1
Huizinga, Johan 12
humanism 4–5
husplex 39
Hutton, Len 114
Huxley, Elspeth, 16.

IAAF (International Athletic Association Federation) 19, 43, 47, 141, 145
Ibbotson, Derek 53

Identity 140–2
idols 32
Iffley Road 44, 48, 51
Igloi, Mihaly 25
Iharos, Sándor 25
imagination 153, 154, 159, 161, 165
Ingold, Tim 10
intentionality 109
interorisation 44–5
interval running 65, 87, 89, 163

Jackson, Ted 92
Jackson, Steven 145
James, C.L.R. 9, 109
Jazy, Michel 96–7
jogging 16
Johnson, Ben 82, 85, 106, 131, 145–6
Johnson, Michael 45
joie de vivre 75
Jokl, Ernst 22, 161, 162
Jones, Charles 30
Jukola, Martti 88
Junxia, Wang 22
Jutel, Annemarie 129

Katz, Elias 146
Keino, Kipchoge 137
Kenya 34, 82, 137, 138, 151
Kidd, Bruce 80
Kipketer, Wilson 143–4
Kipling, Rudyard 15
Kiptanui, Robert Kiplagat 143
Kolehmainen, Hannes 29, 30–1, 68, 88
Korsgaard, Ove 150–1
Kumunya 27
Kundera, Milan 17, 26
Kurgat, Josiah 137, 163
Kuts, Vladimir 53, 55, 89, 113, 114, 118

Laing, Leslie 29
Landy, John 22, 26, 152
landscapes 61, 68–70
lanes 48, 49, 50
Lanzi, Mario 163
Larrieu, Francie 85
Le Corbusier 89
Lenk, Hans 4
Lewis, Carl 19, 118–20, 145–6, 160, 162
Lewis, Kevin 107
Ley, David 132
Leys, Colin 165
Liddell, Eric 68, 147, 150, 154–5
Liquori, Marty 24, 90, 95, 133–4, 159
literature 4-5, 165
Loader, W.R. 43, 51, 52, 63, 66, 79, 107
Lola Rennt, see Run Lola Run
Loland, Sigmund 26, 54, 56, 58–9, 60
loneliness 107

*Loneliness of the Long Distance Runner,
   The* 67, 125–8
Louis, Joe 84
Lovelock, Jack 23, 51, 91, 98, 103–4, 105,
   123, 135
Lowe, Douglas 86, 87, 112, 123
Lowenthal, David 96
Lundberg, Knud 91–92, 95, 165
Lydiard, Arthur 12

machines, athletes as 85–96
Mackenly, Herb 9
Madison Square Garden 45
Magnan, Pierre 148, 153
Maitland, Sara 102
Maiyoro, Nyandika 25, 117–18, 130, 143
Major, John 18 151–2
Mäki, Taisto 68, 117
Mangan, J.A. 72, 152
Maree, Sydney 142–3
Marey, Etienne-Jules 87
masculinity 112, 119–20
masochism 99–100
McDonald's 39
McKechnie, Elsa 154
McNeish, James 23, 35, 51, 91, 98, 105,
   135, 156, 159, 165
McWhirter twins 45
Messner, Michael 101, 110
Metcalfe, Adrian 99
Metcalfe, Ralph 164
migration 132–9
Mimoun, Alain 117
Montherlat, Henry de 102
Moorcroft, David 27
Moore, Kenny 157
moral fibre 150
morals 74, 147, 149, 153
Morgan, Bill 130
Mosse, George 82
muscular Christianity 149–52
Muybridge, Eadweard 87
Myers, Lon 133

nakedness, *see* nudism
National Curriculum 18, 165
National Socialism 82, 89, 110, 112, 155–6,
   162
nature 75, 81
Nazism, *see* National Socialism
NCAA (National Collegiate Athletic
   Association) 127, 152, 160
Nesterenko, Eric 3
Neugass, Herman 155
Nielsen, Gunner 143
Nike 121, 143, 160
nostalgia 29
nudism 14

Nurmi, Matti 34
Nurmi, Paavo 16, 20, 24, 29, 30, 34, 45, 68, 69, 88–9, 93–4, 112, 117

O'Connell, Colm 143
Oates, Joyce Carol 3, 106
Okorokov, Vladimir 27
Ollander, Gösta 62, 65
Olsson, Gunner 25
Olympia 10, 14
Olympic Games, 2, 15, 36, 37, 42, 46–7, 48, 52, 68, 70, 82, 83, 85, 86, 88, 97, 100, 101, 112, 113, 115, 116, 117, 132, 135, 140–1, 142, 144, 145, 155, 156–9
orienteering 50, 70, 72–3
Ormsby, Kathy 127–8, 130, 150, 156
Osendarp, Martinus 164
Ovett, Steve 35
Owens, Jesse 83–4, 164
Oxford University 46, 105, 114, 135, 162

pacemaker 26, 35
pain 96–9, 107
paper-chasing 71–2
Paralympics 18
patriotism 56, 143–4
Peltzer, Otto 99, 111, 112, 113, 146, 154
Penz, Otto 19
Peters, Jim 97, 139
pets, athletes as, 77–96
Peyker, Ingo 42
Phillips, Adam 55
Physical Education 18, 82
Pickles, John 4
Pirie, Gordon 24, 42, 63, 69, 74, 78, 80, 84, 85, 86, 99, 103, 106, 107, 113–14, 115, 116, 118, 130, 131, 134, 135
place 51
placelessness 38–9, 46, 134
play 10–14, 25, 79, 160, 162, 165
Plotin, Stephanie 103
pornography 22
Portsea 65–9, 131
post-Fordism 71
power 80, 119–20
Prefontaine, Steve 31–2, 58, 120–1, 130, 157–8, 159
pride 153–4
progress 165
professional era 113
professionals 40
Pullen, Jim 103
Puma 143
purdah 129
Pyker, Ingo 42

quantification 22–4.

race and racial groups 24–5, 30, 34
racism 56, 117, 118
Radcliffe, Paula 121–2, 130, 148
rebels 111–16
records, quantitative 21–5; non-quantitative, 28–34
recruiting 137
Redmond, Derek 144
Rees, Ronald 44
Relph, Edward 7, 38
resistance 109–30
Rhoden, George 29
Riefenstahl, Leni 14, 135
Rigauer, Bero 71, 89
road running 70–1
Robinson, Matthew 164
Rodaway, Paul 76
Roessler, Kirsten 55
Rohé, Fred 14-15, 16
Rono, Peter 74, 138
Rose, Gillian 70
Roth, Esther 157
Rover, The 122, 123
rowing 3, 99
Royal Military Academy 40
Rózavölgyi, Istvan 25
Rudd, Bevil 123
Rudolph, Wilma 85
Run Lola Run 1
runner's high 103, 105–6, 134
running as work 34, 35
running track 37-50, 51, 57
Ryun, Jim 151, 152

Sack, Robert 7, 49, 147
sadism 162
Salazar, Alberto 73
sameness, *see* placelessness
Sands, Robert 80, 96
Sauer, Carl 76
Schama, Simon 2
Schultz, Dr Bruno 92
Schumacher, Jack 68–9
Seamon, David 51, 90
Segrave, Jeffrey 98
self-denial 74
sensuousness 103, 107
sex 3, 78, 102
Shearman, Montague 25, 26, 40, 41, 46, 47, 48
Shilling, Chris 17, 85
Shorter, Frank 131, 157
Sibelius, Jean 29
Sillitoe, Alan 67, 79, 125, 159, 165
Simpson, George 43
Skydome 45
Slaney, Mary, *see* Mary Decker
slowness 25–8, 75–6

Slusher, Howard 87
Smith (Colin) 67, 75, 125–8
Smith, Red 157
Smith, Tommy 110
Solnit, Rebecca 76
Sorley, Charles Hamilton 12–13
space, frontal 20–1, 37–8; back, 29
space-ballet 51
spectators 48, 54, 56, 58
speed 19–21, 43, 44, 54, 75
Spino, Mike 150
spirituality 149–53
Sport und Rasse 92
St. Patrick's High School 143
stadiums 3, 47, 50–4, 55, 58, 59
Stampfl, Franz 87, 96
standardisation 46, 47–9, 70, 73
starting blocks 22, 43
statistics 5, 24–5
statues 29–31
steeplechase 46–7
Stein, Jeremy 23
stereotypes 84, 135, 164, 165
Stoller, Sam 155
Stone, Laurie 102
stopwatch 50, 88, 89
stotan 66, 81
Strand, Lernnart 61
Strode Jackson, Arnold 123
style 147–8
Sudhaus, Norbert 131
Sweden 61–3
Sykes, Devon 103
synthetic tracks 22, 43–4

Tabori, László 25
Tännsjö, Torbjörn 55–6
territoriality 49
Thrift, Nigel 105
time-space compression 22–3
topophilia 2, 7, 50–2, 56, 154
totalization process 109–30
training 77, 97–8
tracks 38–42
transgression 109, 116, 118
Tuan, Yi-Fu, 1-2, 3, 4
 on statistics 5
 on the approach of the cultural-humanist
  writer 7
 on children and the experience of play 12,
  14, 25
 on space and sport 19, 20–1, 25
 on aspiration 35
 on human power and design 37
 on culture and nature 40–1, 69
 on dominance 41, 109
 on segmentation 49

on social reality and data collecting
 49–50
on patriotism 56
on the edenic 61
on escape 69, 109
on the good life 74–5, 147, 152–3, 162,
 164, 165
on pets 77, 79, 96
on play 79
on bodies as machines 86
on the geographer 131
on migration 132, 136, 139
Tupper, Alf 122–5, 130
Tykwer, Tom 1

Ullman, Edward 28
University of Iowa 31
University of Texas, El Paso 138

Vaatinen, Juha 61, 68
Vålådalen 62, 69, 131
Van Gool, Wilma 157
Vance, Norman 152
Victor, The 123
Viren, Lasse 36, 68
vitality 3, 10, 25
von Halt, Karl Ritter 112, 163

Waern, Dan 62
Wagner, Philip 37
Waitz, Grete 30, 31, 65
Wales 63–4
walking 1, 75, 76
Walton, Theresa 120
Warren, Patricia Nell 55, 66–7, 79, 103, 165
Webster, F.A.M. 15, 26, 78, 88, 107
Weis, Kurt 19
Weiss, Paul 19, 38, 58
welfare running 16–17
Wheeler, Ted 31, 34
wilderness 61
Williams, Archie 163
Williams, Willie 80
Willumsen, Jens Ferdinand 11, 14
Wilson 125, 130
Wint, Arthur 29
Winters, Christopher 71, 74
Wizard, The 121, 122, 125
Wooderson, Sydney 27, 62, 163
Woods, Tiger 3

Yegorova, Olga 121–2

Zátopek, Emil 86, 89, 117, 134, 147–8
Zelinsky, Wilbur 140
Zeller, Robert 127–8
zen of running 14–15